As I went out a Crow
In a low voice said, "Oh,
I was looking for you.
How do you do?
I just came to tell you
To tell Lesley (will you?)
That her little Bluebird
Wanted me to bring word
That the north wind last night
That made the stars bright
And made ice on the trough
Almost made him cough
His tail feathers off.
He just had to fly!
But he sent her Good-by,
And said to be good,
And wear her red hood,
And look for skunk tracks
In the snow with an ax —
And do everything!
And perhaps in the spring
He would come back and sing."

"The Last Word of a Bluebird"
ROBERT FROST

HarperCollins books may be purchased for educational, business, or sales promotional use. For information please write: Special Markets Department, HarperCollins Publishers Inc., 10 East 53rd Street, New York, NY 10022.

FIRST EDITION

"The Last Word of a Bluebird," by Robert Frost, from THE POETRY OF ROBERT FROST edited by Edward Connery Lathem. Copyright 1930, 1939, 1969 by Henry Holt and Co., copyright 1944 by Robert Frost. Reprinted by permission of Henry Holt and Company, LLC

Library of Congress Cataloging-in-Publication Data has been applied for.

ISBN 0-06-273743-0

04 05 10 9 8 7 6 5 4 3

A CORNELL BIRD LIBRARY GUIDE

The BLUEBIRD MONITOR'S Guide

by Cynthia Berger, Keith Kridler, and Jack Griggs

HarperResource
An Imprint of HarperCollins*Publishers*

Acknowledgments

PRODUCTION AND LAYOUT
Jack Griggs

INTERIOR DESIGN
Stuart L. Silberman

PREPRESS
John E. Griggs
U.S. Color

COVER DESIGN
Stuart L. Silberman and Peter Martin

COVER PHOTOGRAPHS
Front: Richard Day/Daybreak Imagery
Back: Steve and Dave Maslowski

COPY EDITOR
Virginia Croft

PROOFREADER
Helen Garfinkle

ILLUSTRATIONS
Paul Carrier

PHOTOGRAPHERS
Names of photographers are followed by the page number
on which their work appears. L = left, C = center, R = right,
T = top, B = bottom.

Jerry Beauregard: 76T
Kay Bongers: 64, 65
Shirl Brunell: 61, 62
Bruce Burdett: 51
Veronique Conolly: 8
Ervin Davis: 52, 53, 54
Richard Day/Daybreak Imagery: 9, 70, 76B, 93
Jack Finch: 30, 58T, 58B
Fort Sill Photo: 59, 60TL, 60TR
Steve Gilbertson: 23, 26BL, 26BR, 31, 77, 79B, 103, 109
Don Hutchings: 118
John Ivanko: 7B
Kevin T. Karlson: 56, 93
Ron Kingston: 115
Jane Kirkland: 27TL, 71
Keith Kridler: 27TR, 99L, 99R, 104T, 105, 108, 110L,
    110R, 111, 112T, 112B, 113, 117, 122
Harry Krueger: 26TR, 29, 74TR, 74BL, 74BR
Wendell Long: 6, 12, 20T, 78, 93, 94, 100, 106
David Magness: 121
Steve and Dave Maslowski: 19, 72, 73, 75, 90, 91, 119
Malinda Mastako: 32-44ALL
Dan McCue: 50
Jeff Milton/Daybreak Imagery: 79T
North American Bluebird Society: 7T
Kevin Putman: 55
Haleya Priest: 63
Marie Read: 27BL, 47

Jeffrey Rich: 1, 15T, 16, 22
George Schackel: 26TL, 116
Gregory K. Scott: 20B, 21, 45
Brian E. Small: 14, 17
Hugh P. Smith, Jr.: 15B, 18, 49, 93
Connie Toops: 10, 11, 24, 25, 27BR, 28T, 28B, 48, 57, 69,
    81, 82, 83, 84, 85, 89, 102, 104B
Tom Vezo: 13
Linda Violett: 66, 67
Bob Wilson: 107
Terry Whitworth: 87
Paul Zimmerman: 5

SPECIAL THANKS TO
John W. Fitzpatrick
    Louis Agassiz Fuertes Director
    Cornell Lab of Ornithology
Tina Phillips
    Project Leader, The Birdhouse Network
John Ivanko and Lisa Kivirist
    Co-Executive Directors, North American Bluebird Society
Ann Wick
    Board Member, North American Bluebird Society
Doug LeVasseur
    President, North American Bluebird Society
Dorene Scriven
    Chair, Minnesota Bluebird Recovery Project
Megan Newman
    Editor in Chief, HarperResource

VERY SPECIAL THANKS TO
All the bluebird monitors who generously shared their
experiences and knowledge to make this book possible.

The bird monitoring techniques and suggestions made
herein are not necessarily the recommendations of the
North American Bluebird Society, The Birdhouse Network,
or the Cornell Lab of Ornithology.

The Bluebird Monitor's Guide

CONTENTS

Wing Wave
A handsome male
eastern bluebird
attracts the attention
of females by waving
his wings.

A male eastern bluebird hunts from atop a post. "Every time you see one, it takes your breath away like the first time," says Diane Slavin of Vernon, New York.

Bluebirds of Happiness

Bluebirds and humans have always had a special relationship. Native Americans hung up dry gourds to encourage bluebirds to nest near their settlements, and the earliest European settlers welcomed bluebirds to their fields and yards just as enthusiastically. In the 1800s, Henry David Thoreau celebrated "His Most Serene Birdship," while naturalist John Burroughs proclaimed, "Thy azure coat and ruddy vest are hues that April loveth best."

Bluebirds have become the very symbol of happiness because of their uncanny power to bring joy to an onlooker. The symbolism was sealed in the early 1900s, when Maurice Maeterlinck wrote a fairy-tale play about two children who search for the "blue bird of happiness," only to find, after many adventures, that it has been in their own backyard all along. Since then the bluebird has been celebrated in countless songs and poems. The 1939 movie *Wizard of Oz* saw Judy Garland longing for a happy place where bluebirds fly "somewhere over the rainbow." After World War II, the tenor Jan Peerce made *Bluebird of Happiness* a nationwide hit; the lyrics promised, "Life is sweet, tender and complete, when you find the bluebird of happiness."

To the Brink and Back

Ironically, just as the bluebird was being celebrated on stage and screen, people noticed that eastern bluebirds were disappearing from their fields, dooryards, and lives. House sparrows, imported from Europe in 1851, had multiplied rapidly in America. By the early 1900s, these aggressive newcomers were overwhelming bluebirds in their competition for nesting cavities. Bluebirds needed help.

Thomas E. Musselman of Quincy, Illinois, was the first person to spread the gospel of bluebird conservation. In 1934, he wrote an article for the National Audubon Society magazine *Bird-Lore* urging the establishment of bluebird trails throughout the country. Musselman also wrote a monthly column for *Nature Society News,* called "The Bluebird Trail," in which he worked to increase public awareness of the plight of bluebirds and to tell readers how they could help.

Musselman was not alone. Across the U.S., many other dedicated bluebird enthusiasts were helping in the effort to restore bluebird populations, including William Duncan in Kentucky, Amelia Laskey in Tennessee, Art Aylesworth in Montana, Philip J. Hummel in Wisconsin, and John and Norah Lane in Manitoba, Canada, to name just a few of the earliest.

In 1969, Musselman relinquished his monthly column to Dr. Lawrence Zeleny, who wrote it for another 12 years. Besides reaching out to people in his monthly column, Zeleny brought Musselman's original cry of alarm for the future of the bluebird to a much larger audience through his book *The Bluebird — How You Can Help Its Fight for Survival,* published in 1975.

Three years later, Zeleny met with a group of friends in Chevy Chase, Maryland, to discuss the idea of a continent-wide program that would restore the dwindling bluebird population. When some of those attending expressed doubt that the public cared enough to make the effort worthwhile, Zeleny produced paper grocery sacks filled with letters he had received from bluebird enthusiasts over the years. Dumping the sacks on the floor, he gave everyone at the meeting a handful of letters to read.

Each letter was a passionate account of enchanting encounters with bluebirds, expressing the joy that this small bird — which "carries the sky on its back and the earth on its breast" — had brought to the writer. And each letter writer expressed dismay that their own children's lives would not be touched by the magical little birds. In letter after letter, people asked, "Where have all the bluebirds gone?" and "What can I do to help them?"

The letters had the same enchanting effect on Zeleny's committee as the bluebirds themselves had on the writers. Under their spell, the North American Bluebird Society (NABS) was born.

Dr. Lawrence Zeleny in a photograph from the 1980s. Zeleny's concern for bluebirds began in 1918 when he noted invading house sparrows outcompete bluebirds for nesting cavities. "I wondered how bluebirds could possibly survive without human help," he wrote.

Letters of solicitation went out to everyone who had written a letter to Zeleny, inviting the recipients to join together in an organization dedicated to reversing the decline of bluebirds. Remarkably, about 350 of these "grocery sack people" responded enthusiastically. Rallying to the cry "Where have all the bluebirds gone?" the charter members of NABS, under Zeleny's gentle leadership, gave themselves up to the task of ensuring that bluebirds would be here to enchant people for generations.

They're B-a-a-a-ck!
Today the organization that Zeleny started has an answer for all the people who asked, "Where have all the bluebirds gone?" Doug LeVasseur, current NABS president, says, "The bluebirds are back!" In the quarter century since NABS was launched, countless volunteers have set out thousands upon thousands of bluebird nestboxes and monitored them solicitously. Today bluebirds are once again a cheery fact of everyday life for many people.

To maintain this happy status, the nonprofit organization (which is committed not only to bluebird conservation but to public education and research) continues to coordinate the efforts of more than 15,000 nestbox monitors through affiliated

state, regional, and provincial organizations in the U.S. and Canada. NABS also publishes a journal, *Bluebird,* that disseminates bluebird research results and other information. And to reach those people not already under the delightful influence of bluebird sorcery, NABS has long maintained a speakers bureau. It now includes over 350 veteran bluebird-monitor volunteers who give talks, slide shows, and workshops.

NABS reaches out on behalf of bluebirds in many other ways. If you buy a well-designed nestbox, chances are it will carry the "NABS-approved" label; each year over 100,000 such nestboxes are sold. The Boy Scouts' bird studies merit badge book includes material provided by NABS, and countless elementary and secondary science teachers make the NABS award-winning bluebird poster and *Pocket Field Guide for Kids* part of their curriculum.

The Longest Trail
On May 20, 2000, NABS — in partnership with the retail birding supply company Wild Birds Unlimited — launched a new long-term program of far-reaching significance: the Transcontinental Bluebird Trail (TBT). As its name indicates, this project comprises a network of nestbox trails across North America. And despite its name, boxes on the TBT aren't necessarily intended for use only by bluebirds; NABS support and research has always included all native cavity-nesting birds.

On June 10, 2001, just over a year after it was first established, the TBT already spanned the North American continent with 18,587 registered nestboxes on 360 trails across the U.S. and Canada — making it the largest coordinated network of bluebird trails in existence.

Charlie Zepp from the North American Bluebird Society helps a young girl construct a nestbox at one of many NABS-sponsored workshops. Making nestboxes from scrap lumber is a popular project for workshops and high school shop classes.

But there's plenty of room for the TBT to grow. If this book inspires you to start your own trail of five boxes or more (and we hope it will), you can make it part of the TBT simply by registering it at the NABS Web site (see Resources, p. 123). This interactive Web site is a prime resource for bluebird nestbox monitors, helping them keep track of their own records and to review the statistics of all the other participants.

Of the 360 trails on the TBT, 20 are not privately managed but are operated by NABS affiliate groups as "Adopt-A-Box" trails. The Adopt-A-Box program makes it possible for everyone to participate in bluebird conservation — even those who can't monitor a nestbox themselves. The program also provides a way for garden clubs, church groups, and environmentally conscious corporations to directly assist in supporting bluebirds.

Bird Science for Citizens

Another organization that has devoted significant effort to the study of cavity-nesting birds — including bluebirds — is the Cornell Lab of Ornithology, based in Ithaca, New York. The oldest and perhaps most prominent bird research institution in the U. S., the Lab directs several "citizen-science" programs in which field research is carried out not by university scientists but by ordinary folks who care about birds. Participants in the Lab's flagship citizen science program, Project FeederWatch, have been collecting data on the birds that visit backyard feeders since 1987.

With the assistance of thousands of amateur researchers who collect data in the field across the continent, Lab ornithologists have been able to assemble — and analyze — unique sets of data. "We can address questions that we have never addressed before," says Dr. André Dhondt, director of CLO's Bird Population Studies program.

The Birdhouse Network

In 1995, Dhondt, with the help of Cornell researcher Dr. David Winkler and education specialist Rick Bonney, created a citizen-science program for the study of cavity-nesting birds. Though this program, now named The Birdhouse Network (TBN), has been in existence only a few years, it has already collected numerous useful statistics — and a few surprising bits of information — about cavity-nesting birds, many of which are cited throughout this book.

The data accumulated by TBN's citizen scientists are particularly valuable because the location of each nestbox monitored for the study can be pinpointed precisely. When participants log on to the TBN Web site (TBN is an Internet-based program) to provide data, they use maps provided by TBN to establish the latitude and longitude of each of their nestboxes to within about 30 meters!

While TBN, the Lab, and science in general benefit from the information provided by nestbox monitors who participate in The Birdhouse Network, TBN returns the favor by allowing participants to access the entire database for their own research.

Bluebird monitors with Internet access will want to check out one of the most popular features of the CLO Web site, Nest Box Cam. In operation since 1998 and receiving millions of hits every year, this site receives continuous video feed from several small cameras installed inside nestboxes. You'll get a true "bird's-eye view" of the nesting cycles of such birds as eastern bluebirds, tree swallows, Carolina chickadees, and even larger cavity-nesters such as American kestrels and barn owls. Minute-by-minute updates during the nesting season let you follow the activites in real time. For access to the Nest Box Cam — and all of TBN's Internet resources — see Resources, p. 123.

One final feature of TBN that is available to anyone who cares to participate is the listserv called Bluebird-L. Maintained as a collaborative effort by CLO and NABS, this listserv connects bluebird monitors across the continent and allows them to exchange information and advice. If you have a bluebird question that isn't answered in this book, you can subscribe to Bluebird-L and get personal answers from many of the same experts whose advice you'll read in these pages.

André A. Dhondt uses the data submitted by TBN participants to study bluebirds and other cavity-nesters. "Everyone who monitors just a box or two wonders if their small amount of data matters," Dr. Dhondt worries. "The answer is, it does!" The data are not just lumped together like votes — each bit has geographic importance.

Attracting
BLUEBIRDS
To Our Yards

by Cynthia Berger

Standing Guard
A male eastern bluebird
keeps a sharp lookout
from atop his Peterson
nestbox while his mate
prepares to exit the box.

Nestboxes for Bluebirds — A Helping Hand

Steve Garr lives near a big city — Nashville, Tennessee. "When I first moved here 15 years ago," he says, "I'd be lucky if I saw a bluebird once in a while. Now it's unusual if I don't see a bluebird every day."

The pair of colorful eastern bluebirds that Steve and his wife watch from their bedroom window didn't show up in the Garrs' backyard just by chance. The birds are there because the Garrs have welcomed them and provided for their needs — especially with regard to a nest site.

Across North America, dedicated bird lovers like the Garrs are inviting nesting bluebirds into their backyards by providing essential nesting sites. All three bluebird species (eastern, western, and mountain) are what scientists call "cavity-nesters." They build their nests in cavities — holes in dead trees and similar sheltered places. But though primary cavity-nesters such as woodpeckers can excavate their own cavities in decaying wood, secondary cavity-nesters, including bluebirds, lack the sturdy beaks and powerful muscles needed to chisel out a nest site. Instead, they use abandoned woodpecker cavities or find tree holes created by the natural action of decay.

The trouble is that these days natural cavities are rare. Across much of North America, cities, residential areas, industrial parks, and "industrialized" farms have replaced natural habitat and small family farms. Also, where forests are managed for timber, trees are harvested before they die, so there are no standing dead trees to provide nest sites for cavity-nesters. In residential areas, no one wants a dead tree in the backyard.

And in places where nesting cavities remain, they are the target of increasingly fierce competition among the birds themselves. In the last century, two cavity-nesting species introduced to North America from Europe — house (or English) sparrows and European starlings — have multiplied to be among the most abundant birds on the continent, making it harder and harder for bluebirds to find a natural nest site.

No wonder cavity-nesting birds need a helping hand. This book explains how you can help bluebirds — and other cavity-nesting birds — by providing "nestboxes" where they can safely raise their young. While the birds benefit from your generosity, you'll enjoy the sight, the song, and the fascinating behavior of these beautiful wild creatures right in your own backyard.

Nestbox (or nest box) is the accepted ornithological term for a structure that most people simply refer to as a "birdhouse" — a small, frequently house-shaped structure that is usually (but not always) rectangular and made of wood, with (again, usually but not always) a round entrance hole. Nestboxes come in many sizes and shapes, in designs that accommodate birds as small as a chickadee and as large as a wood duck. This book focuses on nestboxes that are sized to accommodate the three species of bluebirds. Because a number of other cavity-nesting species readily nest in bluebird-sized boxes, the book also covers the needs and habits of those birds. You'll find it can be just as fascinating to watch chickadees or tree swallows raise a family as it is to fledge a box of bluebirds.

This book could not have been written without the generous contributions of dozens of nestbox monitors from across North America — people who put up homes for the birds and monitor, or check regularly, to help protect the birds from predators and competitors.

In these pages, the experts tell you, in their own words, what has worked for them: how to build or buy a nestbox the birds will flock to, how to prevent predators from raiding your boxes, how to evict or deter competitors, and all the other ways that you can help cavity-nesting birds to have a successful nesting season.

The Ten Most Commonly Reported Cavity-Nesters:

Eastern bluebird
Tree swallow
House wren
House sparrow
Mountain bluebird
Western bluebird
Carolina chickadee
Black-capped chickadee
Tufted titmouse
Ash-throated flycatcher

Source: The Birdhouse Network

Eastern bluebirds pass food as a courting gesture. The male has a bright blue back; notice that the female is much grayer on the head, back, and wings.

If You Build It, Will They Come?

You say you've never seen a bluebird in your neighborhood? Welcome to the club! Many successful nestbox monitors say they'd never seen a bluebird until they set out their first nestbox.

But will you have similar success in your yard? Chances are, wherever you live, at least one species of cavity-nesting bird lives in or near your neighborhood. Note that **different birds prefer different kinds of habitat,** so a yard that's ideal for chickadees may not attract bluebirds, and vice versa.

To find out what birds you might attract to backyard nestboxes, your first step is to become familiar with your neighborhood habitat and the local bird population. If you don't know much about birds, suggests Arlene Ripley of Dunkirk, Maryland, "get a simple field guide to help you identify them." Arlene certainly knows her birds; she's the Calvert Bluebird Council county coordinator.

Your next step, says Arlene: "Go out and observe! Look for boxes in other yards. Ask those neighbors if they are getting bluebirds or other cavity-nesters."

And of course, scan for the birds themselves. Have you seen chickadees at a backyard birdfeeder? Do swallows perch on an overhead power line? If you are hoping to attract bluebirds, Arlene says, it's fairly easy to tell if they're already in your neighborhood. "They're not hard to spot because **they like to hunt out in the open,"** she says. "You'll see them sitting on fence posts or flying down to look for insects on lawns."

"Open space" was the phrase we heard over and over again when we asked the experts what kind of habitat bluebirds prefer. "Eastern bluebirds need mowed meadows," says Barbara Chambers of Annandale, Virginia. "Unless your house is located near fields and meadows that are mowed or where the grass is low, you won't get bluebirds. These birds are ground-feeders. They like to sit on a perch, look for insects on the ground, then fly down and get that grasshopper or caterpillar. That's how they do it."

Erv Davis, who sees both western and mountain bluebirds on his trails in northwestern Montana, says, "Pine trees with open areas — that's prime habitat for westerns. They seem to like areas with trees, along the gulches, as opposed to the wide-open, barren sagebrush areas at higher elevation." On the other hand, says Erv, "pasture lands, open areas with a few scattered juniper trees and sagebrush — that seems to be choice habitat for mountain bluebirds." Western and mountain bluebirds usually forage the same way as eastern bluebirds — they choose a lofty place to sit while they eyeball the ground, looking for food.

Note that because bluebirds need those perches, truly wide-open spaces don't make great bluebird habitat. Look for areas that have fences, scattered

A family of eastern bluebirds perches on a fence. Notice that young eastern bluebirds have spots on their breasts, backs, and shoulders. After two or three months, they gradually molt to adult plumage. Juveniles from a second or third brood molt sooner.

trees, or utility lines. "You don't want four acres of pastureland, and you don't want heavy woods," says Ron Kingston of Charlottesville, Virginia. "But you need *some* trees so bluebirds can perch and search for insects down below."

If there are no trees or other perches nearby, Dorene Scriven of the Minnesota Bluebird Recovery Project advises that you erect some kind of perching post so the bluebirds will have a place from which to scout when they hunt for food. Some nestbox monitors attach a tree branch to the top of the nestbox.

You don't have to live on a farm to attract bluebirds. Across North America, bluebird enthusiasts are challenging the accepted wisdom that you must live in a rural area on a property with acres of open space to attract these striking birds to your yard.

EASTERN BLUEBIRD

SUMMER
WINTER
ALL YEAR
MIGRATION

TUFTED TITMOUSE

Dick Walker monitors several nestboxes in postage-stamp-sized yards in the small town of Loogootee, Indiana. He says, **"Bluebirds will nest in town.** I'll put a box up in a yard if there's a clearing of at least 50 feet all the way around the nestbox."

Nashville, Tennessee, is hardly a small town, yet eastern bluebirds are thriving there, practically in the shadow of skyscrapers, thanks to the efforts of Steve Garr. Fifteen years ago, Steve recalls, he would see bluebird boxes only in rural areas, on farmland, or perhaps in subdivisions with large lots. "Then new subdivisions were built, and the birds needed cavities to replace the ones they had lost," Steve says.

As he convinced folks in the new subdivisions to put up nestboxes, the bluebirds moved in. And the birds have continued to expand their range. "The next thing you know," Steve says, "people were getting bluebirds 5 to 10 miles from the place where they were originally found" and the birds were nesting in smaller and smaller yards. "This year we had 16 eastern bluebirds fledge from seven nest starts in downtown Nashville, and we also fledged 4 tree swallows and 23 chickadees," he says with glee.

Nestbox monitor Ann Wick also sees bluebirds in suburbia. Near the small midwestern town of Black Earth, Wisconsin, where she lives, new subdivisions seem to be sprouting everywhere. The rows of houses replace farm fields and open areas, yet Ann says she's noticed that the spacious yards can make good bluebird habitat. "The birds have adjusted," she notes. "They use gutters and swing sets as perches to hunt insects from."

Even if your house is on a very small lot with practically no usable bluebird habitat, Ron Kingston says, "it's still very possible you could attract bluebirds if there is some kind of wild area or buffer zone nearby — an industrial park or federal complex where the lawns are mowed, or a big cemetery."

"If you saw my yard," says Arlene Ripley, "you would never think that bluebirds nest here." But they do, even though Arlene's backyard in suburban Maryland is completely surrounded by trees, with

This tufted titmouse is easy to identify — notice the prominent crest. Males and females look alike. Titmice are members of the chickadee family.

very little open space. "I don't think your yard necessarily has to be open in order to attract bluebirds," Arlene says. "I think the main thing is that you have to know that bluebirds are in your area."

Tree swallows often use the same habitat as bluebirds, but open spaces near water — a lake or marsh — are especially attractive for this species. If your yard is heavily wooded or borders on forested land, your backyard nestbox may attract chickadees or titmice. Areas with thick underbrush or shrubs provide a haven for wrens.

The sidebar (left) provides more specific information on the habitat preferences of the common native cavity-nesting species that use bluebird-sized boxes (other than the three bluebirds already discussed).

When They Come, Will They Be Safe?

So you've established that you *can* attract bluebirds to your backyard nestboxes. The next question to ask is whether you *should.* And the answer to that depends greatly on the presence or absence of a chunky little bird introduced from Europe and parts of Asia — the **house sparrow.** As the name suggests, house sparrows thrive around houses; they're also common around barns and outbuildings and in the center of many cities.

"If you live in a neighborhood with a lot of house sparrows, I just don't recommend putting up bluebird boxes," says Arlene Ripley. "Even if you're willing to be very vigilant about removing the sparrows from

Nesting Habitat for Some Common Cavity-Nesting Birds

- *Tree Swallow: Open fields near water such as ponds and lakes, expansive open areas, marshes, meadows, wooded swamps*
- *Tufted Titmouse: Deciduous forests, thick timber stands, woodland clearings, forest edges, woodlots, riparian and mesquite habitats*
- *Black-capped Chickadee: Forests, woodlots, and yards with mature hardwood trees, forest edges, meadows*
- *Carolina Chickadee: Deciduous and mixed deciduous-coniferous forests, rural woodlands, swamps, thickets, parks, suburban areas*
- *House Wren: Farmland, open forests, forest edges, hedgerows, shrub lands, suburban gardens, parks, backyards; avoids heavily forested habitat*
- *Ash-throated Flycatcher: Desert scrub, piñon-juniper and oak woodlands, chaparral, thorn scrub, woodlands near water*

Source: The Birdhouse Network of Cornell Lab of Ornithology.

your nestboxes, other sparrows will move right in. You'll be inviting bluebirds into a box to die."

House sparrows (they're not actually sparrows but members of the "weaver finch" family) were deliberately released in the U.S. in the 1850s. It was thought that they would gobble up insect pests, but instead they turned out to be pests in their own right. On farms they especially damage grain and fruit crops. House sparrows also pose a serious threat to native birds because they compete aggressively for nesting cavities.

Ann Wick tells the cautionary tale of how house sparrows discovered the very first nestbox she mounted in her yard. "I thought I had *no* chance of getting bluebirds in town, but I put up a nestbox, and lo and behold, in a few days I had a pair!" Ann says. "The nestbox was right outside the window, so we could see what was going on. My son was little at the time. We were all so excited.

"The bluebirds pulled off a first nesting," Ann continues. "One day when the nestlings were about nine days old, I looked out the window and saw a male house sparrow go in the box. Not knowing what I know now, I didn't intervene. I said, 'Let nature take its course.'"

The male house sparrow killed two of the five bluebird nestlings and seriously injured the others. When Ann took them to a wildlife rehabilitator, the rehabber had to euthanize the birds — their beaks were so badly damaged, they would never have been able to feed on their own.

"After that experience, I decided I couldn't go through such a disaster again!" Ann says. "You draw the birds into your yard, your small children are fascinated, and then you watch the birds die. After that, I read every book I could find so I wouldn't make the same mistake the second time."

The most obvious way to keep house sparrows away from your boxes is to keep your boxes away from house sparrows. If house sparrows are in the area but your yard is spacious, position your box well away from your home or any outbuildings, and sparrows will be less likely to move in.

However, if house sparrows are everywhere on your property, you are in for a battle if you decide to attempt to attract bluebirds. The North American Bluebird Society (NABS) divides house sparrow control measures into "passive control" (you discourage the birds from nesting) and "aggressive control" (you interfere with the nesting process or the birds themselves). You'll find more details on sparrow control measures in Chapter 4; sparrow traps are described in Chapter 5.

Unlike house sparrows, house wrens are a native species, and you may consider them to be welcome backyard visitors because of their melodious songs. But be aware that, just like house sparrows, **house wrens routinely take over nestboxes** occupied by

House sparrows claim a nestbox. The black bib and head markings of the male house sparrow are distinctive identifying marks. Female house sparrows are more nondescript. Look for a clear (unspotted) breast, a single bar of white on each wing, and a plain head with only a pale line behind the eye to distinguish it.

bluebirds, swallows, or others. The house wrens will puncture or discard the eggs and sometimes remove young nestlings from a box in order to take it over.

"I once saw a wren leaving the box with a bluebird egg stuck on its beak!" says Bill Reddy of Galena, Illinois. "They're tough little birds." It was a house wren that Bill saw, not just any wren. Carolina wrens and Bewick's wrens are not a threat to other cavity-nesters and are welcomed by nestbox monitors.

House wrens like brush and hedges — any thick, low cover. They nest in much of the U.S. and southern Canada where they can find suitable habitat, although they avoid the hot summer weather of the southeastern and south-central states (see range map, p. 14). House wrens do most of their damage where they compete with eastern bluebirds. They are less of a problem west of the Rockies.

You cannot use the same techniques to control house wrens that you use on house sparrows because, as a native species, wrens and their eggs are protected under federal law. The only way to keep house wrens from taking over your nestbox is to place the box well away from that ornamental hedge or the tangle of raspberry canes at the back of the garden that they prefer.

"Wrens don't seem comfortable out in the open," says New Hampshire nestbox monitor Bruce Burdett. "It's good to place the boxes at least 100

HOUSE SPARROW

HOUSE WREN

feet out from the nearest thicket," he advises. That's the standard recommendation, but Dorene Scriven says 100 feet isn't always enough. In some areas, she says, "wrens have been seen to go more than 200 feet out into the open to cause havoc at bluebird boxes."

If you have house wrens around your property and you don't have a large open area well away from shrubs and underbrush, you might still be able to safely attract bluebirds to a nestbox. It's a matter of timing. In many locations, bluebirds return from migration weeks before house wrens do. By the time the house wrens arrive, bluebird eggs have usually hatched, and wrens aren't much of a threat to nestlings. Once the bluebirds have fledged their first nestful of young, you should close up the box or remove it. If you don't take these steps, you are likely to find your box stuffed full of twigs — the sure sign that a house wren has found it. (See p. 26 to learn how nestbox monitors deal with nestboxes taken over by house wrens.)

If your yard is not fit for bluebirds because of house sparrows or poor habitat, you can still find ways to enjoy bluebirds and help them prosper. Ann Wick, the nestbox monitor who had such a devastating experience with house sparrows, didn't give up. "I decided to seek out areas away from house sparrow habitat that would be safe for bluebirds," Ann says. Her father-in-law had just purchased an old farmstead with grassland areas bordering woods, so Ann went over the property and put up a series of boxes, creating a nestbox trail. "With more boxes," Ann says, "I decided that even if I had a disaster once in a while, at least some of the birds would make out OK."

Getting Started...by the Book

"Two years ago," says Diane Bingeman, "I didn't know if I could get bluebirds here or not. I'd never seen a bluebird in my life!" Today Diane, a registered nurse who lives in Beech, North Dakota, is a brand-new nestbox monitor.

Diane says, "When I was considering the idea of attracting bluebirds, the first thing I did was check the range maps in my field guide to see if I was even in an area where they would come." She learned that North Dakota is at the extreme western edge of the eastern bluebird's range. "I also wasn't sure if I had the right habitat," Diane continues. "According to what I read, bluebirds like to have space around the nesting area where they can find food, on the ground with short grass."

Initially Diane wanted to put up bluebird boxes in her own backyard. Armed with information about the birds' habitat preferences, she instead decided to place the boxes in a vacant lot next door. "They're in the far end of the lot," she notes. "There's quite a lot of space between our house and the boxes." The nearest trees are about 200 feet away.

Diane says she set her boxes out early in spring, and it took only three weeks for bluebirds to find one of them. "When I saw the pair I couldn't believe it," says Diane. "I had to have my husband, Michael, come out and take a look. He said, yes, that's two bluebirds!" Diane's birds did well their first season: they laid five eggs, hatched four chicks, and all four chicks fledged.

This house wren has caught a spider to serve to its nestlings. Male and female house wrens look alike. The male wren has a distinctive loud, bubbling song.

Dick Purvis of Anaheim, California, also encourages people to look beyond their backyards. "There are hundreds of locations that are ideal for bluebirds but have no nestboxes," he says. "Consider setting up a trail on a golf course, in a park, or in a cemetery where there are no wrens or house sparrows."

Barbara Chambers, the educational vice president of the Virginia Bluebird Society, is another nestbox monitor who has opted for a trail rather than backyard boxes. The reason, explains Barbara, is that she lives close to the Beltway that encircles Washington, D.C. "I'm in a suburban neighborhood on a cul-de-sac; my yard is wooded; and there's not enough lawn," she says. So Barbara monitors trails on area golf courses. When she found bluebirds in a small park near her house, she got permission from the Fairfax County park authority to put up boxes there. Now, Barbara says, she can enjoy the beauty of bluebirds — and she knows the birds are safe. (For more ideas on how to start a bluebird trail, turn to Chapter 3.)

If house sparrows roam your yard and you're too busy or physically unable to do the sometimes arduous work of monitoring a trail, there are other ways you can make a difference for cavity-nesting birds. Ann Wick points out that "many bluebird organizations, including the North American Bluebird Society (NABS), have 'Adopt-A-Box' programs." Alicia Craig, senior manager for nature education at Wild Birds Unlimited, suggests you consider donating a box to a nature center.

"One of the things we should all do," Alicia adds, "whether we are putting up nestboxes in our own yards or on public lands or donating a box, is to share the experience with children. I think all of us who have a passion for birds owe it to future generations to share our passion with them."

Selecting a Nestbox — And a Place to Put It

You've established that you have good bluebird habitat in your yard and house sparrows aren't a problem. Now you are wondering exactly **what kind of box** to put up. Some of the nestboxes on the market today are intended to be decorative rather than functional. A box that is elaborately painted or covered with decorations is probably not constructed to specifications that will work well for real birds — enjoy it in your living room rather than in your yard. Also avoid boxes with a perch below the entrance hole. Bluebirds and other native species don't need a perch; it only helps house sparrows to clamber inside.

Most of the truly functional bluebird boxes are approved by NABS, and manufacturers prominently display this approval. But even among these well-designed boxes, the choices can be bewildering. Which is the best? All of the manufacturers will be happy to explain in detail why the boxes they make are the best ones available.

In Chapter 5, Keith Kridler will help you make your nestbox choice. He describes the range of boxes available and the advantages and disadvantages of the different models so that you can make the best choice for your circumstances. Depending on your locale and preferences, certain features will be more desirable than others. For example, good ventilation will be more important if you live in a hot climate, and a side-opening box may be preferable to a top-opening box if you plan to monitor frequently. Keith also provides details on how to build your own nestbox.

Most often, however, **"It's not the box that counts, it's where you put it."** That's the title of

A male western bluebird at his nestbox. Western males often have a patch of red on their backs, an identifying mark that is not seen on eastern males.

WESTERN BLUEBIRD

an article that Dean Sheldon of Greenwich, Ohio, once wrote for the quarterly newsletter of the Ohio Bluebird Society. Even though proponents of different style boxes sometimes argue loudly over their relative merits, nearly all agree that proper positioning of the boxes is critical. We've already discussed how a box that is too close to house sparrow or house wren habitat will not be safe for bluebirds.

Bluebirds are most apt to occupy a nestbox that is in or near the short-grass areas where they like to feed. Exceptions to this rule are rare, although Linda Violett of Yorba Linda, California, says she's

Western bluebirds enjoy a snack at a mealworm feeder. Where eastern and western bluebird ranges overlap, a sure way to separate the birds is by throat color. Eastern bluebirds of both sexes have reddish throats. Western bluebird males have a blue throat and upper breast; females have white throats.

had western bluebirds fledge successfully from a box hung over a parking lot. "To forage, the birds had to fly across the lot to get to a nearby baseball field, where they had to compete with ballplayers

Mountain bluebirds are larger and more elongated than eastern or western bluebirds. Male mountain bluebirds are almost entirely sky blue. Females are mostly gray, with blue feathers only in their wings and tails. Some have dull reddish tones on the breast.

and dozens of starlings for insects in the grassy outfield," she notes.

Your first impulse may be to **mount your nestbox where you can see it:** for example, outside the kitchen window or close to your porch or deck. It truly is delightful to have a close-up view of your backyard guests. It's also practical. Haleya Priest of Amherst, Massachusetts, says she tries to put her backyard boxes where she can easily see them from her windows — "both for the pleasure of seeing the birds and for the ability to watch out for trouble. I had one box that was so far from the house I didn't have a good view," she says, "and I had a couple of predator problems that I might have been able to prevent if the box had been closer to the house."

To encourage bluebirds to choose the box that's visible from his bedroom window, Steve Garr says he leaves an offering of tasty mealworms (p. 70) near the box.

The presence of house sparrows or house wrens may make it necessary to place your nestbox some distance from the house, however, or even out of sight. Your first consideration should be the birds' needs rather than your own.

Placing a nestbox in **sun or shade can make a big difference** to the birds inside. Which location is better depends on local conditions. If your spring weather tends to be chilly, placing a box in full sun can help keep the nestlings comfortably warm inside. On the other hand, if your summers are especially hot, try to position boxes so that they're shaded by nearby trees. "That's the perfect situation," says Don Hutchings, who lives in east Texas, where summer temperatures can hit 106 degrees. For extra protection from the sun, Don collects old shingles, preferably white, and attaches them to the top of each box with silicon cement. White shingles reflect the sunlight, so he feels the box stays a bit cooler with the reflective roofing.

Sun and storm conditions play a role in choosing **the best direction to face the entrance hole.** In the early 1980s, Ohio nestbox monitor Dick Tuttle showed that when the sun shines directly into a nestbox, it can raise the temperature inside by as much as 5 degrees — maybe more. Whether this elevation in temperature is helpful or harmful depends upon your local conditions.

Recent findings from Cornell's Birdhouse Network suggest that birds residing in cooler areas, where morning temperatures are often low, have better nesting success in boxes facing east or northeast, where they can most benefit from the early morning sun warming up the nestbox.

It's never a good idea to position a box so that wind or driving rain can blow in through the entrance hole, however. If your bad weather generally comes from one direction, make sure the entrance hole faces a different direction.

Compare this young mountain bluebird to the juvenile eastern bluebirds on p. 11. Note that it lacks spots on its back, and the breast spots are very faint.

A major concern with regard to the orientation of the entrance hole is the needs of the young birds when they fledge. When fledglings make their first fluttering flight, they need a convenient perch where they can pause and rest safely. It's a good idea to position the box so the entrance hole faces a tree, shrub, or fence line about 100 feet away.

Another consideration with regard to box orientation: can bluebirds that are scouting for a nest site see the entrance hole? Imagine yourself as a bluebird flying across the yard. Is the dark entrance hole easy to spot, or is it hidden?

To make your boxes even more alluring, Don Yoder, the program director for the California Bluebird Recovery Program, recommends a bluebird-attracting strategy that he calls **"the attraction spot."** It's a black spot, an inch and a half in diameter, painted on the upper part of each side of the box. Says Don, "We believe the bird sees it from a distance and thinks, 'Perhaps that's a cavity! I should go look,' and then goes closer to the box and finds the real entrance hole. Some people say putting the spot on doesn't make a bit of difference, but I do think it makes the box more easily found." Instead of painting a spot on the box, some nestbox monitors make an attraction spot out of black electrical tape, which is easy to remove once the box is occupied.

Finally, do your planning for perfect box placement early in the year — birds won't be able to find your nestbox if the nestbox isn't there for them to find. Make sure you **get your box up before the birds start scouting** for nesting sites. In southern parts of the United States — in fact, even as far north as Ohio — the first male bluebirds may be busily inspecting possible nest sites as early as mid-February. In areas where bluebirds are resident year-round, put the boxes up anytime; don't wait for spring. Nestboxes with their vents and most of

their drain holes plugged can serve as roost sites in winter — cozy places where bluebirds can sleep warm and safe from predators.

If you put up a single box and it doesn't attract bluebirds, try putting up two boxes...or three or more. Multiple boxes may increase your chances of attracting a pair of nesting bluebirds. Even if there is only enough habitat available to support a single pair of bluebirds, Steve Garr says, go ahead and put up two or three boxes. "You never know which box a bluebird is going to decide that it likes the best," he says. "So you have a better chance of bluebirds nesting if you put up more than one box."

Note that unless the boxes are far enough apart, you won't get more than a single pair of bluebirds. Bluebirds are territorial; both males and females will fight vigorously to defend a territory from other bluebirds. As a rule of thumb, to attract more than one pair of bluebirds to your property, you need to place the boxes at least 100 yards apart.

This guideline makes it sound like small yards can hold only a single box; sometimes, however, boxes can be placed closer together if the occupants can't see each other — for example, if boxes are placed on opposite sides of a house. Co-author Keith Kridler suggests that if your property is surrounded by good bluebird habitat, you can try placing a box in each corner even if your lot is smaller than an acre. "The bluebirds will feed in the outlying areas beyond your property rather than compete for foraging rights in your backyard," he says.

Not only are you more likely to entice a bluebird with a choice of boxes, notes Steve Garr, but multiple living spaces also means you could end up with a variety of bird tenants. "If a bluebird does nest in one corner," he notes, "you might get a titmouse or

Bluebirding...by Murphy's Law

So you're a new nestbox monitor, and you're worried that you might make a few mistakes. Consider Doug LeVasseur's story. Doug had no idea that eastern bluebirds nested on his Ohio farm until the day a neighbor came looking for a lost cow. "We both heard this pretty song from the top of a walnut tree," Doug remembers, "and the neighbor said, 'Oh, I see you've got bluebirds down here.'" That's when Doug decided to put up his first bluebird box.

"I was sort of on my own that first year or so," he says. "There were no local bluebird organizations. So, like anybody starting out on their own, I did absolutely everything wrong!" First, he mounted the box right at the top of the walnut tree, where he had seen the bluebird. "It was a difficult place to monitor," Doug remembers. "I had to climb up on a real long extension ladder. And of course I'd built my box very solidly, so I couldn't open it to look inside. Also, I didn't protect the box from any kind of predators — anything I could possibly do wrong, I did do wrong."

Fast-forward almost two decades. Doug knows a lot more about bluebirds these days. He monitors an 18-box trail with all the boxes built and mounted to NABS specifications. And incidentally, he was recently elected president of the North American Bluebird Society. Everyone has to start somewhere.

a chickadee in the other corner." These birds prefer to nest far from other members of their same species, but they will tolerate a neighbor of a different species.

Mounting a Nestbox — For Convenience and Safety

You've chosen the spot; now it's time to mount the nestbox. You'll probably be tempted to nail it to a support structure that's already in your yard, such as a tree or fence post, says Ray Briggs of Cobleskill, New York. "A lot of people, when they get their first nestbox, will nail it to a tree because it's so easy," he notes. "But that's the wrong place to place a box." Most of the animals that prey on eggs and nestlings can climb trees with ease. So unless you know that raccoons, snakes, and other nestbox predators are rare in your area, avoid the temptation to use tree trunks and posts as mounts.

Most experts recommend that you **mount boxes on smooth metal poles.** Among the nestbox monitors we talked to, the preferred metal mounting post is ½- or ¾-inch electrical conduit, which is inexpensive and readily available at building supply stores. Raccoons, most snakes, and other nestbox predators have a hard time scaling the slippery surface.

"I like to make the pole even slicker by rubbing it with steel wool," says Steve Gilbertson of Aitkin, Minnesota. For the finishing touch, he polishes the metal pole with carnauba wax (an auto paste wax) to make it extra slippery. (See Chapter 5 for more details on conduit and other recommended mounting methods. We'll even tell you how hanging boxes from tree branches turns out to be a *good* idea under certain conditions.)

Most bluebird monitors we talked to mount boxes at a height that's convenient for monitoring. The magic height seems to be eye level — about 5 feet off the ground, maybe a little lower for top-opening boxes. Note that bluebirds aren't fussy about the height of their nests; they will happily nest anywhere from a few feet above the ground to high up in a tree. The other small cavity-nesting species are similarly versatile, although swallows seem to show a preference for higher boxes and wrens often prefer lower ones.

If cats are a problem, put boxes out of their reach. Clay Billman of Stillwater, Oklahoma, initially mounted his backyard box with the entrance hole about 5½ feet off the ground. Clay and his wife, Ginger, were enjoying the sight of their first pair of nesting bluebirds when one morning Ginger was horrified to discover blue feathers in the yard. Clay immediately suspected the neighbor's cat. "Sure enough, there were signs of fur around the box," he says.

To keep your nestbox safe from cats, you must mount your boxes as high as 7 feet above the

Ash-throated flycatchers bring food to their nestbox. Rusty red in the wings and tail is an identifying mark that is most obvious in flight. In the East, the great crested flycatcher is similar but slightly larger.

ground. Some cats will leap 6 feet to snatch a bird, and 5 feet is a gimme!

When a box is mounted more than 5 feet high, however, it can be difficult to carry out routine monitoring. Gary Springer of Carnesville, Georgia, keeps a lightweight fiberglass stepladder handy for his nestbox checks. "It's really easy to carry," he says. Some other monitors use a mirror mounted on a long-handled pole to get a reflected view inside boxes mounted above eye level. But the most convenient solution is to mount your box on a telescoping pole (p. 108) so you can raise it out of the reach of predators and lower it easily for monitoring. Hatch Graham of Eldorado County, California, says, "I use an elevator pole that puts the box up 9 feet. It is still easy to monitor." Telescoping poles are easy to make and inexpensive.

Besides cats, you may have to prepare for other predators. Raccoons are common in suburban neighborhoods, and black rat snakes are the bane of nestbox monitors in southeastern states. Opossums and squirrels have been known to take eggs from nestboxes just about anywhere; starlings, crows, jays, and magpies can also be nestbox predators. In New Mexico, Rob Yaksich has even had black bears demolish his nestboxes.

Although a polished conduit mounting pole will deter most raccoons and other climbers, they have less trouble scaling other kinds of mounting poles, including metal water pipe or PVC pipe. The classic way to **baffle climbing predators** such as 'coons and snakes is with devices called, appropriately enough, "baffles." Some nestbox monitors start out without any baffles because they take time to make and install and are an extra expense. But you might instead think of baffles as insurance policies. You may get through repeated nesting seasons without them, but when a predator finally turns a nestbox into a coffin, well... "I am sick with guilt because I could have prevented this" were the words of one nestbox monitor who lost a clutch of nestlings to a raccoon.

One especially popular and effective baffle is made from a length of stovepipe or PVC pipe suspended below the nestbox over the mounting pole. This and many other baffle options are described in detail in Chapter 5.

Jim Walters of Iowa City, Iowa, has used stovepipe baffles since the early 1990s. "We use them on our pole-mounted houses, and they have eliminated all raccoon predation," he says. If you're not convinced that baffles keep 'coons away, Ron Kingston has solid evidence. When his backyard birdfeeder was being raided each night by a large raccoon, Ron took one of the stovepipe baffles he uses on his nestboxes and put it on the feeder pole. "That night we got beeped by our backyard motion detector," says Ron. "And there was the raccoon at the bottom of the pole. It was looking around, trying to get up!" But no such luck.

An alternative to a pole-mounted baffle is a hole guard attached right to the box itself. Some prefabricated nestboxes come with a built-in "raccoon guard" consisting of a flat piece of wood mounted on the front of the box so that the entrance hole passes through an extra inch or so of wood (p. 118). In theory, the extra thickness prevents a raccoon or cat from sticking its paw inside the box.

In practice, says Dr. Kevin Berner, the NABS research chairman who has tested predator guards with a captive raccoon, "by no stretch of the imagination does the extra thickness of wood keep raccoons out." What's more, he says, this kind of guard sometimes seems to discourage birds from using the box.

Wood-block hole guards *are* useful in limiting the distance that birds such as starlings, jays, and crows can reach into a nestbox. Although these birds are too large to actually enter a bluebird nestbox, they will stand on its roof, stick their heads inside, and lunch on bluebird eggs or young. Once a single bird masters the trick, it can do great damage on a trail. And other birds may learn from it. Note that raids by birds other than house wrens or house sparrows are not normally a problem for backyard nestbox monitors. This kind of predation is more common along nestbox trails. But if such a problem does develop, the wood-block hole guard is worth a try.

Tree swallows display at a nestbox. The male (right) is calling and performing a gaping display as part of courtship. Note how the female is a duller color and has less sheen than the male.

Nestbox monitors told us that the way they most often use a wood-block hole guard is to repair a box after its entrance hole has been enlarged by woodpeckers or squirrels. (You don't want to leave a damaged box in this condition because, when the hole is larger than 1 9/16 inches in diameter, starlings are able to squeeze inside and take over the box.) Since a wood-block hole guard has a predrilled entrance hole of the proper diameter, you can quickly repair a box with a chewed-up entrance hole by tacking the hole guard on the front of the box. It's easier than replacing the entire front board.

Although a wood-block hole guard will not deter raccoons and cats, other kinds of box-mounted guards do exist that will make it difficult to impossible for raccoons and cats to reach through the guard and down into a nest. Hole guards are described in Chapter 5.

Box-mounted predator guards make a lot of sense if for some reason a nestbox is mounted on a post, a tree, or some other object that can't be baffled. But most nestbox monitors agree with Dan Sparks of the Brown County Bluebird Society in Nashville, Indiana, who says, "I prefer to prevent the predator from reaching the nestbox in the first place." Raccoons will rip apart all but the sturdiest boxes to get to the birds inside. "Would you want to put a female bluebird that is sitting on eggs through the trauma of having a raccoon or cat trying to claw its way into the box every night?" asks Keith Kridler. A pole-mounted baffle that keeps predators away from the box is really your best bet.

TREE SWALLOW

Several species of chickadees use nestboxes. The most commonly reported are the Carolina chickadee (above) and the nearly identical black-capped chickadee. The two species have separate ranges with only a narrow band of overlap.

CAROLINA CHICKADEE

BLACK-CAPPED CHICKADEE

More Than Nestboxes — Food and Drink for Bluebirds

Once you've got your boxes mounted and ready for the bluebirds to arrive, consider adding other features to make your yard even more hospitable.

Says Arlene Ripley, "I think **water is another big attraction,** even if it's just a small birdbath." Birds need water both for drinking and for bathing. Home-and-garden stores and birding supply stores now offer a wide range of attractive birdbaths that not only complement your garden decor but are easy to keep clean and also safe for birds to use (look for baths that are shallow — just an inch or two deep — and that offer places to perch).

"My birdbath overflows with baby bluebirds,"

says Kerry Sweet of Talala, Oklahoma. "I see them four and five at a time all day. It's like a swim party!"

If bluebirds live in your vicinity year-round, use an inexpensive outdoor electric heater to keep the water from freezing in winter. Your birdbath will become a "bird magnet," says Koby Prater of Seneca, Missouri. "Since I went ahead and got a new birdbath with a built-in heater, I've seen gobs of birds — six or seven bluebirds at a time!"

Trees and bushes that provide **berries also attract birds.** When a stretch of cold spring weather temporarily knocks out the insect population, bluebirds turn to berries to tide them over. Steve Garr, who often leads seminars on how to attract box-nesting birds, says, "We encourage people to plant an assortment of trees and shrubs so that something is producing berries in the spring, summer, and fall and so that berries are also available in the wintertime."

Many nestbox monitors provide mealworms to bluebirds, both as a supplement during hard times and as treats. A favorite trick is to whistle to the birds when the mealworms are set out. Fawzi Emad of Laytonville, Maryland, says, "The bluebirds are used to my whistle and will come to feed as soon as they hear it." Fawzi also provides a birdbath and a dripper, which he says they seem to enjoy with abandon.

Jane Beauregard of West Monroe, Louisiana, feeds mealworms to her bluebirds year-round. And the bluebirds know who provides their treats. "I've had them follow me when I walk around the neighborhood," she says.

You'll find more information about feeding bluebirds in Chapter 4.

Eastern bluebirds enjoy a refreshing dip in the birdbath. Young bluebirds are especially enthusiastic bathers.

How We MONITOR

Our Backyard "Blues"

by Jack Griggs and Cynthia Berger

Keeping Records
An important part of nestbox monitoring is keeping good records.

The Importance of Monitoring —
For Nesting Success and for Science

What, exactly, is monitoring? It's simple, really. On a regular basis, you peek inside a nestbox — or you watch the activity around the box — to see how its residents are doing. If there's a problem, you try to solve it. It's also a good idea to take a few notes while you're monitoring, either for your own information or to send to TBN or NABS, where your data will add to the sum total of scientific knowledge about birds.

Must you monitor your boxes? Experienced nestbox monitors agree: if you put up a nestbox, you should monitor it. "If you can't check regularly, we would say don't put up a bluebird box," says Dorene Scriven, chair of the Minnesota Bluebird Recovery Program. Regular monitoring is especially critical for backyard boxes because of the risk that house sparrows will claim the bluebirds' boxes or interfere with their nesting.

Many first-time monitors worry they will scare their bluebirds away if they get too close to the box while the birds are around. As one beginning monitor told us, "I worry about opening the box and finding a female sitting on a nest. Is this a problem?"

Some birds are quite sensitive to disturbances while nesting, but bluebirds are fairly tolerant of people. They do sometimes abandon their nests or even their eggs, but not because of humans. "In years of monitoring thousands of nests, I have never had bluebirds abandon a nest because of my interference," says Dick Purvis of Anaheim, California. "I always lift the incubating female to count the eggs or chicks," he notes. "Many times, when I replace her, she will stay on the nest."

Some new monitors fear that if they touch the nest or chicks, the human scent will make the parents desert the clutch. Though it's true some birds have a well-developed sense of smell, bluebirds (and most other songbirds) do not. So you don't need to worry that a whiff of "eau de human being" will send the parents packing.

An ash-throated flycatcher exits a box. Flycatchers seldom stay on the nest when a box is monitored.

Monitoring is important for more than house sparrow control. Problems can arise during nesting that you can correct or help prevent. Exactly what problems might develop depends on what stage of the nesting cycle your birds are at. In this chapter, we'll describe the possible problems at each stage and offer solutions from experienced monitors.

Regular monitoring has benefits for you, as well as for the birds. "That's how you learn about bluebirds, by monitoring the boxes on a regular basis," says Don Hutchings of Winfield, Texas.

Besides regular monitoring, says Dorene Scriven, "the next most important thing you can do is to keep records." Scientists need and want the data you'll collect so that they can learn more about bird biology and behavior. Nestbox data can be valuable for the study of such topics as geographic differences in clutch size and the effects of weather on hatch date.

The monitoring schedule for a backyard nestbox is very flexible. You can visit whenever you are curious, for the most part. A minimum once-a-week box check is the "industry standard" for trail operators, but monitors of backyard bluebirds typically check their boxes much more frequently.

"I think the more often you check, the more you learn and the more fun it is," says Bill Reddy of Galena, Illinois. "If I am in my yard and see a bluebird exit the box, I like to go have a peek," agrees co-author Keith Kridler. It's unlikely that brief visits bother the birds.

"You don't necessarily have to look inside a box to know that all is well," advises Don Wilkins of Park Rapids, Minnesota. If you can see your

---

Bluebirds of Happiness

Experts agree: regular nestbox monitoring is critical for the benefit of the birds. But for Nathan Jennings, age 19, monitoring brought an unexpected personal benefit — it's how he met his girlfriend. Nathan has been monitoring nestboxes since he was in seventh grade. "My middle school teacher, Dick Tuttle, was always talking about bluebirds, so I set up a box in my yard and got a pair of bluebirds the second season," Nathan says. Since then, Nathan's interest in bluebirds has grown — and so have his monitoring responsibilities. Last year he monitored more than 250 nestboxes in and around his hometown of Sudbury, Ohio. And now that he's the head volunteer at Sharon Woods Metro Park, Nathan also trains the group of volunteers who check boxes on the park's 40-box trail. That's how Nathan met Julie. "They asked me to train a new volunteer, and it was her," he says. Now Nathan and Julie do their monitoring visits together. Says Nathan, "It gives a whole new meaning to the idea that bluebirds symbolize happiness!"

nestbox from your house window, you are monitoring the box every time you spend a few minutes watching the activity around it. "If I see normal activity, I don't even go up to the box," Don says. "If the parents are sitting up on the power line or feeding nearby, then even if they're not going in the box, I figure everything's OK."

If you have nestboxes you don't see routinely, make sure to check them every week. "If you wait and check every two weeks, an entire part of the nesting cycle could be completed between your visits," says Dorene Scriven. "The eggs take about two weeks to hatch; the babies take about two weeks to fledge. You can't deal with any problems that come up if you check only every two weeks."

Your visits don't have to be precisely seven days apart, however. In fact, if your schedule says "time to monitor" and it's pouring rain, it's a good idea to change your plans. "I don't ever monitor when it's raining," says Ann Wick of Black Earth, Wisconsin, "because the birds are stressed enough about trying to find food without me complicating their lives by opening the nestbox."

It doesn't take long to complete **a monitoring visit.** "Once you are used to the procedure for monitoring, it should take you less than a minute to check a box," says Elsie Eltzroth, who coordinates the monitoring activities for a whole cadre of bluebird volunteers in Corvallis, Oregon.

If you are monitoring an active nest in your backyard, watch and wait until both adults are out of the box before you go up to it and open the door. When you monitor a remote box, keep your eye out for bluebirds as you approach it. If your records show that there is an active nest in the box, try to spot both the male and the female, just to assure yourself that they are still alive and tending the nest. Many monitors warn of their approach by whistling, and some bring along a treat of mealworms. Once the birds learn to expect mealworms, they will come readily to a whistle.

A whistled call also warns any adult inside a nestbox of your approach. Elsie suggests tapping gently on the box if you think it might be occupied. That will alert the adult so it can leave the box if it wishes. Elsie also reminds her monitors to open a box slowly and not to stand directly in front of the entrance hole — instead, stand off to one side in case an adult bird flies out suddenly.

If an adult bird remains on the nest when you open the box, Elsie recommends that you gently close the door, move away, and wait for it to leave the nest. This is the suggested approach; however, some monitors routinely lift incubating females from their nest without incident to check the eggs. When Dick Purvis of Anaheim, California, has a group of school kids monitoring boxes with him, he'll even take an incubating female around for all of them to see. "Needless to say, the children are spellbound," Dick says.

What should you look for when you peer inside a nestbox? In addition to checking for any problems,

A female eastern bluebird continues incubating her eggs while being monitored. Some bluebirds will leave a nest while they are being monitored; others, like this bird, remain tight on their eggs.

Julie Kutruff of Lorton, Virginia, says, "We record the following: when we see the beginnings of a nest, the kind of nest it is, and the materials used to build the nest. We also record when egg laying begins — or we try to figure out when egg laying began." You can also take notes on the growth of the nestlings and record when they fledge.

Julie suggests you keep written records instead of just making mental notes. Careful records will help you to do a good job monitoring. For example, if you've made a note of the date on which the babies hatched, you can check the table on p. 29 and be able to predict when they will fledge. That way, you can be extra careful on your monitoring visits near the fledge day so the young birds don't try to take off prematurely.

Many nestbox monitors create their own "data forms" — check-off boxes or fill-in-the-blank spaces that make it easy to collect all the necessary information. The Birdhouse Network makes "field data forms" available online; you can print and use these data forms even if you do not register with the project. (But please register — they need your data!)

Before Bluebirds Return —
Late Winter/Early Spring

Just as you check the guest bedroom before your company arrives to **make sure all is ready,** you should check any nestbox that has been up all winter. "Check your boxes in the spring to make sure everything is ready to go for the season," advises Julie Kutruff. Early spring is the time to replace a roof that has split or a floor that has started to decay. In rainy Corvallis, Oregon, Elsie Eltzroth notes, "Boxes *have* to be maintained, repaired, and weatherproofed because spring weather can be devastating to our bluebirds. Sometimes we have rain into June, and we lose a lot of first broods."

Also check to make sure that the entrance hole

An introduced species, the European paper wasp, is spreading rapidly in eastern states. Dr. Eugene Morton, a scientist at the Smithsonian Institution, reports that these European invaders (Polistes dominulus) are much more aggressive than native wasps. First discovered in Cambridge, Massachusetts, in 1980, European paper wasps have now been spotted in New Jersey, upstate New York, Connecticut, Vermont, Pennsylvania, southern Michigan, and northern Ohio, as well as isolated locations in Maine and Maryland.

A wasp nest is suspended from the ceiling of a nestbox. Wasps often invade nestboxes in spring.

hasn't been "re-engineered" by a winter tenant. Bill Reddy says downy woodpeckers often use his nestboxes for shelter on winter nights. "Now, I don't know if it's out of boredom or what, but the woodpeckers start pecking on the bottom of the entrance hole and enlarge the opening," he says. "Then starlings can get in the box during the nesting season." If woodpeckers or squirrels enlarge the entrance hole, you may need to add a hole protector (p. 117) to the box. Gary Springer of Carnesville, Georgia, puts screws around the entrance hole. He places them so that the heads are very close to the hole. "They do seem to stop squirrels from chewing on the entrance," says Gary.

It is important that entrance holes be smooth, as well as the right size. Entrance holes on nestboxes that have been up for a couple of seasons are often ragged. Check them each spring by running your finger over them. If the surface has weathered and feels rough, then it will tear at a bird's feathers. Keith Kridler says hardware stores sell small expandable drum sanders made for use with battery-powered portable drills. A small sander will polish an entrance hole as smooth as glass in less than a minute.

Trail operators whose boxes are mounted on fence posts or utility poles need to look for mice in their boxes come spring — mice like to overwinter in bluebird boxes, and they can make quite a mess. But mice can't climb conduit or water pipe, and they can't get around baffles, so if you are a backyard bluebirder with a properly mounted box, you shouldn't find mice in your box in the spring. If you have fence-post-mounted boxes, read about mice (p. 49) before giving your boxes their spring check.

If this is your first year as a nestbox monitor, your new boxes should be in place shortly before the bluebirds return. Once the bluebirds arrive (or in places where bluebirds overwinter, once they are actively inspecting your box), most experts suggest that you commit to regular box checks. That could mean you start monitoring as early as February or March in many parts of North America.

One reason it is important to regularly monitor an empty box is to **check for paper wasps.** "This year some of my favorite boxes — the ones that have always had bluebirds — were empty," says Betty Darrell, who lives in northwestern Illinois. "I checked the ceilings, and there were some wasps building nests. Bluebirds will not use a box if there's a wasp nest in it." Which, from the bird's point of view, seems like a sensible decision.

After David Magness expanded one of his bluebird trails in Maryland, he returned to check the recently mounted boxes. "Ninety-five percent of the boxes had paper wasps," he says. "If I hadn't monitored my boxes, I wouldn't have had any bluebirds." Besides paper wasps and yellow jackets, you might also find a queen bumblebee occupying a box.

How can you get rid of insects that occupy your boxes? Actually, you have several choices. Betty Darrell's solution is the simplest. "I just use a gloved hand to scrape the nest out," she explains. Betty wears heavy plastic gardening gloves to protect her from stings.

If you want more between you and the wasps than the thickness of a glove, you can use a putty knife with a wide blade — or even a pancake spatula from the kitchen — to scrape out the wasp nest.

"By the way," adds New Hampshire resident Bruce Burdett, "if you think wasps are in your box, make sure it's cold out when you check your boxes. They're more likely to come out and sting you if it's warm." Like all insects, wasps are cold-blooded; their bodies take on the temperature of their environment. If the air temperature is cool, wasps will be sluggish and less likely to attack you.

If you shrink from the idea of squashing wasps, you can try to prevent them from nesting in your box in the first place. "I've found if I coat the ceiling of the box with soap, wasps won't nest there," says Bruce Burdett. Dave Magness agrees. "I just do the soap one time, and it knocks out almost a hundred percent of the wasps," he says.

Any special kind of soap? The bar soap from your bathtub will work. "Plain old Ivory is good," says Burdett. Some people swear by Vaseline rather than soap, but because of its sticky nature, it's a little harder to apply. Other nestbox monitors staple a sheet of aluminum foil to the ceiling of the box. All of these treatments seem to prevent wasps from attaching their nests to the rough wood. It's best to apply anti-wasp defenses early in spring because wasps often move into boxes before migratory birds return.

Some nestbox monitors prefer to kill wasps with insecticides. Insecticides made specifically for use with caged birds (see sidebar, right) can be safely used in a nestbox.

Courtship and Nest Building — Boxes Are Claimed

Your box is clean and ready, and now you see a male bluebird perched in a tree nearby! In places where bluebirds are migratory, the males return to the nesting ground a few days to a week before the females to establish a territory. As the females arrive, each male advertises his availability by singing from a high, exposed perch within his territory.

After a male attracts a mate, he performs a flight display that directs her attention to the nesting sites within his territory. It is the female that makes the **nestbox selection.** You may see a male make a slow, almost stalling flight to your nestbox, then cling to the entrance and poke his head inside. Or while clinging to the box, he may do a "wing-wave" display in which he flicks open one or both

Two eastern bluebirds perform a nuptial display on the nestbox they have claimed.

of his wings. He may also pop in and out of the box or fly off to grab some dry grass or other nesting material and bring it to the box.

A female who likes the look of the real estate will fly closer to perch on the box or at the entrance. But if she doesn't go inside, the male may fly off to lead her to another box or nest site. If you see both the male and the female going in and out of your box, that's a good sign they plan to nest there.

Tom Heintzelman of Milton, Florida, recalls the first pair of bluebirds that came to nest in his yard. "After the male showed the boxes to the female, it looked like she made her choice known to him by depositing a single long-needle pine leaf in the box of her choice," Tom says. "The fellow went bonkers — hovered 6 feet above the box, then did a hovering circle around the box at box height, and then hovered above it again while slowly revolving 360 degrees." Nest building started the next day, Tom reports.

If your boxes are out of view, you'll miss seeing the birds choose their nestbox. Instead, when you make your regular monitoring visit, you might find a blade of grass, a straw, or perhaps a feather left by birds investigating the box.

Safe Insecticides for Bluebird Nestboxes

Pyrethrin is a naturally occurring insecticide extracted from flower petals. It kills insects on contact but does not harm birds or mammals. It breaks down rapidly after application and so must be sprayed directly on an insect to be effective. Look for "caged bird spray" containing 0.1 percent pyrethrin or less at a pet store, or check a garden store for pyrethrin-based sprays designed for use on vegetables.

Dick Walker of Loogootee, Indiana, has experimented with a newer compound, cypermethrin, a synthetic form of pyrethrin. "I was searching for something that would be nontoxic to birds, and several firms came up with the same recommendation," he says. The spray he uses contains 0.1 percent cypermethrin and costs $18 for a 15-ounce spray can. Dick says the compound kills wasps on contact. "Then I just pull the nest out," he adds. He's had good results with the treatment: "This year my computer says I'm going to fledge 786 birds," he says proudly.

Carolina chickadee nestlings in a soft cup of downy feathers, hair, plant down, and fine dry grasses built on a base of moss.

Tufted titmouse nest with dried leaves and other matter, including snakeskin, worked into the moss base; the soft cup, resembling a chickadee's, is not yet built.

If you find **a completed nest** when you monitor, you may be able to determine what species of bird built it. The nest illustrations on these pages will help. But to be sure of your identification, you should try to spot the birds that built the nest. Sometimes one species will take over another's nest and simply add nesting material to it. "If you're not sure who the nest belongs to, just watch and wait," Julie Kutruff advises.

If you come upon a **house sparrow nest** (picture, p. 81) in one of your nestboxes, refer to Chapter 4 for advice. We recommend that you decide what strategy you are comfortable using to control sparrows *before* you find your first sparrow nest.

House sparrow nests can resemble bluebird nests, but they tend to be larger than the neat cups of grass constructed by bluebirds. Often you'll see some seed heads on the grass stems woven into a sparrow nest (seed heads are rare in a bluebird nest). Sparrow nests also contain materials and bits of junk that bluebirds seldom use — animal hair, cigarette butts, gum wrappers, or feathers.

If you find a jumble of twigs inside a nestbox, that's proof a male house wren is staking claim to the box. Typically, **a male wren will stuff twigs into boxes** in his territory to keep other birds from moving in. The twig jumbles are called "dummy nests." The male will lead a prospective mate on a tour of his real estate so she can chose the final nest site. Then she builds a softer nest cup among the twigs.

To keep your box open for bluebirds instead of wrens, check it often. If you find a dummy nest or a wren nest that is still under construction, it's OK to pull it out and discard the sticks. Destroying a real or dummy nest, however, is not likely to discourage a wren from continuing to fill boxes with twigs. Although other small cavity-nesters often tolerate neighbors of different species, house wrens don't want *any* songbirds — including their own as well as other species — nesting in their territory. They will persist in filling a box with twigs so that other birds cannot use it, and if they nest in your yard, there will always be the risk that they will sneak into other nests and puncture or remove the eggs.

Jane Grant of Pound Ridge, New York, recalls what a house wren did to the two nests — bluebird and chickadee — she was monitoring in her yard. The bluebird nest had five eggs, and the chickadee nest had seven; a house wren ravaged both nests on the same day. "I know it was a house wren because I saw him leaving one of the boxes," Jane says. When she checked the bluebird box, only one egg remained. Another egg lay broken on the ground, directly under the entrance hole. Jane says the chickadee box had one egg missing, and one of the six remaining eggs had a tiny puncture in it. Both the bluebirds and the chickadees abandoned their nests.

Jane says she wondered at the time if she could have put up another box for the wrens and prevented the tragedy. This strategy — erecting a "decoy" box — often works with house sparrows

(L) **House wren eggs** in a woven cup of feathers, hair, and fine grass buried in a jumble of twigs. (R) **Black-capped chickadee eggs** in a soft cup like the Carolina chickadee's; the moss base is concealed.

Tree swallow eggs in a cup of feathers on dry grass.

Two cowbird eggs in an eastern bluebird nest.

(p. 81), and in the short term it can work with house wrens, says Ted Ossege of Cincinnati, Ohio. House wrens kept harassing a pair of bluebirds in Ted's yard — "They even pulled out a partial nest" — until he gave them their own box away from the bluebirds. Unmolested any longer, the bluebirds fledged two broods, says Ted.

But Ted's house wrens also fledged young, and that's why experienced bluebird monitors avoid erecting a box just for house wrens. House wrens that are allowed to use your nestboxes will multiply. Each succeeding year the growing number of wrens will make it increasingly harder for bluebirds — or any other songbirds — to nest successfully in the vicinity of the wrens' nestboxes.

To avoid attracting house wrens, most monitors simply try to keep their boxes away from thickets

and brushy areas. "House wrens are slow fliers, and they hate being caught in the open by a blue-bird or other cavity-nester," says Joe Huber of Venice, Florida. If you've misjudged how close is "too close" and see a house wren taking interest in a box, simply move the box into a more open area. Even if bluebirds are in the process of building a nest, you can still move the box a short distance to safety and the bluebirds will not abandon it.

If you feel that your only practical solution to an immediate house wren threat is to provide an extra nestbox for the wrens and hope that they will leave your bluebirds or other cavity-nesters in peace, try putting the wren box very close to the box you are protecting. According to recent research, house wrens seem to avoid entering boxes placed within 10 to 15 feet of their own nestbox.

Tree swallow nestlings in their feather-lined nest.

An eastern bluebird nest made of pine straw. The twigs over the eggs indicate that a house wren has taken over the nestbox.

House sparrow nest built on top of a bluebird nest.

Pairing — placing boxes 10 to 15 feet from each other — is a common way to settle disputes between bluebirds and tree swallows. But pairing a box for wrens with a box for bluebirds (or any other small cavity-nester) is a relatively new idea. If you try it, you should monitor the boxes closely to help avert any problems.

If you're a backyard bluebird monitor with only one prime spot in which to mount a nestbox, pairing means that you don't have to give up hope of attracting a bluebird if, for example, chickadees claim your box before the bluebirds are ready to nest. "Put up another box," advises Diane Slavin of Vernon, New York. "Please don't disturb the

chickadees. You will get enjoyment watching that momma raise her babies." And meanwhile, the nesting chickadees will not permit another pair of 'dees to take over the newly paired box, so the second box should be open for bluebirds when they return.

Chickadees and bluebirds usually coexist peacefully, but it is always a good idea to place a hole restrictor (p. 117) with a 1⅛-inch-diameter hole on a chickadee's box. Who knows, the bluebirds might otherwise prefer the chickadees' box to the one reserved for them — and proceed to evict the chickadees. Keith Kridler tells of the time that he and Harry Krueger came upon a pair of eastern bluebirds evicting a family of Carolina chickadees from a nestbox. "We watched the male bluebird enter the box and then come out carrying a five-day-old chickadee baby in its bill. It flew 70 to 100 feet and dropped the nestling along a barbed wire fence." Keith and Harry scared the bluebirds off and hurriedly drove 3 miles to get a hole restrictor to protect the remaining five chickadee nestlings. "By the time we got back, bluebirds and chickadees were fighting over an empty box," Keith says.

Shortly after bluebirds begin nesting, tree swallows arrive over much of the continent. Bonnie Baker of Summit County, Colorado, reports that tree swallows will dive-bomb the bluebird nests they want to take over. "If the bluebirds have not started laying eggs, sometimes the swallows succeed," says Bonnie. "If eggs have been laid, it's harder for the swallows to drive off the bluebird pair. It depends on the maturity and feistiness of the bluebirds involved." Indeed, bluebirds that are attempting a second nesting may even try to evict tree swallows from a box.

Pairing nestboxes so that bluebirds and tree swallows each have one can help resolve a conflict. You might want to start the nesting season with paired boxes if you expect both bluebirds and tree swallows in your yard. If bluebirds claim one of the paired boxes, they might be possessive of the second one also, but when tree swallows want the second one badly enough, they can usually claim it. (For more on box pairing, see p. 49.)

Haleya Priest of Amherst, Massachusetts, says she has seen bluebirds nesting in one box of a pair guard the second box until their eggs hatched. "Then they had to be more concerned about feeding five hungry mouths than about whether tree swallows would get the second box," she says. "I finally have tree swallows nesting in the second box instead of getting kicked out for the umpteenth time by the bluebirds."

Egg Laying and Incubation — Life Begins Anew

Egg laying usually starts shortly after the female bluebird completes her nest. At least, that's typically

A pair of nestboxes hosts neighboring pairs of tree swallows and eastern bluebirds.

A dwarf eastern bluebird egg rests with normal eggs in a typical grass bluebird nest. Dwarf eggs are not fertile and are extremely rare.

when egg laying happens with second or third clutches, but **females may delay** starting their first clutch for weeks after the first nest is complete. In Fairview, West Virginia, Patty Haught faithfully monitored a box with an empty nest. "Whenever I checked that box, there were no bluebirds in the area; usually, they will fly nearby to watch what I'm doing at 'their' box, but in this case, nothing," she says. It was two weeks before the birds returned and Patty found eggs in the nest.

"The female *usually* will not begin to lay her eggs until she is confident the eggs will not be harmed by the cold," suggests Betty Nichols of Middletown, Maryland. It may be the weather that makes the female decide when to lay eggs, or it may be the availability of food or the length of the day — all are interrelated. In any case, the nest will wait until the female is ready...and females differ greatly in deciding when the time is right to lay eggs. Trail monitors note that two females in boxes a few hundred yards from each other may start laying eggs several weeks apart.

Birds in warmer southern areas start laying eggs earlier than birds in colder northern locales, but the date when the first egg is laid can change significantly from year to year at any location. Bluebird monitors in the southern tier of states can expect a first egg around early March; those in the middle tier will wait several weeks longer. In Wisconsin, Mary Roen says unhappily, "I have to wait until the end of April!" Monitors in southern Canada commonly wait until the end of May or early June before they see their first eastern or western bluebird eggs. Mountain bluebirds start laying eggs about a month earlier than eastern or western bluebirds where their ranges overlap.

Sometimes a bluebird makes a perfect nest but never lays eggs. If this happens in your box, Betty Darrell recommends you "remove the nest from the box and save it for a rainy day." She means that literally! "I had one nest full of eggs get quite wet," Betty recalls, "and I'd kept a dry, unused nest, so

Species	Color	Clutch Size (Mean Size)	Days of Incubation	Days to Fledge	Broods per Season
Eastern Bluebird	Blue, sometimes white	3–5 (3.84)	12–14	16–22	1–3
Mountain Bluebird	Pale blue, rarely white	5–6 (4.55)	13–14	17–22	1–2
Western Bluebird	Blue, sometimes white	4–6 (4.16)	13–14	19–22	1–2
Tree Swallow	White	4–7 (4.11)	14–15	16–22	1
Black-capped Chickadee	White to pinkish white; small red, brownish red, or purplish red spots	6–8 (4.16)	12–13	14–16	1
Carolina Chickadee	Like black-capped chickadee's; spots on eggs of both often heavier at large end of egg	5–8 (4.30)	11–14	13–17	1
Tufted Titmouse	White to creamy white; fine speckles of chestnut red, purplish red, or brown — sometimes lilac	5–6 (4.04)	12–14	15–16	1–2
Ash-throated Flycatcher	Ivory, creamy, or pinkish white; densely streaked, scrawled, and blotched with red, purple, brown	4–5 (3.41)	13–15	16–17	1
House Wren	White or tinted pink or buff; extensive small to very fine specks of red, brown, purple	6–8 (3.58)	12–16	15–19	1–2
House Sparrow	White or greenish white; variably spotted and blotched with gray, blue-gray, brown, black	4–6	10–13	14–17	up to 4

Source: The Birdhouse Network of Cornell Lab of Ornithology.

Sometimes a bluebird will surprise you by laying white eggs instead of blue ones. In 1997, 4.3 percent of the bluebird clutches reported to Cornell's Birdhouse Network had white eggs. In 1998, the percentage was about the same, at 4.5 percent. An additional 1.7 percent of nests have both blue and white eggs.

I brought the dry nest over, put the eggs in that, and put it back in the box." A spare nest can also be handy to replace a nest that is infested with blowflies (p. 84). Plastic baggies are convenient for storing nests till you need them.

The nest becomes "active" when the first egg is laid. That's a good time to give the nestbox another quick inspection. Do any cracks or seams need caulking? Check that the drain holes haven't become clogged. In southern states, several tiny species of solitary wasps may plug these holes with mud. Some spiders will also plug drains.

Also check that the nest has not been built up so high that the eggs (and later on, the nestlings) are dangerously close to the entrance hole. Keith Kridler says, "It is best if the nest cup is at least 3 inches below the entrance hole." If the nest has been built on top of an old nest, it is easy to lower the active nest by removing the nest underneath it. "Make sure to leave at least an inch of nesting material between the eggs and the floor of the box," advises Keith.

The timing of your monitoring during the egg-laying period is important, says Hatch Graham of Somerset, California: "During egg laying, it's best not to visit too early in the morning, as this is when the actual egg delivery takes place." If you disturb the female while she is in the process of laying an egg, she may desert the nest. As long as you follow Hatch's advice and wait till the afternoon to check the box, it's fine to take daily peeks.

If you see a single egg when you check the box, expect to see two eggs the next day, three eggs the next, and so on until the clutch is complete. See the table on p. 29 for the typical range of clutch sizes for common small cavity-nesters. The first clutch of the season is usually a female's largest, and experienced females usually lay more eggs than first-timers.

Although the eggs are laid on subsequent days, they eventually hatch on the same day. The eggs don't start to develop into chicks until the female starts to incubate, and the female doesn't normally start to incubate until the clutch is complete.

Sometimes it can be a challenge to **count the number of eggs** in the nest. The quality of your view will depend on whether your box is top open-

This bluebird nest with nine eggs was found in the spring of 2000 in one of Jack Finch's nestbox pots.

ing, side opening, or front opening and also on the way the bird has constructed the nest. A mechanic's mirror with a long handle is a helpful tool to get a better view; some monitors count the eggs very carefully by feel or slide the nest out to get a better look.

"When we monitor our boxes, we use a mechanic's inspection mirror," says Steve Garr of Mt. Joliet, Tennessee. "It's a 2-inch mirror on a flexible pole. You can use it to look at the nest from above — it gives you a very good view." Steve says you can purchase an inspection mirror at most auto supply shops, although some birding supply stores also carry them.

When chickadees and tree swallows leave the nest to feed or drink, they often cover the eggs with down or feathers to keep them from chilling. Katherine Wolfthal of Weston, Massachusetts, says she would never have found the first egg in her chickadees' nestbox if she hadn't searched carefully. "It was buried under at least ½ inch of nesting material, and I had to feel around," she says. "Looking with a mirror showed nothing." Katherine says she carefully tucked the egg back under its insulating cover when she finished monitoring.

Even if they have a beautiful view of the eggs, some monitors **touch the eggs gently.** Are the eggs warm or are they at ambient temperature? If the female has not started incubation, the eggs will be at ambient temperature and feel cool. Once the clutch is complete and incubation has started, the eggs will feel warm. Eggs can stay viable for several weeks if incubation is delayed.

The female bluebird does all **the incubating of the eggs.** (This is true for the other small cavity-nesters as well.) Only she pulls out feathers on her

How Many Eggs Does a Bluebird Lay?

Rarely monitors find one or two more eggs in a clutch than indicated in the table, p. 29. Eastern bluebirds may lay 6 or even 7 eggs. Mountain bluebirds sometimes have 8 eggs. But clutches that are several eggs larger than expected don't mean the female is extraordinarily prolific. Chances are, another female has engaged in "egg dumping" — laying her eggs in someone else's nest. Ray Briggs of Cobleskill, New York, once found a nest with 10 eastern bluebird eggs. Esther Leck of Woolwich, Maine, tells of a clutch of 12 chickadees. "They all fledged too!" she says. Jack Finch of Bailey, North Carolina, didn't have such good fortune with the nest of 9 eggs illustrated above. Only one bluebird fledged.

lower abdomen to create a "brood patch," a bare area that allows heat to be transferred from her body to the eggs. She nearly always starts incubation when the last or next-to-last egg is laid. During the day, she takes frequent short trips away from the box and her incubation duties, but she spends all night sitting on her eggs. Often the male brings her food while she is on the nest during the day.

Many monitors avoid disturbing a female during the first few days of incubation, though some trail operators handle the female during this time and report no bad effects. For backyard bluebird monitors, it's easy to wait until you see the female leave before you check an active nestbox.

Chickadees, titmice, and swallows are as tolerant of monitoring as bluebirds are. Shelly Ducharme of Auburn, Alabama, says, "Mom titmouse is quite tenacious about sitting on her eggs — she will *not* leave the nest when I open the box, and she 'curses' me as the box is opened." Hatch Graham says that ash-throated flycatchers seem to be less tolerant of disturbance during nest building and egg laying than other small cavity-nesters. "Later during incubation, monitoring the nest doesn't seem to drive them away, but they are wary and usually — not always — leave the nest on your approach," Hatch says.

Bluebirds and the other common small cavity-nesters normally spend about two weeks incubating their eggs (see table, p. 29). While the female incubates, she repeatedly turns the eggs and rearranges them in the nest. The eggs gradually become shiny because of all the moving about.

The rate of development of the embryo varies with temperature. One scientific study found the average incubating temperature of eastern bluebird eggs in warm weather to be about 92 degrees Fahrenheit. The optimum temperature for incubation is probably about the same as it is for chicken eggs — 95 degrees.

Some females incubate their eggs more diligently than others do. Female eastern bluebirds spend an average of about two-thirds of their daylight hours on the nest. Experienced females often incubate more diligently than first-timers. Eggs that are poorly incubated and allowed to cool are not harmed, but they can take up to five or six days longer to incubate than eggs maintained at optimum incubating temperature.

A wet nest loses its power to insulate. Rain that leaks into a box on a cold spring day is absorbed by the nest and may chill the eggs enough to threaten the developing embryos. Linda Inlow of Pendleton, Indiana, had a nest get soaked because of a leaky box. She replaced the wet nest — which had one egg in it — with a nest she made. "The female accepted this and laid her second egg in it," Linda says. "In the meantime, the sun came out, and I laid the old nest in the sun to dry." When

A female tree swallow sits tight on her nest and continues to incubate her eggs while her nest is monitored.

the old nest was dried out, Linda and her husband quickly replaced the leaky box with a tight, dry box, put the old nest in it, and added the two eggs. "Next day there were three eggs!" Linda exclaims.

If an egg becomes seriously chilled, the embryo may continue to develop when it is incubated again, but the chick may not hatch successfully. To peck its way out of an eggshell, a chick must be able to move around inside the shell. A slick mucous membrane lines the inside of the shell, allowing the chick to move, but if it is subjected to very cold temperatures, the membrane can become sticky and trap a chick so that it can't get out.

In summer, when temperatures may stay in the 90s in some regions, **hot air temperatures will start eggs incubating.** Barry Whitney of South Carolina relates that the June heat where he lives once incubated a clutch of eggs he was monitoring; at least, that's what Barry deduces from the staggered hatching. "One of the eggs hatched one day, two hatched the next day, and a fourth hatched on the third day," he says. This pattern suggests the heat may have started incubating the eggs as each one was laid. Barry reports that all four nestlings developed normally and fledged, but not all on the same day.

In the foothills of the Sierra Nevada range in California, Wendy Guglieri saw a clutch of western bluebirds incubated by the heat of the day. The female was seldom on the nest, Wendy says. "At first, I thought the five eggs were abandoned, but the female waited 5 days before even starting incubation, and she incubated for only 10 days!"

Keep an eye on the adult birds during incubation. Are both of them entering and leaving the box — or are they nowhere to be seen? A cold snap can cause so much stress that **a female will abandon her eggs.** But she and her mate won't necessarily leave the area. Jill Miller of Natick, Massachusetts, tells of bluebirds abandoning four eggs because of two weeks of nasty weather. "They built a new nest in the next box to the east and began laying eggs in it," Jill reports. The late Harry Krueger had many records of color-banded bluebirds that built second nests right on top of abandoned eggs. Krueger determined that it took the female at least 10 days before she was able to lay new eggs.

Sometimes eggs are abandoned because they are infertile or because the embryos don't develop for some reason. Kelley Coppens of Bridgman, Michigan, noted that the five beautiful blue eggs in one of her nestboxes didn't hatch when they were supposed to. "The female continued to sit, and the male continued to feed her and 'run off' anything that got close to his territory," Kelly says. Eventually the pair became aware that something was wrong. Kelly watched them act confused for a couple of days and then abandon the eggs.

If the female dies during egg laying or incubation, the male will not be able to incubate the eggs on his own; he will have to abandon the nest. What to do with the abandoned eggs? If you conclude that a box is abandoned, you can remove the nest and its contents so other birds may claim the space.

"I once found a bluebird female dead on the ground," relates Dorene Scriven, "and inside the box, the eggs were still warm. Dorene says she took the eggs, marked them very softly with pencil, and distributed them in other nests (she has the

Six bluebird eggs in one of Malinda Mastako's backyard nestboxes. Only 3.5 percent of eastern bluebird clutches contain as many as six eggs, according to data from Cornell's Birdhouse Network.

permits to do this legally) where the eggs were about the same age. Because she had marked the eggs with pencil, she could confirm that they did eventually hatch. "That was very successful," Dorene says with pleasure.

"The important thing in this situation is to place the eggs in a nest where the eggs are the same age so they will hatch at the same time," Dorene emphasizes. However, if you are a backyard bluebird monitor with only a few boxes, you will be very fortunate to have nests at the right stage of development to accept abandoned eggs. Your chances of salvaging abandoned eggs are improved if you network with other bluebird monitors in your vicinity.

Once eggs are laid, **climbing predators** become interested in a nestbox. The box develops a scent that grows stronger as the eggs hatch and the young birds develop. The scent is what attracts some predators, especially snakes. Raccoons and opossums can also learn to recognize nestboxes by sight.

If your backyard box is properly mounted and baffled, you have nothing to fear from climbing predators. If you have any doubts about how well protected the box is, remember to check for scratch marks that would indicate a predator is trying to climb your mount. "You won't usually see a predator at your box," says Elsie Eltzroth, "but you may find evidence after the fact." A thin layer of grease on a pole will reveal any raiding attempts by snakes or other climbing predators.

If a clutch of eggs seems to have vanished, look in and under the nest materials for broken eggs or

Meet Malinda...and Fred and Ethel

In her backyard near Detroit, Michigan, Malinda Mastako had been monitoring bluebirds for five years when she shot the photos of developing nestlings shown on the following pages in spring 2001. Malinda knows the parent bluebirds well. "'Fred' was hatched here in the backyard in 1998," Malinda says. "He was the kid who would not leave home no matter how much they chased him. In 1999, he nested in the front yard while his parents used the backyard. After his father was killed by a hawk during the third nesting that year, Fred took over the backyard as well."

"Ethel" is Fred's second mate, Malinda says. "This is their second year together. Last year they nested four times and fledged 17 young. They were here all winter in a group of 20 or so that lived in the nearby woods. They visited my yard daily to drink and bathe, and to dine on peanut butter mix and mealworms. In spring, they chased off the other bluebirds, and on March 25, Ethel began laying eggs."

Before the first clutch of four had fledged, Malinda says that Ethel had chosen another box in the backyard (Malinda provides a choice of four) for her second nesting. She built her second nest and started laying eggs just five days after the first clutch had fledged. On the morning of May 24, 2001, the first chick in Ethel's second clutch of the season began pecking its way out of its shell...and Malinda began to document a most unusual nesting.

DAY 1, 7:45 A.M.

The first chick emerges on a gloomy, rainy day. The weather will make it difficult for the parents, Fred and Ethel, to find small soft insects for the newly hatched chicks.

DAY 1, 10:30 A.M.

Only two nestlings hatch on the first day. Already the nestlings can raise their heads and gape in response to Malinda's whistle. Ethel apparently eats the eggshells; she is not seen removing them from the nest.

bits of shell. House sparrows often break eggs and basically trash a nest. Neatly punctured eggs may be the work of a house wren. If the eggs really are completely gone, that may be the work of a house wren or snake. House wrens sometimes remove eggs, and snakes will swallow them whole.

Though broken or missing eggs seem like a tragedy, Erv Davis of Charlo, Montana, notes that birds are resilient and a female will likely lay new eggs if a clutch is lost. "Once, a snake demolished six eggs in a western bluebird box," Erv relates. "I cleaned it out, and Mama and Pop went back in, laid six more eggs, and had a successful fledging."

Nestlings Emerge — Young Birds Develop

When nestlings hatch, it is often during the first two hours after dawn. Sometimes all the young birds hatch out within the space of a half hour; it seldom takes more than a day for an entire clutch to hatch. The chicks manage the escape from their shells on their own; the parents don't normally assist in the process except to remove the eggshells from the nest. Often the female will eat the shells to recycle the calcium.

When you look inside the nest, the little birds will be pressed so close together they might as well be a tangled lump of fishing worms. And it's so dark in the box — how can you tell if they all hatched successfully?

Of course you are eager to get a count, but birds that are just a day or two old are still quite fragile,

and you don't want to disturb them. Keith Kridler suggests a trick that makes getting a head count easier. "You can make the nestlings think their parents are there to feed them," he says. "Just make a series of high-pitched whistle notes. If the little birds are hungry, they will raise their heads and open their mouths to beg for food. It's easier to

Fred guards the yard from his favorite perch — a shepherd's crook near the middle of the yard — while he takes a break from feeding his nestlings.

Each nesting season, The Birdhouse Network provides several nest-box cams for you to monitor the development of bluebirds and other cavity-nesting species in real time. Go to http://birds.Cornell.edu and click on Nest Box Cam.

DAY 2, 7:30 A.M.

A third chick hatches 24 hours after the first two. It is still cold and rainy, and Ethel spends much of her time on the nest. Fred busily brings tiny bugs to the box. Sometimes he is so wet his blue feathers look black.

DAY 3, 8:30 A.M.

And a fourth chick hatches a day later! "Tiny" has flopped over but is gaping, ready to be fed. Having chicks hatched 48 hours apart will make it difficult for the parents to properly feed, brood, and fledge them.

Ethel flies from her nestbox with a fecal sac. Young nestlings produce feces in a gelatinous sac that the adults carry away from the nestbox. By the time the nestlings fledge, they stop producing prepackaged poop. The nestbox is Springer's Chalet (p. 101). Because of the cold weather, Malinda has boarded up the vents. Under the entry hole, she has hot-glued a piece of bark mulch. "As I watched Ethel building the nest, I could see that she was having difficulty getting in and out," Malinda says, "and my scratching up the front of the box wasn't helping."

count the open mouths than it is to count a tangle of bodies."

The parents will start feeding soft insects to the chicks within an hour of hatching. Both the male and the female feed the nestlings. During the first few days, Dad may be especially busy feeding because Mom has to spend much of her time brooding the babies to keep them warm. So if it's a cold, rainy day, refrain from monitoring boxes with young nestlings inside unless you are sure the female is not incubating. If the female leaves the nest when you open the box, the young birds could become chilled.

Keith Kridler also advises that you refrain from monitoring just before dark. "If a female is incubating eggs or brooding young and leaves the nest, she may be too frightened to return before morning, and eggs or young could perish on a cold night."

Nestlings cannot regulate their body temperature for the first six days or so. They rely on their mother to keep them warm. The father can usually keep young nestlings fed if something happens to the mother, but he can't keep them warm because he has no brood patch. As a result, a spell of cold spring weather can be doubly threatening to young nestlings. Food becomes scarce because of the weather, and if the mother leaves the nest to help feed herself and the nestlings, the babies might die of exposure. If she sits tight, they may still weaken or die from hunger.

The first time you check a box of nestlings you may find that not all of the eggs have hatched. "Among bluebirds, **unhatched or infertile eggs** occur in approximately 10 to 15 percent of nests," says Tina Phillips, project leader of The Birdhouse Network for Cornell Lab of Ornithology. TBN participants have reported unhatched eggs in as many as 25 percent of nests in some years.

How can you be sure an egg is not going to hatch? "In my area, bad eggs often have fly specks on the shell," says Keith, "because flies can smell

Tiny lies squished in the middle, next to the two unhatched eggs. In addition to small bugs, Fred and Ethel start bringing some inch-long green caterpillars to the nest, presumably for the older nestlings.

Four hungry mouths demand food, and the rate of feeding picks up, with 13 food deliveries during a 15-minute period early in the morning. The chicks eat caterpillars, small insects, and their first mealworms.

Malinda Mastako reports that she thought Ethel began incubating after the fourth egg was laid, which would not have been unusual for a normal, five-egg clutch. The early incubation would explain the staggered hatchings, as the first four eggs would have been incubating before the final two were laid.

the odor from a bad egg." It's also likely the eggs are bad if you see houseflies or green bottle flies clustered around the box.

Keith advises that you watch and wait for a few days after the other eggs have hatched because the eggs may still contain viable embryos. "However, by the fourth or fifth day, it's OK to remove the unhatched eggs," he says. "Rotten eggs can and do occasionally explode, creating a stinking box and possibly a health hazard for the surviving chicks." Viruses and bacteria may multiply inside an infertile egg, and if the egg breaks, they could infect the nestlings.

If nesting birds are lucky, insects are everywhere. But sometimes bird parents have a tough time **finding enough food** to fill all those gaping mouths. If the weather is unseasonably cold, for example, flying insects won't be active. If there's prolonged rain, it's hard for the birds to get out and forage. And if there's a drought, insects may be less abundant than usual.

How can you tell if the parents are having trouble finding food? Linda Violett of Yorba Linda, California, says one clue is when you see the remains of fruits and berries in a bluebird nest; these items are not the on the "preferred" menu. "If there were plenty of naturally available insects," Linda says, "the birds would be feeding their babies insects, not fruit."

Even if you don't see any juice stains, the birds may still be having a tough time. "In one nest," Linda relates, "I could see that the parents were

feeding the chicks 'last resort' insects, such as pill bugs and earthworms. The next time I checked that box, three chicks were dead."

Linda decided to offer the bluebird parents some supplemental food in the form of mealworms and minced bits of scrambled egg, and they eventually fledged two young. Some monitors also offer supplemental feedings in a situation where one parent bird has been killed. Elsie Eltzroth, who has conducted banding studies on western bluebirds, notes, "A female bluebird can't handle a box by herself if she has more than three young in the nest — that's pretty conclusive from my records."

Besides monitoring to see that they are well fed, **check that the nest is dry.** Cold, wet nests are even more of a threat to young nestlings than they are to eggs. Evaporating moisture can remove heat

The Good Life in the Yard

Fred and Ethel have a regular daily routine, says Malinda Mastako. "They will bring food in a flurry for a while and then take a short break. If it is cold or the young are just hatched, Ethel will brood them and Fred will bring her food before feeding himself and taking his break." After brooding, Malinda says that Ethel will come out and stretch her wings and preen. "During their breaks," she adds, "they will sit on their favorite perches or hunt food for themselves. Sometimes in the afternoon or evening they'll take a bath." Malinda observes that Fred and Ethel spend more time feeding the kids than resting or feeding themselves. And one thing they do at least once every day is check all the other available boxes in the yard. "They do this as a pair," Malinda explains, "and the wing waving and vocalization still go on as in early courtship. Each bird sits at the hole and leans in or enters the box entirely as the other one waits on the roof for its turn."

Malinda removes the unhatched eggs on the sixth day. Candling reveals that they were infertile. On the left, Ethel has just left the nest after brooding, so the nestlings are in a more compact ball than they would be when feeding. The rain has let up and it is finally sunny, but it is still unseasonably cold during the day, and there is a heavy frost both nights. The other nestlings can now regulate their body temperature, but Tiny (recognized by the smaller gape) must still depend on heat generated by its mother or siblings to stay warm. It is not clear whether Ethel is still brooding. The *cheeps* of the nestlings are now strong enough that Malinda hears them from her deck, 25 feet away.

In southern states, the ants you find in your boxes are likely to be one of the introduced fire ant species. "Around here, the biggest problem for nestbox monitors is fire ants," says Don Hutchings of Winfield, Texas. These ants pose a danger to you when you monitor your boxes — their bites sting like fire. The ants are also a threat to the nestlings in the box. "I have seen five 12-day-old bluebirds reduced to skeletons in 48 hours by fire ants," says Keith Kridler.

from a nest faster than a brooding female can generate it. As a Nebraska nestbox monitor notes, "Birds have oils in their feathers to keep the 'life-sapping' cold water from their skin. Baby birds do not have their 'lifesaving' feathers yet, so they need a *dry* nest."

"When I monitor a box and see the babies sleeping," says Haleya Priest, "I always touch each one gently to make sure by body temperature that they are alive and well. If one of the nestlings is dead, I can feel it because it will be cooler than the others."

The bluebird mother will usually remove any young nestling that dies before you notice it. Experiments done by James Hartshorne and pub-

lished in the Cornell Lab of Ornithology journal, *Living Bird,* in the early 1960s showed that the female carried off a dead nestling as soon as she discovered it if it weighed less than half her own weight. She would usually manage to remove heavier nestlings as well. If you do find a dead nestling, remove it from the nest before it starts to decompose.

The odor of **decomposition and fecal matter may attract ants to a nest.** Ants usually aren't a problem until after the eggs hatch. The major exception is when birds build a new nest on top of a used nest. The detritus and feces in the old nest can attract ants long before eggs hatch in the new nest. "In my experience," says Dean Sheldon of

One of the first nestlings to hatch naps after being fed and brooded. The dark areas are feather tracts developing under the skin. The small points at the edge of the wing are feathers just beginning to emerge.

"Tiny," who hatched 48 hours after the first nestling, looks exactly like its older sibling did two days earlier. Tiny isn't "catching up" to its more developed siblings, as some monitors believe happens.

DAY 8, 7:45 A.M.

DAY 9, 1:30 P.M.

The difference in development of the wings of the nestlings is obvious in the picture at the left. Tiny is in the middle, gaping, with one wing draped over an older nestling below; the intermediate chick is to the right. In the right-side picture, the wing feathers — wrapped in individual sheaths — look like quills. One nestling's eyes started opening on the eighth day. After three clear days and plentiful bugs, it rains all morning and part of the afternoon of Day 9. Fred and Ethel feed the nestlings heavily in spite of the rain. Malinda checks the nest for blowflies in the afternoon of Day 9. None are found, but she does find bits of eggshell, which would seem to confirm that Ethel ate the shells.

Greenwich, Ohio, "the biggest problem with leaving nests in the box after the young have fledged is the ants they attract."

To avoid an ant infestation, nestbox monitors use a variety of defenses. Maynard Sumner of Flint, Michigan, uses Tanglefoot. This sticky, nontoxic compound is available at most home-and-garden stores (landscapers use it to protect trees and shrubs from climbing insect pests). It takes only a small amount of Tanglefoot applied in a ring on a metal pole to stop ants. Apply it close to the bottom of the nestbox, where birds and other animals won't come in contact with it accidentally.

Other nestbox monitors apply a ring of Vaseline or axle grease to their poles. Tape wrapped sticky side out is also an effective ant barrier; in fact, any greasy or sticky substance will work, but you should check it regularly to make sure that it hasn't hardened or worn off. Make the barrier ring wide — if it's narrow, only an inch or two, waves of ants may sacrifice themselves to form a bridge so that other ants may cross.

Whatever ant barrier you employ, it should be in place by the time the eggs hatch. If you are late or your barrier proves inadequate, you might open your nestbox and see an army of ants. Dean Sheldon has to deal with ant problems regularly because he monitors a trail of boxes mounted on utility poles that have no ant barrier. He removes the nest and nestlings and sprays the bottom of the box with pyrethrin (see sidebar, p. 25). "Then I make a new nest, put that in the box, and replace

the nestlings. The spray will not hurt the birds," Dean says.

Kathy Bennett of Durhamville, New York, says she dealt with ants by zapping an infested nest in the microwave (after removing the nestlings). She put the nest in a plastic baggie and put it in a microwave oven at 50 percent power for two minutes. "The ants came out real fast and were zapped dead! I let the nest cool off a couple minutes, gave it a fluff, and put the babies back in it," Kathy says. "They were as snug as a bug in a rug."

Other insects can be a problem for nestlings too. Gnats, blackflies, mites, and bird blowflies are the most common pests that threaten young birds.

Fights and Challenges for Fred and Ethel

On Day 6, Fred has a small fight with a kingbird that was gathering nesting materials that Malinda had set out. Tree swallows show up on Days 8 and 9; Fred spends a lot of time and energy defending the empty boxes in the yard from their attempts to claim one. After disappearing on Days 10 and 11 — perhaps because of the unrelentingly bad weather — the swallows reappear with the sunshine on Day 12. They are interested in the nestbox closest to Ethel's. "This time Ethel is the aggressor in all the fights," Malinda says. "She literally pulls a tree swallow out of the box by its beak and pins it to the ground, belly up, for several seconds." The tree swallows persist, and in several days they are allowed to begin nesting in a box in Malinda's side yard, out of direct sight of Ethel's nestbox.

On Day 13, a sharp-shinned hawk spends 20 minutes in the nearby woods. "Fred hides in the side yard spruce tree and never stops giving his fast, three-note, whistled alarm call the entire time," says Malinda. The nestlings hear it all and have a chance to learn the calls that signal danger. Malinda hopes the experience helps prevent them from being killed by a hawk as Fred's father was.

The nestlings no longer gape for Malinda. On Day 5, Malinda has to switch from a whistle to a kissing noise to coax them into gaping, but now that their eyes are opened, they can't be fooled. They know when Malinda is opening the box, and they all hunker down and close their eyes. In both pictures, Tiny is at the bottom right and the intermediate nestling is at the bottom left. The rain persists until noon of Day 11. Fred and Ethel feed mealworms to the nestlings during the rain but happily hunt bugs when the sun comes out.

Earwigs may also show up in boxes, sometimes in great numbers, but they don't appear to bother the bluebirds and are easy to evict.

Gnats and blackflies are biting insects that may hang in a cloud over a nestbox, particularly near a wetland. In extreme conditions, gnats and blackflies can draw enough blood from a nestling to kill it. Natural insecticides (see sidebar, p. 25) will kill gnats and blackflies on contact, but the box (not the birds) must be sprayed frequently because the insecticide dissipates rapidly.

A wet and bedraggled Fred stands on Malinda's deck on Day 10, holding three mealworms taken from the bowl on his right. Fred and Ethel took several hundred mealworms that rainy day, Malinda says. During the previous three days — all clear and sunny — they hardly touched the mealworms. Since she started providing mealworms as an emergency food, Malinda says she has not had a nestling die.

Mites are tiny biters that seldom pose a risk to nestlings. Monitors generally discover them after nestlings have fledged. The hungry mites crawl onto the monitor's hands while the box is being cleaned. They can't live on humans, but they can bite and cause discomfort. Soap and water removes them.

Bird blowflies are a common parasite that can be a serious threat to nestlings. They are described in Chapter 4, where you'll find more information on how to monitor for them and control them.

Briefly, to monitor for blowflies, it's best to have boxes that open from the side or front so that you can get at the nest. Blowflies may be visible when the nestlings are six or seven days old. "Look closely near the bottom of the nest for small oval-shaped larvae or pupae along the wall and on the floor of the box," advises Crystal Davis in Ohio. "You may want to slide a putty knife under the nest to raise it a tad and get a better look underneath. If the nest looks dry and fluffy, you probably do not have a problem. If the nest looks dark, stained, or moist, you may have blowflies," she says.

What should you do if you see a house sparrow hanging around a box with a nest full of baby bluebirds? We provide those answers in Chapter 4 as well. It's upsetting to check a box and find nestlings or a parent bird that has been **wounded by a sparrow.** There's not much that you can do for a wounded bird. It's a personal decision as to whether you should take an injured bird to a licensed wildlife rehabilitator. None of the species covered in this book is in danger of extinction, and when birds lose a clutch, they often nest again quickly.

The sheaths enclosing the wing feathers are starting to disintegrate, and the wing feathers are beginning to emerge. At first, only the gray feather tips are visible, but by Day 13, there is no question that the oldest nestlings (at the bottom of each picture) have the bright blue wing feathers of males. The weather is cold but clear, until clouds roll in and rain resumes on the afternoon of Day 13. Malinda notes that Fred and Ethel are so distracted by tree swallows (see sidebar, p. 37) that they feed the nestlings notably less often than usual.

Still, it's only human to want to help, and it's natural to feel responsible for birds you've invited to make a home on your property. If you're not the kind of person who's prepared to let nature take its course — if you want to see an injured bird get some help — then Haleya Priest says, "I recommend you find out who your local rehabbers are *before* an emergency takes place."

How do you find a local rehabber? Call your local nature center, a bird specialty store, or your local animal shelter and ask for a referral. "An animal shelter is probably your best bet," says Mary Penn of Stanton, Virginia, who is herself a rehabilitator. "The folks there are usually already working very closely with rehabbers."

When tragedy strikes your backyard box, it's time to reassess your situation. Could the problem have been prevented? Can you relocate the box so it is far away from sparrow habitat? Can you monitor more often? Are you ready to commit to trapping sparrows (p. 82)? Or should you reconsider whether your yard is a safe place for cavity-nesters?

Sometimes it happens that both parent birds disappear, leaving nestlings orphaned. Perhaps they were taken by predators — a sharp-shinned hawk that patrols the local birdfeeder or the neighborhood cat. Nestlings can live about 24 hours without food, and because you are making regular monitoring visits, you may find the **orphaned nestlings** before they succumb to starvation. If you are not certain whether nestlings are orphaned or not, you can wedge a stem of grass into the entrance hole and then check back in an hour to see if it has been disturbed by parents coming and going or if it is still blocking the entrance.

Your first impulse may be to hustle the nestlings to a wildlife rehabilitator. But in a case like this, says expert rehabber Mary Penn, "the nestlings will actually have a better chance if they never come in to rehab." She strongly advises that you try to locate a box with nestlings of about the same age and place your orphans with a foster family — or two. Elsie Eltzroth, who lives in Corvallis, Oregon, where spring weather is generally cold and rainy, sees a number of orphans each season, and she

"I have noticed that the closer we get to fledging, the more testy Fred and Ethel get with me," Malinda says. *"They really have an investment going now. Check on eggs, and they could not care less; the older the kids, the more concerned they are."*

The bright blue feathers protruding from the wing sheaths on Day 13 are evidence that this nestling — one of the two oldest — is a male.

The intermediate nestling is at the top left. The developing wing feathers reveal that this is a female (compare to the older male on the lower right). It is still cold and dreary, but Fred and Ethel had a good "bugging" day. This is the last day that the nestbox will be opened to be photographed.

agrees that this strategy really works. "I often foster between boxes during bad weather in springtime," Elsie says.

Sure, it's easy enough for someone with a 200-box trail and a banding permit to find some suitable foster parents. But what do you do when all you have is a single backyard box? Get to know other nestbox enthusiasts in your area, suggests Mary, or join your local or state bluebird organization. "That way, if you get orphans, you can call around and say, 'Hey, do you have a nest of nine-day-old bluebirds?' As long as they're the same age, the parent birds really can't count." Mary says.

For safe transport of the orphans to their new nest, Mary makes an artificial nest out of a plastic margarine tub with some tissues in it and puts it in a shoebox with some holes in the top for ventilation. "That's nice and quiet and dark," she says. "And I

put rice in a little cloth bag — some people use a sock instead of a bag — and microwave it for a few minutes. Then I put it under the nest for heat."

Although it probably seems logical to look for an adoptive nest with only a few nestlings, Mary says it's better to place orphaned birds with parents that have a large clutch because that's a sign the mother and father are experienced parents. "Especially when orphans are a little bit older, I can add one or two birds to a nest of five without over-taxing the parents," she says.

Tennessee bluebird expert Steve Garr says neighbors often ask him for help in finding a foster nest for orphaned bluebirds. When he makes a placement, Steve likes to give the adoptive parents a helping hand. "We put a bluebird feeder close to the nestbox and supplement with 50 to 100 mealworms each day," he says. "That makes it easier on the parents."

Mary notes that there's one situation of apparent "orphaning" where neither nest monitor nor expert rehabber should step in. "If you see a fledgling sitting on the ground, and it appears to be healthy, bright, and alert, don't intervene," she emphasizes. "If you take that healthy fledgling to a rehabber, the bird will know the rehabber is not its parents, and it will be extremely difficult to get that bird to eat." It's better, she says, to leave the fledgling alone so its parents can come and care for it. Mary concedes that you can do one helpful thing for the fledgling: shoo away any curious cats.

Fledging — First Flight

With good care from their parents and diligent monitoring from you, the young birds have grown big. They are almost ready to fledge, or leave the nest.

The time it takes for the young birds to reach fledging age depends on several factors. Of course, birds of different species take different amounts of time to mature (see table, p. 29). But the number of days till fledging also depends on whether the weather has been warm or cold; southern nestlings fledge sooner than northern ones, and summer

DAY 12, 4:00 P.M.

One of the oldest nestlings can be compared with Tiny (right) at the same age. Side by side, wing feathers reveal that the older nestling is male; Tiny is female.

DAY 14, 5:00 P.M.

Tiny on her 12th day is nearly identical to her older brother (left). She has not caught up with the other nestlings and won't be ready to fledge when they are.

DAYS 15 AND 16

Fred stands guard while Ethel delivers food to the nestlings. In the right-hand photo, he wing-waves, assuring her that it is safe, even though she isn't looking. Malinda notes that when Ethel enters the box to deliver food or get a fecal sac, she will often wait for his wing wave or call before leaving. The food deliveries are slowing. Fred and Ethel take breaks of almost an hour. Increasingly they only lean in the hole to deliver food. The nestlings are able to scramble to the hole to get the food, but they don't show themselves in the hole yet.

broods fledge sooner than spring broods. The number of days till fledging also depends on how well the parents have fed the young birds.

Keith Kridler recalls the day he found a little group of bluebird nestlings on the ground below the box, days before they were expected to fledge. Why had the birds bailed out so early? "A snake was in the box," Keith explains. Predators aren't the only things that can stimulate what scientists call **"premature fledging."** When you open the box to monitor, that simple step may be enough to make the birds jump ship. And if the birds bail out before they can fly, that can be a problem. The ability to fly is a young bird's main defense against predators. Birds that find themselves out in the wide world before their feathers are sufficiently developed to support flight will still get food from their parents, but they'll be easy prey for a cat or a hawk.

For this reason, says Ray Briggs of Cobleskill, New York, "we do not monitor the boxes after the nestlings are about 12 days old." In other words, after you determine the sex of the nestlings on the 12th or 13th day (males reveal bright blue wings; females' wings are blue-gray), lay off the monitoring. For western bluebirds, which take a few days longer to mature, Elsie Eltzroth says it is "usually inadvisable to open a box after the nestlings are 14 days old."

But other nestbox monitors say the risk of premature fledging is overstated and that continued monitoring is a good idea — you're more likely to notice and deal with any problems. "Parent birds are as likely to die the last 5 days the young are in the nest as they are the first 12 days!" exclaims Keith Kridler.

"I have saved a good number of birds from trouble by continuing to monitor — and that should make up for any minor losses to premature fledging," argues Dick Purvis.

To illustrate the value of continued monitoring, Joe Huber told us about the time he noticed that the bluebird parents at his backyard box were not behaving normally. At the time, the nestlings were 12 days old. "When I opened the box, I saw two dead nestlings," he says. "Two live nestlings were standing up in the corners of the box. I knew immediately the problem was blowfly larvae. I went to the house for a paper bag and a towel, put the towel in the bottom of the bag, and put the birds in the bag while I replaced the nest. Four days later I watched from my porch as the birds fledged."

"I've had only two or three true cases of premature fledging," says Hatch Graham. "Usually I can gather up the chicks, stuff them back through the

Diversionary Flying

"If other birds are in the yard when Fred or Ethel feeds the babies," Malinda relates, "they use a diversion tactic; they take a mealworm, fly in the wrong direction, then at the last second zoom back to the nestbox and dart straight into the hole." Malinda says they often use this tactic when they are feeding fledgings in a tree to avoid directing predators to the nestlings. They pause on a branch a few trees away from the nestlings, look around, and if all is safe, make a quick, inconspicuous flight to the fledgling waiting to be fed. "It doesn't do much good because the kids are so loud anyone could find them," Malinda says with a laugh. "But the parents do try."

DAY 17

DAY 18

DAY 18. 7:19 P.M.

On Day 17, the nestlings begin to peek out the entrance hole. Malinda sees that they are jumping and fluttering a bit, trying to get up to the hole to look out. There are long gaps between feedings, and on Day 18, Malinda counts only 59 food deliveries between 6:30 A.M. and 6:45 P.M. (Ethel, 44; Fred, 15). The parents seldom enter the box except to remove fecal sacs. Day 18 is a long day of nestlings peeking and leaning slightly out of the hole. Finally, at 7:19 P.M., a nestling leans far out of the hole and almost without pause, flies off.

Note that Day 1 is the day the first nestlings emerge. Those nestlings are not actually one day old until Day 2. So the oldest pair of nestlings were 17 days old when they fledged on Day 18.

entrance hole (Hatch says it's too risky to open the door), plug the entrance hole with my bandanna, and wait for them to quiet down."

If the young birds won't stay put, you can try putting a 1-inch-diameter hole restrictor over the entrance hole. At this point, the birds are so big they won't be able to squeeze through. Leave the restrictor on for only a few hours — at most, overnight — just until the young birds have calmed down. Then remove the restrictor. "I have seen this method used on hundreds of nestlings with no damage and no premature fledglings," says Keith Kridler. "The parents will continue to feed the young through the hole reducer."

Koby Prater of Seneca, Missouri, describes how he had a nestling jump ship early. It was nearly dark, and Koby couldn't find where the early bird had landed. He worried about whether the little one would make it safely through the night by itself. Up by six the next morning, Koby found the fledgling in a thick bush. "The parents were feeding it," he says. The four nestlings remaining in the box didn't fledge until evening, Koby reports.

Finally, note that you may not need to open the box to determine that your close-to-fledging birds are doing fine. When you approach the box for your monitoring visit, tap gently on the side of the box instead of opening it. Young birds at this age will come forward to the entrance hole, so you'll be able to see if they seem alert and unstressed. Also, look around for the parent birds. "If they are behaving normally," says Keith Kridler, "probably nothing bad is happening in the box."

You may have fond hopes of giving your **fledgling birds** a warm send-off as they emerge from the box into the wide world. But don't count on throwing confetti at the big event, says

Betty Darrell. "In all the years I've been doing bluebirds, I've never ever seen the babies fly," she says.

"Three to four days prior to fledging, you'll be able to glimpse the birds' faces inside the entrance hole," says Linda Violett, who monitors western bluebirds. "About two to three days prior to fledging, the nestlings will be clinging to the inside, looking out the hole. Fledging will happen within a day or so if you see a nestling start to stick its head way out the hole to look around. And when you see a nestling actually sitting in the hole with its toes on the outside, quietly get in a comfortable position in a place that's somewhat secluded from the nestling's view — and be patient!"

If you miss the momentous launch, how can you tell for sure the young birds did indeed fledge and weren't taken by a predator? For one thing, you won't see any evidence of predation — the nest will be intact. It will usually be flattened, but it won't be torn apart. You may also see a telltale streak of "whitewash," or fecal streaking, down the front of the box, below the entrance hole, deposited by the nestlings as they fledged.

Once the babies have left the box, many nestbox monitors experience the true meaning of "empty nest syndrome." But the birds will still be in the neighborhood, even if they are not very conspicuous. "Normally fledglings fly to a high place in the treetops, where they're difficult to spot, even with binoculars," says Bruce Burdett. "Often the only way to spot them is to watch where the parents are going."

Bill Darnell of Savannah, Tennessee, has watched fledglings after they leave the nest. "For the first few days, they stay pretty close to each other, fairly high up in trees," Bill observes. "During a cool twilight, you can find them in a limb crotch, piled on top of

Only Tiny remains in the nestbox. The intermediate nestling has just fledged and joined her older brothers in the woods. Tiny finally summons her courage and fledges successfully at 7:08 P.M., one day younger than her older brothers were when they took off.

each other just as they were in the nest.

"As time passes, you will notice the young birds coming down lower," Bill says. "I see them sitting on guy wires while the adult catches food. Then the adult flutters on the ground, tempting the young to come and get it. They finally do, and before you know it, they are losing their spots, the yellow 'lips,' and they're catching their own food." Experts at the Cornell Lab of Ornithology report it takes 10 days to 2 weeks after fledging for the young birds to start drop-feeding like adults.

While the fledglings from the first nesting are learning about life in the big world, the female usually starts nesting for a second time. If another nestbox is available nearby, she will often prepare her second nest before the nestlings in the first box fledge. The female bluebird in Nancy Bocian's backyard in Newtown, Connecticut, had a second nest prepared in advance, Nancy reports. "Within a day of the fledging, the female began laying eggs in the second nest."

Before the female bluebird starts to incubate her second brood, she can still help with feeding and tending to the fledglings from the first brood. Once she starts incubating, however, raising the kids is mostly Dad's job. By the time the second brood is ready to fledge, the youngsters from the first brood are able to take care of themselves, and the parents often aggressively drive them away. Bruce Johnson of Germantown, Tennessee, says, "Most times they just deliver a good peck. Sometimes it looks like they have declared full-scale war on the little ones."

Fledging Day(s) for Fred and Ethel's Kids

DAY 18, 7:19 P.M. The first nestling leans out of the hole and takes off. "There is no standing in the hole, then going back in, only to do it all over again," Malinda says. "On the first big lean, he takes off." But instead of heading for the woods, he flies about 200 feet to a neighbor's house. "He is too low, only about 10 feet in the air, when he hits the house and tumbles to the ground," Malinda says. "Fred dive-bombs the kid and he gets airborne again. He flies over my house to a tree in the front yard, where he sits crying for a few minutes. Fred sees him, lands next to him, then leaves and returns to the backyard."

7:25 P.M. A second nestling peeks out, "then it goes back in and cries that plaintive wail for several minutes," Malinda says. Ethel heads for the wood line at the back of the lot; Fred sits mid-yard on the shepherd's hook.

7:33 P.M. The second nestling leans out and takes off, flying toward the woods. "Ethel meets him and flies alongside," Malinda says. "He lands on a branch about 40 feet up a tree — perfect aim, perfect landing."

7:34 P.M. "Then the first fledging takes off from the front yard and flies straight to the woods alone," Malinda continues. "He lands about 20 feet away from Ethel and the second fledgling."

7:55 P.M. A third nestling leans out the entrance hole. "Ethel heads back to the woods; Fred heads to the deck, where I am, most likely to stop the fledgling from heading to the front yard like the first one did." But the nestling retreats back into the box. Through the entrance hole, Malinda can see wings flapping in the box and nestlings coming to the hole, but neither of the remaining nestlings fledges. Fred and Ethel feed them in the box and leave the yard at dark.

DAY 19, 5:45 A.M. Fred is up and singing. "He and Ethel feed the kids in the woods and check out one of the backyard nestboxes until 7:20, when they start feeding the kids in the box," Malinda says. "They continue feeding until 9:00 A.M. and then both leave the yard."

10:53 A.M. The intermediate nestling appears about to fledge, Malinda thinks. After much crying and peeking out the hole since 9:30, she is sitting in the hole with her toes wrapped around the edge. Malinda describes the scene: "She cries for over two minutes while Ethel sits across from the box on a shepherd's hook. At 10:56, she leans way out and takes off like a rocket straight to the woods as Ethel flies alongside. Perfect takeoff and landing."

11:12 A.M. Ethel is feeding the kids in the woods, and Fred has left the yard. Malinda takes the opportunity to peek in the nestbox to see if Tiny's wings are developed enough to fly. Malinda is concerned that Tiny will attempt to fledge before she can fly and simply fall to the ground. That's what happened with a late-hatched nestling in Fred and Ethel's previous brood. Tiny looks as if she is developed enough to fledge. Malinda says, "goodbye, good luck, and thanks for the experience. I hope I see you again soon."

12:11 P.M. Fred and Ethel finally bring food to the crying Tiny. She has not been fed since the previous nestling fledged. "Ethel has been concentrating on building a new nest in a nearby box," Malinda says. Tiny cries and peeks out of the box much of the afternoon. She is fed only sparingly. "She hangs out of the hole to meet Fred or Ethel when they come to feed her," Malinda says. "She is so hungry."

7:05 P.M. "Tiny hears Fred and Ethel in the yard and appears at the hole, crying," says Malinda. "Fred feeds her, and Tiny remains at the hole. She falls back into the box but scrambles up to the hole again. Toes appear at the edge of the hole. Tiny leans farther and farther out and at 7:08 P.M. takes off!" But she flies between the trees and hits the neighbor's house like the first fledgling did. She sits on the grass for 15 minutes while Fred feeds her. Ethel is nowhere around. "Then Tiny takes off again and lands on the neighbor's roof," Malinda says. "Fred feeds her and then leaves her alone at 7:50."

8:08 P.M. Fred returns with a very wet Ethel, who has been taking a bath somewhere. "Tiny has been walking on the roof crying before her parents return and sit with her," Malinda says. "Then after a few moments, Ethel takes off for the woods. Fred follows her, showing Tiny where to go. Left alone, Tiny takes off screaming and flies right to the woods where her parents are. I jump for joy."

A pair of young eastern bluebirds — one male, one female — check the mealworm bowl on Malinda Mastako's deck. The young birds are in the process of molting from their spotted juvenile plumage to their adult attire.

Post-Fledging —
Getting Ready for Winter

It's a good idea to monitor one last time in the fall as you did in the spring to make any necessary repairs to the box and remove the old nests if you choose to do so. If the box is mounted on a post or other structure that mice can climb, you can prevent them from using the box as a winter home by taking the box down, propping the door open, or plugging the entrance hole.

On the other hand, you might not want to block that entrance hole. In southern states in particular, bluebirds routinely overwinter, and they will use nestboxes as nighttime roosting sites. That's why Don Hutchings of Winfield, Texas, always makes sure his backyard boxes are in good repair before winter comes. Several eastern bluebirds may share a single box for extra warmth, says Don. "I've gone out a lot of times when it's 20 degrees and sleeting, just to see what's in my boxes. One night we found six birds in one box," he says. "They just kind of packed in there. That's one reason I like to clean the old nests out at the end of the season — to give the birds a good place to roost."

Don notes that bluebirds spend the night inside the boxes only when the weather is at its worst. "On a clear night, 30 degrees, you won't find them in there," he says. "It's got to be pretty bad weather for them to roost in a box."

Even in northern locations, you may find that you have bluebirds overwintering. "All three species of bluebird overwinter in many of the northern states and even parts of Canada," says Joe Huber. The birds feed on wild fruits and berries.

"I see too many overwintering bluebirds investigating my boxes to justify closing them," agrees Dean Sheldon. And not only bluebirds but also woodpeckers and chickadees will take refuge in his Ohio nestboxes to stay a bit warmer. Dean notes that by making boxes available as roost sites in winter, you'll be helping the birds in spring, because they can make an early start in locating a nest site.

You should consider winterizing your boxes if they are going to serve as roost sites. "The box design we use here in Virginia has a lot of ventilation because we get pretty hot summers," notes Julie Kutruff. "So in the fall, we winterize our boxes by stuffing little pieces of foam in the ventilation holes." Julie uses the soft black foam designed to seal the space around portable air conditioners — you can find it at most hardware stores.

Bluebirds in Fall — East and West

All summer long your backyard bluebird pair has pretty much kept to themselves. But in the fall, you may see eastern bluebirds forming flocks, notes Jane Kirkland of Downingtown, Pennsylvania. "The bluebirds seem to start to join together in one place — you just see blue everywhere!" she says. "It's not uncommon for us to see as many as 20 or 30 bluebirds together at certain times of the year."

Western bluebirds do things a bit differently come fall, according to Dick Purvis of Anaheim, California. "They don't flock together in big flocks the way eastern bluebirds do," he says. "I see smaller flocks of western bluebirds — two to eight birds. And they associate with other birds to form mixed flocks. The main species in these flocks is the yellow-rumped warbler. I've seen 8 to 10 species in a flock, including goldfinches, juncos, and chipping sparrows, all of them feeding on the ground, perching on low branches, or flying back and forth." What a colorful sight!

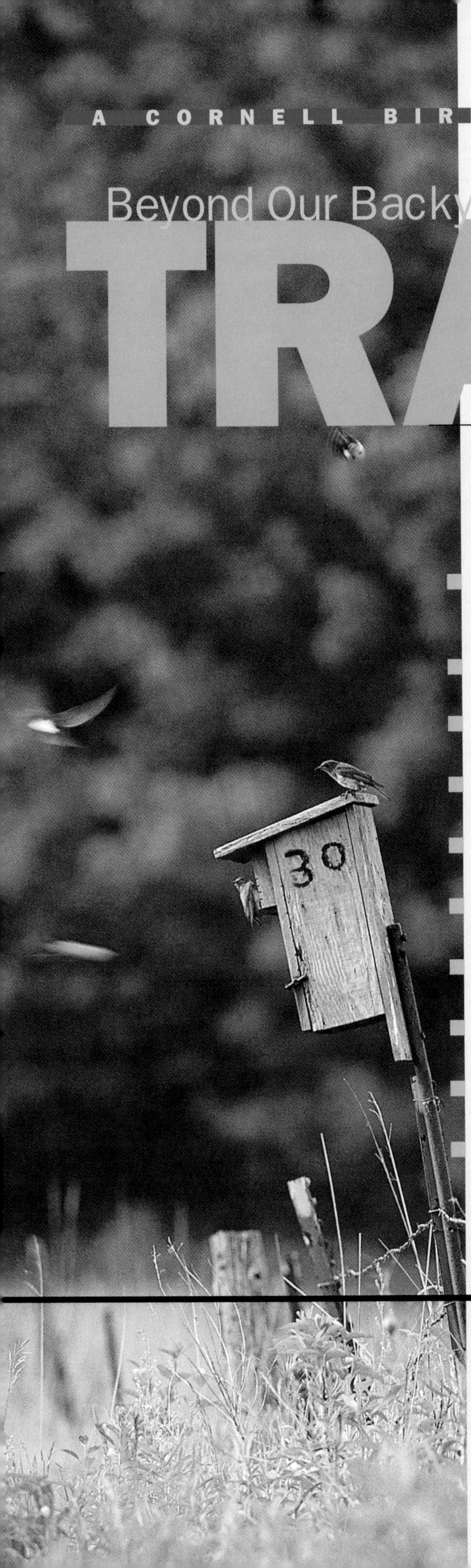

Beyond Our Backyards:

TRAILS

For Bluebirds

by Cynthia Berger

Nestbox Fight
Tree swallows gang up
in an attempt to evict a
pair of eastern bluebirds
from their nestbox.

Starting a Bluebird Trail —
And Making It Grow

Perhaps you've concluded that your backyard simply can't be made safe for bluebirds. Or perhaps you have backyard bluebird boxes and they're quite happily occupied, but you'd like to do even more to help cavity-nesting songbirds. You're ready to set up your first nestbox trail.

In this chapter, we'll introduce you to some special friends — experienced trail operators across North America who will tell you about their unusual and creative approaches to the challenges of monitoring a bluebird trail. But before we make those introductions, we'll provide you with some background information about the unique concerns of trail operators. It's a big world beyond the backyard.

The term **"bluebird trail"** may be confusing to folks who are unfamiliar with the jargon, probably because the word "trail" makes them think of a footpath that leads over rough terrain. But operating a trail doesn't necessarily mean one is in for some heavy-duty hiking — in fact, many bluebird trails lie along well-traveled roads.

There's no single way to define a bluebird trail, but we'll try. According to the North American Bluebird Society, "a bluebird trail is a series of bluebird boxes placed along a prescribed route." Note that bluebird trails don't have to go in a straight line — the boxes can be placed in a figure eight, a circle, or whatever arrangement makes sense to the operator. Bluebird researchers in particular often lay "trails" out in a regular grid pattern.

Most people consider five or more boxes to constitute a trail, but that's not a hard-and-fast rule, according to no less an authority than NABS president Doug LeVasseur, who says, "For years

I've defined a bluebird trail as walking from your back door out to a clothes pole in the backyard with a box on it." At the other end of the spectrum is Jack Finch (p. 56), who in 1979 maintained a trail with 2,280 boxes!

Most trail operators monitor 20 to 200 boxes. The exact number on your trail will depend on the amount of bluebird habitat in your area and the amount of time and money that you want to invest in building or buying boxes, setting them up, and making weekly monitoring visits.

But be forewarned: once you get involved in trail monitoring, you may get hooked. Trail monitors are to backyard monitors as "birders" are to bird-watchers — they're the ones keeping track of the numbers: how many boxes monitored, number of birds fledged, and that most important number of all, "number of birds fledged per box."

Assuming that your goal is to fledge bluebirds (as opposed to tree swallows, chickadees, or ash-throated flycatchers, all birds for which some monitor at some time has set up a special trail), the **best place for your trail** is obviously in good bluebird habitat. Rural roads that border pastures or mowed fields are ideal locations for bluebird trails; so are golf courses, cemeteries, and any other place that offers short or mowed grass interspersed with trees for perching sites, providing pesticide use is minimal. Enterprising trail monitors like Bruce Burdett of Sunapee, New Hampshire (p. 51), and Linda Violett of Yorba Linda, California (p. 65), have established trails in the yards and greenbelts of towns and cities.

Your local park or nature preserve may be a great place to get a trail going. Or perhaps your geographic area offers some unique kind of habitat that would be ideal for a bluebird trail. "Out here in Oregon," says Elsie Eltzroth, a charter member of NABS, "one of the better bluebird habitats is Christmas tree farms — we have many of them here." Also take a look at the corporate parks springing up around many cities — some feature promising expanses of mowed lawn.

Arlene Ripley monitors a trail on the grounds around a natural gas plant near her home in Dunkirk, Maryland. "My boxes are mostly on the cyclone fence that surrounds the property — but they're *inside* the fence, facing the plant," Arlene says. "That's my best trail because it's very protected inside the fence. I've never had a raccoon problem there, and I don't think I've ever had a snake problem." Last year Arlene's 28-box trail fledged almost 130 bluebirds.

Pastureland with grass kept short by grazing animals is often excellent habitat for bluebirds, but you'll have to keep boxes out of reach of livestock so they won't be chewed on or trampled. An extension pole fastened to a fence post (p. 111) will keep a box safe from curious cattle and horses.

Bluebird Trails, Inc.

"I recently got a large company in Columbus, Ohio, to allow us to put up a nest-box trail on their corporate grounds," says bluebird monitor Jackie Gribble. "We have a 13-box bluebird trail plus one box for a kestrel. We plan to add wood duck boxes since the company is on a river here in town."

One of Jackie's colleagues has had similar success setting up bluebird trails at other corporate sites in Franklin County. "Making use of this kind of habitat is important because of all the land development in the county," Jackie says. "These largely unused tracts of open space are a real resource for our cavity-nesters. I even find that with careful work, the corporations are usually willing to foot the bill for the trail materials, do the physical installation with our direction, and cheerfully help with any problems that arise." Of course, companies benefit too when they get a reputation for being environmentally aware.

"I think unconventional trail sites like these are bound to play a bigger part in bird conservation in the upcoming years," Jackie says. "And besides, corporate trails introduce lots of new folks to this aspect of birding. The company put an article in the workplace newsletter, and I've had many employees come and ask about the trail. We plan to have sessions for kids too — we'll take them to see birds on the trail and do some birding education."

A handsome male eastern bluebird hunts from a flowering branch in spring. A good way to establish a trail is to take a walk or drive early in spring and scan the trees and power lines for bluebirds. If the birds are there, chances are they would welcome a handy homesite.

When you're setting up boxes in your own backyard, you put them wherever you wish. When you're setting up boxes on a trail, the fact that you're on public property (or someone else's private property) means you will probably need to **ask for permission** first. "If you can find the owner of the land, it is wise and nice to ask permission," one anonymous trail monitor advises, but he adds, "Sometimes I am neither wise nor nice."

The trail operators we talked to said landowners and property managers are usually delighted to help your bird conservation efforts. Barbara Chambers of Annandale, Virginia, tells about her experiences coordinating the monitoring of three golf course trails for the Virginia Bluebird Society. "Golf course managers are very appreciative of what we do because golf courses are charged with enhancing the environment," Barbara notes. "If they can say, 'We're providing habitat for birds,' it's to their advantage."

Be prepared to be flexible about the details of exactly where or how you hang your boxes, says Arlene Ripley, who monitors trails on two golf courses near her home in Dunkirk, Maryland. "On one golf course, I'm required to mount the boxes on trees," she says. That may mean the birds are somewhat more at risk of predation — but it's more convenient for the golf course because it keeps the boxes out of the way of the mowing machines.

"The other golf course is more environmentally minded, and they allow me to mount the boxes on posts," Arlene notes. "In fact, they use the bluebird boxes as the 150-yard markers!"

Establishing clear communication channels can be helpful, especially in public places like golf courses and parks. "The golf course staff is good about calling us if there's a problem with a box," Barbara Chambers notes. "We have a notebook with names, phone numbers, and e-mail addresses for every person who monitors on that trail. The golf course manager also has a schedule, so he knows which monitors will be coming any given week."

Operating a bluebird trail is different in many respects from tending a backyard box or two. Even the **boxes used for trails** are chosen by different criteria than boxes selected for backyards. The most critical factor influencing box construction for many trail operators is the cost and availability of materials. Many of the trail monitors we talked with locate a source of scrap lumber (or PVC) for building their boxes. "I'm a scrounger," says Don Wilkins of Park Rapids, Minnesota. "I get stuff at the town dump! Did you know that a very, very good source of box-mounting poles is bed rails?"

A young white (leucistic) eastern bluebird perches next to its father at Don Unger's farm in Carroll County, Maryland. White bluebirds are very rare, but Don says that the bird shown had a white sibling as well.

If you are building a few boxes for the backyard, you may indulge in attractive box designs, such as log boxes or slab-front boxes (p. 104). Or you may carefully paint or stain your backyard boxes. But monitors who build 100 or more boxes for a trail tend to keep the boxes simple and quick to construct. Trail monitors also try to ensure that their boxes are durable and assembled in such a way that they are easy to repair if a floor rots or a roof warps. Box weight and size are sometimes considerations for trail operators, especially if the boxes need to be carried any appreciable distance.

For backyard bluebird monitors, we've recommended mounting boxes on electrical conduit (p. 18), which is inexpensive, easy to work with, and repels predators. Conduit has all the same advantages on a trail, but as a trail operator, you may find that you prefer to take advantage of existing structures — **trees, utility poles, or fence posts** — as box-mounting sites. Sometimes the issue behind this choice is cost; if you're planning to set up hundreds of boxes, a pole for each box adds considerably to the total expense. More often

the issue is convenience; why bother to hammer in all those mounting poles when handy wooden utility poles are all along the side of the road?

Trail monitors who use posts for mounts usually experience some predation and will tolerate it if it is not excessive. A trail monitor's purpose is usually to fledge as many bluebirds as possible given the local circumstances. If 10 to 15 percent of nesting attempts end in failure, that means 85 to 90 percent are successful and dozens or even hundreds of bluebirds are fledged.

If you've decided to mount your boxes on preexisting support structures, you'll need to review your options for predator control. Your boxes could end up mounted on quite a variety of posts, poles, and other supports, so you may want to opt for **box-mounted hole guards** instead of baffles mounted on poles. (You'll also keep the cost down if you install the guards only when there's evidence of a predator problem.)

Don Hutchings of Winfield, Texas, has had good success with the guard he developed from a 6-inch length of 4-inch-diameter PVC pipe (p. 119). Another popular box-mounted guard is the Noel guard (p. 119), a rectangular frame of hardware cloth that protects the entrance hole. Dick Walker of Loogootee, Indiana, swears by Noel guards. "One year I lost 137 birds and eggs combined to 'coons," he says. In response, Dick installed Noel guards on all 150 of his boxes. "Now my losses to 'coons and cats are practically nothing," he says.

Don Yoder, program director of the California Bluebird Recovery Program, who monitors 90 boxes near Walnut Creek, California, also favors Noel guards. "After I put the guards on, I had a 37 percent increase in the number of birds fledged," he says.

"You do have to be careful when you put a predator guard on a nestbox," Don Hutchings advises. "If the female is already incubating eggs or

Stopping Fire Ants on a Trail

Fire ants are a major problem on many southern bluebird trails. These non-native ants will attack nestlings and kill them. Ordinary chassis grease (available from any auto supply store) applied to a pole stops ants for a while, but it is heavy and difficult to apply and dries out rapidly in the sun; when the grease hardens, the ants can easily walk across it. To solve this problem, the late Harry Krueger recommended mixing a quart of turpentine with 5 pounds of chassis grease. "Mix well and you have a combination that stays soft all summer and is just the right consistency to apply to poles," he wrote in 1989 in Sialia *(now* Bluebird, *published by NABS). Krueger noted that grease should not be applied if nestboxes are mounted on wooden posts, as it will simply be absorbed into the wood. If your boxes are on wooden poles, he recommended wrapping a narrow band of aluminum just below the nestbox and coating the metal with grease. Krueger gave one other caveat in his article: "If your boxes are located along a fence row where there are cattle," he wrote, "the cows will lick the grease completely off the pole."*

has nestlings, you don't want her to be frightened and stay away so long that they will be harmed."

For this reason, Don says, it's best to install guards in the morning rather than late in the day. "Normally I put the guard on, then back off about a hundred yards with my field glasses and watch to be sure the female goes back in there," Hutchings says. "Last year I put a guard on a titmouse box, and I backed up and watched, and she just didn't want to go in there — so I had to take it off." Luckily, he says, the bird brought off her clutch successfully even without predator protection.

While we're on the subject of predator control, as a trail operator, you'll have to watch out for the one nestbox predator that's far more common on public property than in private backyards: the wily human being. Kevin McCurdy, a biological technician at the U.S. Army's Fort Sill in Oklahoma, examines his raided boxes closely for evidence of culprits. He says, "I'm still not sure *what* predator gets in my boxes, but sometimes I think it's people — someone just pops the lid off the box and jerks the nest out on the ground."

We don't know of any predator guard that will deter a determined human being from opening or taking a box, but some trail monitors have tried using human nature as a deterrent by posting notices on their boxes that explain the conservation activity taking place — and warn of the legal consequences for disturbing a migratory bird. Preprinted signs made from recycled plastic can be purchased from NABS, with a discount for 10 or more signs.

Mice will use nestboxes as cozy winter shelters if the boxes are on a post that they can climb. On your first visit in spring, open the box carefully. "I hate it when you open the box and the mice jump at me," says Betty Darrell of Western Springs, Illinois.

Nestbox monitors have to worry about more than the surprise and inconvenience of finding mice in their boxes. Deer mice and several other common mice species sometimes carry a viral disease called Hantavirus, which can be fatal to humans. The virus most affects rodents in western states but has been identified in every state in the continental U.S. Hantavirus is found in the rodents' droppings and urine. Just breathing in dust or other airborne particles that are contaminated with mouse waste can infect humans.

To protect yourself from becoming infected, experts at the U.S. Centers for Disease Control and Prevention recommend that you make a 10 percent bleach solution (one part bleach to nine parts water), put it in a plastic spray bottle, and use it to wet the nest material thoroughly (not just a light spray). Let the bleach solution soak into the mouse nest for at least 15 to 20 minutes before you try to remove the nest material from the box.

Al Larson's bluebird trail near Prairie, Idaho, has tree swallows too. Tree swallows may take over most of the boxes on some trails and prevent bluebirds from nesting.

Like Betty Darrell, Vivian Pitzrick of Belmont, New York, always wears rubber gloves when she cleans out her boxes — a practice that's recommended by the CDC. After the bleach solution has done its work, she says, "I use a little whisk broom to sweep out the nest and a putty knife to scrape the floor. Then I always wash my hands when I'm done." (That's also recommended by the CDC.)

Although the CDC recommends that you wear a respirator when cleaning out mouse nests and droppings in an enclosed space, such as a cabin, to avoid inhaling the virus along with airborne dust particles, you shouldn't need a respirator when cleaning out nestboxes in the open air. Just the same, CDC experts do recommend that you wait the full 15 minutes for the bleach solution to saturate the nest materials before you clean out the box — and stay upwind of the box as you work.

If you want to be sure mice don't get into your box in the first place, you can leave the box door open come fall — mice won't take shelter in a box that is open to the elements. Or you can seal up the entrance hole. Unfortunately, there's a disadvantage to both of these strategies. Bluebirds, chickadees, and woodpeckers often use nestboxes as roosting sites in winter — boxes provide a safe, warm place to sleep at night. So you'll have to weigh the benefits versus the drawbacks.

Across Canada and the northern half of the U.S., a major concern for many bluebird monitors is that **tree swallows compete for nestboxes.** In a backyard setting, the usual solution is to provide a pair of boxes so that tree swallows and bluebirds can coexist. But trail monitors, as we've mentioned before, often have somewhat different priorities than backyard monitors. Typically, they want to fledge as many bluebirds as they can.

For example, Erv Davis of Charlo, Montana, (p. 52) and like-minded monitors Steve Gilbertson and Don Wilkins of Minnesota say they want their boxes to produce bluebirds, and they measure their success by the number of bluebirds fledged per box. They avoid putting up paired boxes because they don't want to spend half their time and half their boxes fledging tree swallows. And they are getting notable results. Don Wilkins fledges 3.5 bluebirds per box on his trail of 462 boxes — impressive production for an area where bluebirds seldom nest more than twice per season. The average fledging rate for Minnesota bluebird monitors is 1.34 bluebirds per box.

We asked Don the secret to his success. "What I did," he says, "was to head out, early in the spring, with some nestboxes in my pickup, and drive along some roads that I knew went through good bluebird habitat. Wherever I saw a pair of bluebirds on a power line, I'd stop and put up a house. That way I was pretty certain I was going to get almost all bluebirds. And in fact, my trail *is* pretty much all bluebirds. I get some tree swallows, but not a lot.

"The following year I started getting bluebirds coming back," Don continues. "So I started filling in, putting up more boxes." That's how he has worked his way up to 426 boxes — by making homes for the "grand-birds."

Other trail monitors take the opposite approach, saying that they have increased their bluebird production by adopting pairing. "If I didn't pair my houses, I'd get very few bluebirds or none," says Bruce Burdett (p. 51). He feels that swallows are so numerous in his community they would take over nearly every box on his trail if the boxes weren't paired.

Ron Bittner of Saskatchewan, Canada, also pairs boxes to increase his bluebird production. There is a limited amount of suitable bluebird habitat where Ron can mount boxes. "I have about saturated the nearby area," he says. By pairing boxes, Ron has one box available for bluebirds at every suitable site. "Swallows take over both boxes in a pair less than 2 percent of the time," he says. Ron maximizes the number of bluebirds that fledge each spring from his trails in Saskatchewan by pairing his boxes.

Bruce, Ron, and other pairing advocates won't fledge as many bluebirds per box as Don Wilkins, but they argue that the number of bluebirds fledged per site (pair of boxes) is the important number. In many cases, these monitors say tree swallows would take over nearly all their boxes, and very few bluebirds would fledge if the boxes were not paired.

Whether or not you pair your boxes is an individual decision based on a variety of factors, including how much bluebird habitat is available in your area, how big a trail you wish to monitor, whether the local tree swallow population is large or small, and how strongly you feel about focusing your efforts on bluebirds to the exclusion of other species. This is definitely a case in which more data would be welcomed, so if you plan to pair, consider submitting your nestbox records to Cornell or NABS.

Many monitors build their **trails along a roadside** and monitor from a car or pickup. Birds that nest in boxes along a road face one danger that other bluebirds seldom do: traffic. "Don't face the box entrance toward a heavily traveled roadway," says Steve Garr of Mt. Joliet, Tennessee. "I've seen bluebirds killed on the road as they exited their nest." You can minimize the danger to parent birds and fledglings by orienting the box so the entrance hole faces away from the road.

But bluebird monitors with trails in towns and near busy streets say their bluebirds usually don't have problems with traffic. "I have a nestbox in a 10-foot-wide median strip of a four-lane highway that does OK," says Dick Purvis of Anaheim, California.

Roadside monitoring is probably more dangerous for the monitor than for the bluebirds. Co-author Keith Kridler, a veteran of back-road box checks, offers several tips for safe monitoring:

"Position your boxes close to a hard-surfaced driveway so that during the wet season you can pull all the way off the road without the danger of getting stuck in soft mud on the shoulder," he advises. "Later in the summer, when the weather is dry, be aware that tall, dry weeds can ignite if they come in contact with your vehicle's catalytic converter." Don't leave the motor running, even for a quick check.

It should go without saying, but Keith will say it anyway: "Always make sure your brake and tail lights are working — and that they are clear of

Dan McCue of Camden, Tennessee, monitors a box at a cemetery. To make his pickup truck more visible to approaching traffic, Don installed a rotating amber light — the kind used by tow trucks. "It plugs into the cigarette lighter," Dan explains.

A male tree swallow guards a nest and eggs at one of Bruce Burdett's paired nestboxes.

dust, mud, or snow. Check the rearview mirror before you pull over onto the shoulder of the road — and check again before opening your door and stepping into the roadway. You can't help save any bluebirds while you are in the hospital!"

Finally, says Keith, be extra careful if you bring your young children or grandchildren along for the ride. "I almost lost my son Shawn one day when he learned to unbuckle his child seat and decided to 'come help,'" Keith notes.

Don Wilkins has a hint that should be very helpful to anyone whose trail runs along a road. To make data collection easy, he says, "my boxes are all numbered by the mileage on the truck."

Many trail monitors assign their boxes ordinal numbers, with the first box erected as #1, the second box as #2, and so on. But Don numbers his boxes by the distance in miles from the start of the trail to the box. "The first box on a particular trail will be 0.0," he says. "Then the next one will be labeled 0.3, which means ³⁄₁₀ of a mile down the road." And so on.

"That way, if I put up new boxes between existing boxes, I don't have to renumber everything," Don says with satisfaction. When you're monitoring nearly 500 boxes, timesaving tricks really count!

Bruce Burdett
Sunapee, New Hampshire

The modern world seems so complex and filled with so many problems, some folks just throw up their hands and say, "One person can't really make a difference." But this thought seems never to have occurred to Bruce Burdett of Sunapee, New Hampshire. He's the founder, director, secretary,

treasurer, chief executive officer — in fact, the entire membership of the only organization in the Granite State that is dedicated entirely to the study and support of bluebirds. Bruce calls his organization the "New Hampshire Bluebird Conspiracy."

A retired schoolteacher, Bruce moved to New Hampshire from Connecticut in 1988. He enjoys fishing and gardening, working in his wood shop, and serving on the town conservation commission — and he now monitors a trail of nearly 60 nestboxes. But when Bruce first settled in his new home, he says he assumed that bluebirds were, for all practical purposes, extinct. "I hadn't seen one myself for 20 years," he remembers.

When he discovered to his surprise that bluebirds were alive and well in his new hometown of Sunapee, he started reading a few books about them — and putting up boxes. "I have permission from people all over town to put bird houses on their property," he says. Some of his nestboxes are in the yards of friends and neighbors, Bruce says, but often he gets calls from people who've heard through word of mouth that he's the local bluebird expert. They ask him to take a look at their property to see if he thinks they can attract some birds. And in many cases, Bruce says, he has simply knocked on a stranger's door because "I liked the look of their layout.

"I've always gotten a good reception," he adds. "Everyone seems delighted. So I've gotten to know new people through bluebirding."

What does a "good layout" look like? "For the most part, either large lawns or open fields," Bruce explains. He says his unsuccessful boxes — and he has a few — are hemmed in by trees and shrubbery, bushes and thickets. Why does he leave these boxes in place? For good reason, he says: "Sweet old ladies ask me to put boxes in their yards and I can't say no, so I put them up. I know perfectly well there aren't going to be any bluebirds, but I don't have the heart to take them down."

Bruce uses a "NABS-style" box mounted on galvanized pipe. So far, his boxes seem to lead a charmed existence — he hasn't needed to add

The New Hampshire Bluebird Conspiracy

Under the aegis of the New Hampshire Bluebird Conspiracy, Bruce developed and now publishes an information packet aimed at the beginning bluebird monitor. The six-page packet includes a nestbox plan, a troubleshooting chart, and a list of tips for getting started. To get these packets out where they can do their good work, Bruce sends letters each spring to the editors of "carefully chosen New Hampshire newspapers," asking them to let readers know that the packets are available — absolutely free. "I just say, 'If you want this packet, drop me a line,'" he says, "and I ask people to include a few loose stamps." Editors have cooperated, and to date, Bruce has mailed out nearly 2,000 copies of his concise guide to bluebirding in response to requests. "And I've gotten enough stamps that I'm in the black, postage wise," he adds, smiling.

baffles or predator guards. "If I had problems with house sparrows and snakes and starlings and house cats and raccoons, I probably would, but I never have. Just lucky, I guess," he says. The sole time a house sparrow took over a box, Bruce solved the problem by putting a tiny pinprick in the end of each sparrow egg with the corkscrew attachment on his jackknife. The sparrows kept busy incubating the eggs instead of harassing bluebirds.

And his luck continued. "When the sparrows gave up trying to hatch those punctured eggs," he says, "a bluebird promptly came along and rearranged the nest and laid four bluebird eggs."

Bruce says his most significant problem is tree swallows that compete with bluebirds for nestboxes. He guesses that swallows outnumber bluebirds by about 50 to 1 in most neighborhoods where he has boxes. Bruce finds that pairing boxes about 15 feet apart solves his problem. "With paired houses, there is never any competition from the swallows," he says. In 2000, for instance, 18 of his 29 sites fledged bluebirds, and 5 of them had second nestings. He has never had an instance of tree swallows occupying both boxes in a pair.

Whenever Bruce is out and about, he looks at the landscape with an eye to whether it could support some homes for bluebirds. "This summer I found three beautiful new places," he says, "including a 127-acre estate with a $2 million house and the most beautiful bluebird habitat imaginable!" Soon Bruce had helped to enhance the value of the property by adding some bluebird boxes — and he says the bluebirds moved right in.

With no state organization or other nearby blue-birders to answer his bluebirding questions, Bruce has come to depend on the Bluebird-L listserv (p. 8), as his basic source of information. Dedicated trail monitors from across the continent participate in Bluebird-L, sharing experiences and helping each other with specific problems.

After just a short time online, Bruce found that "a good many of my Great Truths were subject to question, skepticism, or even outright contradiction." Practices that worked for him, like cleaning out old nests after each fledging, leaving houses unpainted, pairing boxes, and providing mealworms for bluebirds, all had detractors in some part of the continent. "About the only practices that nobody objected to were omitting perches from boxes and locating boxes well out in clearings to curtail house wren depredation," he says. "I learned this is a very big continent," he continues, "and the conditions bluebirders must cope with vary widely from place to place."

Recently Bruce's one-man band was recognized for its bluebirding accomplishments by being accepted as an official affiliate of the North American Bluebird Society, the nation's pre-eminent

At 74, Erv Davis still climbs fences to monitor his boxes at the National Bison Range in Montana.

organization for the support and study of bluebirds. The enrollment represented an exception to NABS policy because the New Hampshire Bluebird Conspiracy is not really a group or club in the conventional sense. Of course, having a catchy name didn't hurt. Says Bruce, "One of the guys at NABS told me, "We'll accept you as an affiliate if you promise not to change the name.'"

Ervin Davis
Charlo, Montana

The common wisdom is "Don't mount your boxes on fence posts." Yet Erv Davis, a member of the Mountain Bluebird Trails group in northwestern Montana, does put some of his boxes on handy wooden posts; after all, raccoons and snakes aren't much of a problem in this area, with its open expanses of sagebrush and only a scattering of juniper and pine trees. Instead of the usual nest predators, Davis has another concern, and it's literally a big one: he worries that his boxes will get mangled by creatures that weigh more than a ton.

That's because Erv gives birds a home where the buffalo roam. This retired educator maintains seven different trails for mountain and western bluebirds, and one of them is located on the National Bison Range, a 19,000-acre expanse of grassland at the southern end of Montana's Flathead Valley. The U.S. Department of the Interior established the Bison Range in 1908 as a place where Americans could view bison — which at the time were nearly extinct — in their natural habitat. Today the preserve has about 375 head of bison.

On all his other trails, Erv says he likes to mount boxes about "armpit high" so the schoolchildren he recruits to help monitor can easily see inside. But on the Bison Range, he positions his boxes 8 feet up, at the top of the tall, sturdy boundary fences. That's because adult male bison often measure 6 feet tall at their humpy shoulders, and when those shoulders get itchy, the animals like to rub up against the fences. Any boxes mounted at eye level would be crushed in no time.

"The trail on the Bison Range was started by some Boy Scouts without good direction. They went in there and just splattered boxes everywhere, on junipers, on pine trees, on fence posts," Erv says, "and they were a mess." Erv got permission from range biologists to rearrange the boxes in more favorable positions and start a regular monitoring program.

"It's gotten to be a real good trail," he says. "Both western and mountain bluebirds use the boxes." In 1999 Erv's "buffalo bluebirds" were featured on the PBS television program *BirdWatch,* hosted by Dick Hutto. "Now, when tour groups come in and photographers want to know where the birds are, I send them right to a box, and they come back thrilled to death," he reports.

Erv's Bison Range trail has about 40 boxes now — just a small subset of the 400 nestboxes he monitors each summer. Most of his other trails are along roadways and highways, where he mounts the boxes every 1,000 feet or so — a much wider spacing than the conventional "300 feet between boxes" that most experts recommend.

"We've found, over the years, that if we try to space the nestboxes closer together or pair them, tree swallows take over." Erv says. "They hang around while the female bluebird builds her nest, and then a group of them will gang up and harass the poor bluebird until she abandons it."

"Even with boxes placed 1,000 feet apart, I have a 10 to 15 percent tree swallow takeover rate," Erv says. But he doesn't do anything further to discourage them. "I let them nest," he says. "Fortunately, they nest only once a season, so the bluebirds get the boxes after the swallows are done."

In addition to discouraging tree swallows, Erv says well-spaced nestboxes help bluebirds in another way, by ensuring that the parent birds will have a territory large enough to feed themselves plus six baby birds. "You wouldn't put seven people around a table and then put out one sandwich, would you?" he asks.

Other than itchy buffalo and aggressive tree swallows, Erv doesn't have many other problems on his trails. Snakes, raccoons, weasels, and other predators invade fewer than 5 percent of his boxes — a rate he says he can live with. "I don't use baffles or guards at all. If a box attracts a predator,

Bison at the National Bison Range in Montana help keep the prairie grasses nibbled down, creating the short-grass habitats in which bluebirds like to forage.

I simply move it to a new location," Erv says.

"When a box is emptied clean as a whistle, I know it was a snake," he continues. "Weasels will demolish a box and then mark it with a really nasty odor." Although he can't prove it with numbers, Erv feels that raptors such as peregrine falcons probably take more bluebirds than snakes and weasels do.

Erv mounts some of his roadside boxes on fence posts, but he prefers to place boxes on utility poles. He checked first with the local power company, Mission Valley Power, for permission to hang the boxes. "Their regulations prohibit mounting objects that would hinder access for the lineman, so we have a gentlemen's agreement that we will move the boxes if they get in the way," he says.

In order to decide exactly where to position each box, Erv takes into account the afternoon sun, the prevailing winds, and any irrigation sprinklers. "We don't want water going in the hole," he exclaims. But he especially tries to look at the surrounding landscape through a bluebird's eyes. "We often put the box on a pole near a fence line and position it so that if mom and pop want to sit and monitor the box, they can look at the hole," he says.

Teaching the Next Generation

A retired teacher, principal, and school superintendent, Erv still works with kids — only these days the subject is bluebirds. He's helped kids at local schools to build nestboxes for monitoring projects, and in the summer of 1997, he helped the members of the Charlo, Montana, Elementary School's "Buddy Club" not only to build boxes but to set them up, monitor them, and report their observations to the Cornell Lab of Ornithology's Birdhouse Network program. Erv reports that the kids had no problems filling in the computer-readable data forms that baffle many adults. "If anything was difficult for the children," says Davis, "it was checking their nestboxes once a week after the first chicks had fledged and not finding any more eggs."

Ervin Davis, Charlo, Montana

Erv Davis admires a beautiful male mountain bluebird before banding and releasing it.

Stop the presses! Erv Davis reports the first long-distance recapture of a bluebird banded by the Mountain Bluebird Trails group — just as this book goes to press. A western bluebird banded in western Montana by John Citta on July 12, 2000 was recaptured on May 12, 2001 by Laura L. Kendall...in Grass Valley, California.

Putting the box near a fence is also handy when the babies fledge because the little birds will instinctively fly to a perch rather than land on flat ground. If there's no convenient fence nearby, Erv situates the box so the hole points toward a bush or tree, usually a small juniper. One side benefit of positioning boxes close to perching posts, says Erv: "I've had adult birds come up and perch within elbow distance as I check the boxes. It's just beautiful."

Erv notes that he, like many Montana bluebirders, prefers to use a nestbox that the late Art Aylesworth, Montana's "Bluebird Man," developed in 1973. "It really suits the mountain bluebird out here in Montana," he says. Mountain bluebirds, the largest of the three bluebird species, can't rear their six to eight babies in a little Peterson box — Erv says the bottom is just too small! "We make a box that's about 5½ inches square at the bottom," he says, with a 1⁹⁄₁₆-inch entrance hole located about 8 inches above the floor.

Anyone who lives in Erv's corner of Montana can get these NABS-approved boxes for free. "If you will monitor five boxes or more, we (the Mountain Bluebird Trails group) will provide the boxes and help you get started," says Erv. "We go through about 1,500 boxes a year." The boxes are made from trim ends bought from a local lumber mill. Erv pays for them with donations. Local high school shop classes do the construction.

The Aylesworth box comes in both side- and top-opening versions. Bird banders like Erv prefer the top-opening box because the young birds are less likely to fly out and fledge too early when the box is opened for monitoring and banding.

Erv has a master banding permit from the USFWS and supervises eight other subpermittees who also band bluebirds in the area. One mystery he hopes to solve through his banding work is the question of where local bluebirds go in the winter. "Nobody out here knows the answer," he says. "All we know is they disappear around the tail end of October or the first part of November. Then the males show up back here around the 15th of February, and the females follow a week or two later."

Although Erv's crew has banded more than 10,000 bluebirds, he's had no recoveries outside the banding area. Erv has even spent three winters in southern states trying to relocate banded bluebirds. The birds' winter destination remains a mystery.

Erv does know that females that nest in the Flathead Valley often return to raise broods in the same place the next year. He's had great success recapturing banded birds at his boxes using a special radio-remote-controlled trap he designed. In the nesting season in the year 2000, for example, he saw more than 150 banded birds return. Many were birds that had fledged in 1999, but 34 were adult females that had nested in 1999. Of these 34 females, 20 returned to the same trail, and 16 returned to the very same box.

Banding birds is exciting work — sometimes too exciting. Erv tells how, while he was banding birds in the summer of 2000, he looked up and was thrilled to see an unbanded male enter the box where he had just banded a female and her young nestlings. If only he could band the male, Erv thought, he might get some useful information on bluebird family dynamics.

"Well, I hadn't had a chance to set up my radio remote trap," he says. "So when the male dropped into that box unexpectedly, I ran like crazy. I was reaching up to plug the hole with my glove when I stepped in a big hole where a power pole had been removed and fell flat on my face. My arm whiplashed over my head and broke."

Luckily, Erv had a friend along, who loaded him into the car and drove the 25 miles of rough roads back to town and the emergency room. Reflecting on the incident, Erv says, "That's one male bluebird we'll have to trap next year."

Kevin Putman
Yuba City, California

Kevin Putman doesn't play golf much anymore. But on a fine spring weekend, this Yuba City steel machinist is still likely to be found at one of the local golf courses. He's checking his bluebird boxes.

In Sutter County, California, the landscape is mostly rural. Sprawling subdivisions have not yet overwhelmed the patchwork of peach orchards and prune orchards. Many of the farmhouses have a bluebird box right out on the front lawn or next to the mailbox. But even though farms and fruit orchards do make excellent bluebird habitat, Kevin Putman says the most productive sections of his 200-box bluebird trail are on the two local golf courses. "They're spectacularly successful!" he says. Over the course of the nesting season, Kevin (who's a member of the California Bluebird Recovery Program) sees on average more than six birds fledged per golf course box, compared to fewer than three birds per box for trails in agricultural and residential settings.

Kevin has been monitoring nestboxes on the Peachtree Golf and Country Club since 1994. He recalls that he got an inkling the site would be a good one when he spotted six western bluebirds on a quick trip around the links. His next step was to write a letter to the golf course manager describing the bluebird monitoring he was already doing all around Sutter, Yuba, and Butte counties and asking for permission to set up some boxes. Six years and 21 nestboxes later, Kevin says gleefully, "the place is absolutely loaded with bluebirds. They're hopping all over the ground out there!"

In 1997, Kevin added another golf course segment to his trail: 15 boxes on the Plumas Lake Golf Course, which is about 8 miles from Peachtree as the bluebird flies. "The Peachtree course gets exclusively western bluebirds," he says. "But on the Plumas course, I also get ash-throated flycatchers, oak titmice, and tree swallows."

Most of Kevin's boxes are the side-opening NABS design. "Around here, I think that's probably the most widely used box," he says. He favors a 1%6-inch entrance hole because, he says, "some

say that makes it easier for ash-throated flycatchers to use the box. They *can* squeeze through a 1½-inch hole, but it's a tight fit!"

Most experts recommend that you avoid mounting your bluebird boxes on trees. Yet that's where all of Kevin's golf course boxes can be found. This is at the request of the golf course managers, since pole-mounted boxes would get in the way of mowing machines. "But tree mounting is also easier and less expensive for me," Kevin adds.

Kevin uses quarter-inch lag bolts (they look like screws, but the threading stops short of the head of the bolt) to fasten his boxes to the trees. He checked with a local arborist who told him this mounting system would not harm the trees. He avoids putting boxes on young trees or eucalyptus — those Australian imports that have become a ubiquitous part of the California landscape — because they grow so fast. "I'll go to remove a box that's been on a eucalyptus tree for about a year," he says, "and I won't even be able to get my socket wrench on the head of the lag bolt because it's just been sucked into the back of the box. I end up having to tear the box off the tree." To avoid this problem, Kevin tries to put most of his boxes on older, slow-growing evergreen and oak trees.

One typical problem with tree-mounted boxes is their vulnerability to predators, but Kevin says this simply hasn't been the case out on the two golf courses. "I don't find the boxes scratched up or chewed on by raccoons or cats," he says. "Of course, once the birds fledge, I'm sure some get picked off by hawks, but that's the way it is in the natural world."

Often California bluebirders have problems keeping nestboxes cool in the summer heat, but since Kevin's golf course boxes are all on leafy trees, they never get overheated. Instead, one of

Kevin Putman and four-year-old son, Daniel, are ready to install a new bluebird box at Plumas Lake Golf Course in Marysville, California.

Kevin's biggest concerns is avoiding water hazards — not the ornamental ponds but the lawn sprinklers, which can send a chilling spray right through an entrance hole onto a nestful of chicks. "I mount a box on the opposite side of a tree from sprinklers," he says.

Another factor Kevin takes into account when he's putting boxes on a golf course is the direction of play — which way will the golf balls be flying? "You wouldn't want to put a box within 75 or 100 yards of the tee — facing the tee, that is — because a ball could actually crack the box," he says. "I've had that happen." Kevin says the box in question wasn't even at the tee; it was down the fairway, but it faced the direction of play, and when a golfer took his second shot, the ball hit the box so hard the front panel split right in half.

One final aspect of golf course birding has nothing to do with the boxes. "The most important thing is your relationship with the groundskeeper," Kevin emphasizes. Since he started his trail at the Peachtree course, he says, two or three groundskeepers have come and gone. Each time he has worked to build a good relationship with the new groundskeeper. "The main thing is to find out how you can be as little of an annoyance as possible," he advises. He finds it works well to plan his monitoring visits for the day when the course is closed (typically on Monday) or to go early in the morning, before most of the golfers arrive.

Kevin likes to keep the golfers informed about the bluebirds by writing up a summary of each year's nesting successes; the golf course managers distribute the summary to members in their annual mailing or post it on a bulletin board. "I do get some feedback," he says. "A number of golfers tell me they've been noticing the bluebirds."

In addition to his monitoring work, Kevin has been banding his golf course birds (he works under the supervision of a licensed master bander) to try to learn about their dispersal patterns. He remembers one especially surprising find: As he was banding chicks at the Plumas Lake course, he noticed a female bluebird that was already wearing a band. "I caught her in the box when she was feeding her chicks," Kevin remembers. "I expected to find she'd been banded right there at Plumas as a chick. But I looked up the band, and she'd flown over from Peachtree!" — a distance of 8 miles.

"I think that bluebirds, when they're flying over, recognize these golf courses as green oases," Kevin says. The success of his golf course boxes certainly supports that idea.

Jack Finch
Bailey, North Carolina

Like so many bluebird enthusiasts, Jack Finch remembers the galvanizing moment that sparked

his passion for this particular bird. It was in the fall of 1972, and he was working on his North Carolina farm and tree nursery — not far from the place where he'd grown up during the Depression. On this particular day, Jack says, his teenaged son was helping him dig some blueberry plants to fill an order. Just then a bluebird sang. "I realized my son didn't recognize the song," Jack says. "We had plenty of bluebirds around here when I was a boy, but he had never seen or heard one."

Out of that moment, a passion was born, and it grew until in 1979, Jack was single-handedly monitoring 2,280 boxes in locations from North and South Carolina to Virginia and Florida. Of course, he couldn't monitor his many trails every week, but he found that he could get most of the information for his records if he monitored at least once every 40 days. He's sure that he had more than 1,500 bluebirds fledge in 1979. "Thinking back on it," Jack muses, "I don't know how I did all that and farmed too."

Nine hundred of Jack's boxes were in the sandhill area of North Carolina — Southern Pines, Aberdeen, and Pinehurst — where the landscape is dominated by horse pastures and golf courses. "It took me three days to check those boxes," he relates. "I'd go down there, spend two nights at a cheap motel, and be up at first light each morning." With so many boxes to check, there was no time to waste. The time pressure led Jack to develop a box

A black rat snake climbs straight up the side of a house. Snakes are a serious bluebird predator in much of the South because of their climbing ability.

that was quick to open, easy to check, and so durable that it never needed repair.

The box he developed is discussed in detail starting on p. 99. His nonprofit corporation, Homes for Bluebirds, makes and sells it, essentially at cost, to spread the passion for bluebirds to others. Jack estimates that he and longtime employees Desma Perry and Edith Finch (no relation) have provided more than 70,000 homes for bluebirds. Keith Kridler says, "One of these boxes has worked flawlessly for me for the last 16 nesting seasons and looks like it will last another 16!"

One of the common predators that Jack has had to deal with on his trails is snakes. To learn how to deter snakes from climbing a nestbox pole, Jack studied his subjects. He built a backyard "snake pit" 35 feet wide by 75 feet long, with plastic-covered walls 6 feet high. Inside, 30 captive black rat snakes were challenged to scale different kinds of baffles and barriers.

"I built my experiments around the principle that snakes don't like to be out in the bright sunlight — they want to go somewhere and hide," Jack explains. He built a "test pit" in the center of the main snake pit with walls 7 feet high. In the center of the test pit was a pole, and at the top were some lengths of bamboo that the snakes could slither along to escape. "So if the snakes wanted to get out, they *had* to climb the pole," Jack explains, "and that meant they had to figure out how to get around whatever guard or baffle I was testing."

One of the first snake stoppers Jack tested was a commercial sulfur powder called Snake Rid. The directions called for sprinkling some around the bottom of the pole. "They didn't pay that a bit of mind," he laughs. Acquaintances who were Vietnam veterans told Jack they had kept snakes out of their tents with a length of prickly hemp rope, but he found he couldn't replicate their results. "I watched the snakes crawl right over the rope," he says.

How about another widely recommended snake deterrent — greasing the pole? "Well, I already knew they could climb a greased pole," he says. "It just slowed them down a little." Jack also tested various cone-shaped baffles, also to no avail. "I had a snake get around a baffle that was 36 inches in diameter," he says.

In the end, Jack concluded that the most practical snake defense was the mesh trap designed by a fellow bluebird enthusiast, Harry Krueger (p. 116). The only other thing that stopped snakes was a baffle made from a 5-foot length of 4-inch-diameter PVC pipe, used in conjunction with several gallons of clean sand. "If you have your nestbox mounted on a metal pipe," Jack says, "just drop the PVC over the pipe, then put some sand down at the bottom of the pipe and spread it in a circle about a foot in

The red berries of Foster holly (*Ilex attenuata 'Fosteri'*) will stay on this shrub until late spring, when everything else is gone, says Jack Finch. "We're trying to encourage people to plant it."

diameter. When the snake tries to climb the PVC pipe, he has grit on his body, and he can't get any traction. I worked with those 30 black rat snakes for four summers, and I never had one climb a pole as long as I had sand down at the bottom."

One of Jack's more recent bluebirding experiments stems from his lifelong work as a nurseryman rather than his experience monitoring nestboxes. Around 1990, he began planting a new kind of orchard in which the fruit trees are dogwoods *(Cornus florida)* and the crop is intended as winter food for bluebirds. Jack spent several years carefully selecting dogwood trees with fruit that would mature late in the season, after the insects that often infest the berries were all done laying eggs. Free of insect damage, the berries from these trees could be harvested to feed the bluebirds.

On the November day that he was interviewed, Jack had just helped to pick 80 pounds of the firm red berries. "We mix them with dry sawdust in equal parts, store them in cardboard boxes, and keep them refrigerated at about 29 to 30 degrees," he explains. Homes for Bluebirds sells the berries,

Bluebirding Has Got to Be Fun

Doug LeVasseur, the president of NABS, says, "I know Jack Finch used to monitor hundreds of boxes. He had a pretty extensive trail in a state park where the boxes were mounted 10 feet in the air to keep people from messing with them. Jack would get in his station wagon with a ladder in the back, and he'd drive up to a nestbox, pull the ladder from the back, put the ladder up next to the box, climb up, slide out the nest, check it, slide it right back in. Then he'd come down, pick up his ladder, throw it in the back of the car, and drive away. As he was driving to the next box, he would write down his data. Jack used to say, 'I can check a box every 2 minutes and 47 seconds.' And to Jack Finch, that was fun! — you could tell he enjoyed it tremendously. Whereas for me, fun is having 15 boxes within walking distance of the house, and Sunday afternoons my wife and I go out and check the boxes."

mostly at local bird stores, packed in 2-liter soft drink bottles with the tops cut off, for $6.50 a bottle (that's berries only, no sawdust). "This is a *very* nonprofit project," Jack emphasizes. "We hope most people will pick and store their own berries."

In states where bluebirds spend the winter, Jack says a backyard offering of fruits and berries can make all the difference for bluebirds during the lean months when natural food is in short supply or covered by sleet and snow. He says dogwood berries, which have a high fat content, are a bluebird favorite. And naturally, the inventive Jack has designed a special birdfeeder to dispense the berries, one that bluebirds and other cavity-nesters find welcoming but that other birds, including robins, starlings, and mockingbirds, tend to avoid.

"The feeder is a modified nestbox," he says. "We just lower the front by 2 inches to leave a rectangular opening at the top." Inside, an elevated plastic cup holds the berries. "We have put a perch across the top of the box," Jack adds, "to take care of the pecking order." The birds enter the feeder one at a time, and the perch gives the rest of the flock a convenient place to wait their turn.

Jack is careful to emphasize that you don't need to buy a feeder and hand-picked berries if you want to give your bluebirds a winter boost — all you need to do is plant some dogwood trees in your own yard. Dogwood berries on the tree are so alluring to birds they get gobbled up early in the winter.

Rem red honeysuckle *(Lonicera maackii 'rem red')* is another good source of berries that Jack recommends. "In the Carolinas and farther south, that

One of Jack Finch's nestboxes made of wood from the princess tree is mounted on a 1-inch pipe. The lightweight box was in its fifth year of testing when it was photographed. "This box has two or three broods every year," says Jack.

berry tends to fall off, but in northern states, it'll stay on the plant and dry up like a raisin or currant," he says. "Honeysuckle makes an excellent windbreak and provides winter food for the birds, kind of like the Russian olive."

Recently Jack celebrated his 83rd birthday. He says he can't walk very well anymore, but that doesn't seem to slow him down much. He has three new bluebird-related projects underway, including mealworm farming. "That's been one of my 'losing money' projects," he says. Jack has had to learn how to control other insects that get into the mealworm cultures — and twice the crop was consumed by mice. "None of the literature mentioned that mice love mealworms," he says with dismay.

At the same time, Jack and his son, Dan, are experimenting with a tree called *Paulownia elongata,* or princess tree, which is native to China. It is very fast growing and has exceptionally light yet durable wood. Jack figures that if shipping charges keep going up, using lightweight wood for his nestboxes will be very advantageous. "We've got 12 acres of *Paulownia* trees here now," he says. "The wood quickly gets an antique look — after a year, the box looks like it's been out there 20 years, but it's still solid. Maybe in the future we'll be making nestboxes out of it."

Mulberry trees have also captured Jack's attention. One tree that volunteered on his property in the early '90s produces small white berries about the size of a jellybean instead of the typical dark, juicy, messy fruit. After counting 14 bird species,

Jack Finch stands next to the largest tree in a planting of six-year-old princess trees ready for harvest. The lower limbs of the tree are removed because each limb (and the trunk) has a finger-sized hole in the center. If the limbs were not removed, the lumber would be full of holes.

including bluebirds, feeding on those berries one morning, Jack decided to start propogating it. Homes for Bluebirds paid a local nursery to root 1,000 cuttings from the tree, now named the "Finch mulberry," and Jack gives away the rooted cuttings to people who are interested.

Jack also cleared some trees near his house and replanted the area with cuttings from the Finch mulberry. "Bluebirds will feed mulberries to their nestlings," he notes, "after they have pecked and beaten and properly 'killed' them. They are a good emergency food when weather is bad in spring."

Though he says emphatically that he is not in the bluebird business for fame or fortune, a measure of fame has rewarded Jack's good work. In 1990, he appeared with Dan Rather on the *CBS Evening News* as part of a celebration of the 20th anniversary of Earth Day. Rather couldn't have made a better choice. Few people have done as much to help bluebirds as Jack Finch.

Kevin McCurdy
Fort Sill, Oklahoma

Fort Sill sprawls over some 95,000 acres in southwestern Oklahoma. This is the U.S. Army's Field Artillery Center. On three artillery ranges with impact zones that look like moonscapes, recruits learn the skills needed to serve in army artillery units. Fort Sill is also where Kevin McCurdy monitors his bluebird trails.

Kevin is a biological technician with the Department of Army Civilians; he helps manage the extensive wildlife that lives on the reservation away from the impact zones. Many kinds of animals find welcome refuge here. "Because we allow hunting, a lot of our time is spent managing elk, deer, and turkey," he says. "We make an annual deer census, we do prescribed burns to maintain habitat, and we serve as part-time game wardens."

Kevin and his coworkers are also responsible for managing and protecting the endangered species that find refuge at Fort Sill. One of these is the black-capped vireo, a songbird endangered both by loss of habitat and the brown-headed cowbird, a notorious "nest parasite." Female cowbirds lay their eggs in other birds' nests, and the foster parents end up raising cowbirds at the expense of their own offspring.

The endangered vireos find excellent habitat in the rocky hills and canyons of Fort Sill, especially those bristling with patches of scrub-oak. It is Kevin's job to reduce the cowbird threat by trapping as many cowbirds as he can. "By trapping cowbirds," Kevin says, "we've found that we increase the vireo production — and the production of other species too."

Kevin says the Fort Sill nestbox trails were started back in the 1980s when the leadership at the base decided to establish a nongame wildlife program.

A soldier and child at Fort Sill inspect a bluebird box on the West Artillery Range.

There was just enough money to construct a few nestboxes. Those first boxes — some 52 of them, all made of wood — were mounted 100 yards apart on a square grid rather than along the traditional straight line. "We wanted to see if the birds would use them," Kevin says, "and they did — just as readily as boxes on a typical straight-line trail."

Though nestbox monitors who are eager to attract only bluebirds pay careful attention to the habitat around a box, Kevin doesn't worry too much about this detail. His boxes are intended for the use of all small cavity-nesters. "I don't boot out any species except starlings and house sparrows," he explains. "Wherever a hundred yards ends, that's where a box is — within reason."

On much of Fort Sill, the dominant vegetation is mesquite, Kevin says — perfect habitat for bluebirds. Six other bird species have also nested successfully on his trails. Besides eastern bluebirds, Kevin often attracts Carolina and Bewick's wrens, tufted titmice, and Carolina chickadees. Sometimes a woodpecker or a gnawing squirrel will enlarge the entrance hole on a box, and in these boxes, he's seen successful nestings by red-bellied woodpeckers and great crested flycatchers. Red-headed woodpeckers have started nests in a few boxes but have never brought off a clutch.

Of course, boxes with enlarged holes also attract starlings, but Kevin diligently chases them off. "I get tired of doing it," he admits, but he doesn't repair the big-holed boxes; he likes having some nestboxes available for larger cavity-nesters.

If Fort Sill is like a wildlife refuge, aren't predators a problem? "We do have raccoons and skunks," Kevin says, but not enough to cause concern. His nestboxes are mounted on long PVC sleeves, 2 or 3

Carol and Dennis Stayer place a PVC bluebird box mounted on a section of 4-inch-diameter PVC pipe over a T-post at Fort Sill.

inches in diameter, that slide down over metal T-posts to cover them completely. The small-diameter PVC sleeves may help discourage some predators, Kevin suspects, but they are used primarily for convenience. Habitat management plans call for regular controlled burns, and before a burn, it's easy to slide a box and sleeve up and off a post and remove it to a safe location. The metal T-post can stay in place.

"Weather can be more of a problem for the birds than predators," Kevin relates. It's not the heat that's so dangerous, he says. Summer temperatures do sometimes top 100 degrees for days at a time, but in such hot weather, Kevin says, "the birds just quit nesting." Instead, it's spring cold fronts that cause the most serious problems. One year cold weather cut the production of eggs and nestlings on Kevin's trails in half.

There's really nothing Kevin can do about cold weather, but he can do something about the cowbird eggs he sometimes finds in his nestboxes. "When I find one — well, it's gone," he exclaims. Kevin says he's more likely to find the reddish-speckled cowbird eggs in bluebird nests than in the nests of other species. "Sometimes I've seen two or three cowbird eggs in a nest," he says, "but a single egg is more common."

Most bluebird trail monitors never get to see a Bewick's wren, but Kevin does find these somewhat rare birds in his nestboxes fairly often. At one time,

this species was common across much of the southern part of the continent. But Bewick's wren has been almost extirpated east of the Mississippi, and it's becoming increasingly scarce in the West. Experts think the more aggressive house wren has played a major role in the decline of Bewick's wren. Fort Sill lies just south of the house wren's range, and here — as well in as the Southwest, where house wrens aren't common — Bewick's wrens are actually increasing in numbers. Over the years, Kevin has seen more than 100 of them fledge from his boxes.

"They start nesting in June," Kevin says. He's noticed that Bewick's wrens often choose boxes next to mesquite trees. "But there are also some boxes in open areas that they use all the time," he adds. Sometimes Bewick's wrens and bluebirds will alternate nesting in the same box, but Kevin has never seen evidence that one evicts the other.

Although the original bluebird boxes on the Fort Sill trail were made of wood, today Kevin uses mostly PVC boxes. And he's made an interesting discovery about box dimensions. His original PVC boxes were made from 6-inch-diameter PVC pipe for the simple reason that he got some for free. When his supply ran out, he went shopping for more and discovered that 4-inch-diameter pipe and caps (which he uses for the tops of his boxes) were priced much more reasonably than 6-inch pipe and caps. Kevin's trail now has many PVC boxes in both sizes, and he says, "The size makes no difference to any of the birds. They lay as many eggs and fledge as many young in 4-inch boxes as they do in 6-inch boxes."

Kevin currently monitors a total of 140 boxes on several different trails at Fort Sill. He says his favorite trail is probably the one he set up in 1993 for the kids at the base school where his wife, Shirley, teaches fifth grade. "We started with six boxes," he says, "but we've added more, and we've planted things — now it's more like a nature trail." You won't have to worry about heavy artillery on this trail if you ever decide to visit, but be careful just the same. The kids do the monitoring when school is in session, and they take the responsibility very seriously. "I have to warn people," Kevin says, "don't mess with the kid's boxes, because you'll really get harassed if you do."

Dr. Shirl Brunell — Trails of Hope in Arkansas

Experts agree: a trail of nestboxes can offer "learning experiences" for school-aged children. The most obvious lessons are about bird biology and behavior — and about developing an ethic of conservation. But according to Dr. Shirl Brunell, a clinical psychologist in Texarkana, Arkansas, bluebirds can also help children (and adults) who have experienced trauma or abuse learn to cope with tragedy and loss.

Dr. Shirl Brunell feeds the rescued bluebirds that she named Samson and Little Sister.

Dr. Brunell, who works full-time in private practice, is also a popular inspirational speaker, thanks to the success of her book, *I Hear Bluebirds* (Vantage Press, 1988). The slim, eggshell-blue book, which sold out in its second edition, is a deeply personal narrative of a season spent hand-rearing two orphaned bluebird nestlings.

Dr. Brunell says she got the idea for her book in the early 1970s after noticing that in her office waiting room, which is stocked with storybooks and picture books of all kinds, children seemed to prefer one little book about cats. Clearly, stories about animals had special appeal. Around the same time, Dr. Brunell put up her very first bluebird nestbox — a gift from a friend. In short order, a pair of eastern bluebirds moved in. "I quickly learned that these are very family-oriented creatures," reflects Dr. Brunell. "I could see the nestbox from my picture window at home, and I began to take a lot of pictures of the birds and study them."

From those observations came the idea for a "picture storybook," she says, "one that told the developmental history of the bluebird in picture form and also pointed out how the family operates. I felt little children who had been badly abused might benefit from that."

I Hear Bluebirds tells the story of Samson and Baby Sister, two tiny nestlings that were the sole survivors after a clutch of five was attacked by a house sparrow. Dr. Brunell explains in detail how she painstakingly cared for wounded Samson and his sibling, watched them grow, and finally had the bittersweet satisfaction of seeing them fly free to make their way in the wild world. There the birds faced further challenges and tragedy. Yet the overall message of the book is uplifting.

"The birds' experiences closely paralleled the work I do here at the office," Dr. Brunell says. "The message of the book is 'Only when you finally let go of your grief do you begin to develop a new life.'

"In my office," she adds, "I often see people who have been hurt and think the best way to prevent any future pain is to go home, pull down the shades, close the drapes, and stay in the dark." The message of *I Hear Bluebirds* is that you can't avoid life's risks. "To get involved has risks, but to do nothing also has risks," she says. "The story of how Samson responded in the face of tragedy has appealed to so many people in my office — in the most soft and gentle way."

In addition to writing her inspirational book, Dr. Brunell has incorporated birds into her daily practice. "I've got birdfeeders outside my office waiting room window," she says, "so you always see squirrels and birds. I get the children to learn which bird is which, and then I encourage them to go home and set up a bluebird box. Often a kid needs that kind of character-building project. And it's also important for the parent to do something productive with the child. So I talk with the parents and help them follow through."

Dr. Brunell says children who observe the birds' "family" experiences often gain some insight on their own experiences. "Kids will tell me, 'We saw a bluebird family, and the babies flew!'" she says. "Maybe they've learned that the runt of the litter needs a little more time to learn how to fly. Maybe they've worked with the young bird, learned to pick it up and put it somewhere safe and let it try again. And they see that in a few hours it goes from being a baby that can't fly to a bird with full flight. Children apply those lessons in their own world."

While birds have been a successful tool for therapy and learning in the office, Dr. Brunell says she also spreads the message to children who are not "official" clients. "Living out here in the country," she says, "I'll often see a kid walking along the road with a BB gun. And naturally the main target is birds." Without being accusatory or confrontational, Dr. Brunell says, she likes to quietly ask the child, "Whatch'all doing?"

"And he'll say, 'We're shooting birds,'" Dr. Brunell relates. "And I'll say, 'You are? Did you know that birds travel in families? And when you shoot a bird, it's either a mother or a father or a sister or a brother who dies?'

"And the child's little eyes will get all big, and he'll say, 'No!' And I'll say, 'How do you know that

Samson and Little Sister "nest" in Dr. Brunell's hair.

the bird you shot isn't a mama who's got babies back in the nest? Wouldn't it be awful if those babies starve to death?' And he'll say, 'Yes!'

"Then I'll say, "Listen, I've got a team of kids

Bluebirds for the Blind

Darlene Sillick of Dublin, Ohio, has brought the magic of bluebirds to students at the Ohio School for the Blind in Columbus. "It was a real challenge, deciding how to present the programs," she notes; Darlene often talks to school groups about bluebirds, but she usually relies on visual aids, such as pictures and slides.

To help kids who might never have seen a bird get a sense of size and shape, Darlene arranged to borrow study skins, bird nests, and eggs from the museum at Ohio State University. "First we passed the study skins all around," she says. "I'd have them compare a bluebird and a blue jay, then a house wren and a robin. I also brought a nestbox and put a nest inside," she says, "and I had a section of a tree with a nest cavity, which they could feel. We passed around the tree section and the nests and talked about how each species nests in a different habitat and uses different materials to construct their nest."

In the end, Darlene did use one visual aid — a bird video — as part of her presentation. "I didn't expect the students to see it, but I wanted them to hear it," she says. "I was amazed with the kids' listening skills and with how much they picked up from the video." To wrap up the program, Darlene says, "the shop teacher wanted the kids to build nestboxes. I had the wood precut and predrilled, and the students constructed about 18 boxes. They did a really good job. I went out with some of the teachers and staff, and we put the boxes up. Then the kids monitored them."

The program was a success not only with the students but with the local bird population. With satisfaction, Darlene relates, "The nestboxes attracted bluebirds and tree swallows and house wrens."

out here in the country who understand this real well. They know to shoot only fence posts and cans and things that won't die when you shoot them. Do you want to be on my team and help?' And he'll say '*Yeah!*'

"It just turns these children on to the world of birds," Dr. Brunell concludes. "I've had kids come back later, when they're grown up, and tell me what that meant to them."

Dr. Brunell takes a similar approach when she finds that a child has destroyed one of the bluebird boxes on the trail that she monitors. "That's disheartening," she says. "But if I can find the kid who did it, I offer to pay that kid to be my nestbox monitor for the summer. I say, 'You can earn an easy $10 if you keep other kids from touching that box!'" The child comes to learn that protecting birds is more rewarding than harming them.

Often, says Dr. Brunell, the children who tamper with boxes are from transient families and move away at summer's end. But her attitude here, as in her book, is one of hope. "You don't know what they carry away in their hearts," she says, "from being exposed to even a little bit of bluebirding."

Haleya Priest
Amherst, Massachusetts

"How do you balance work and family?" It's a modern problem, much debated by the media. The question of how you juggle all those competing responsibilities is even tougher for bluebird monitors, who must make time for weekly nest-box checks. Haleya Priest has to do more juggling than most. Not only is she a mom who works from her home as a psychotherapist and a nestbox monitor who maintains a trail of 30 boxes for eastern bluebirds, but she also serves as a local community service coordinator, and she's the founder and president of the Massachusetts Bluebird Association. Oh, and did we mention she's an avid gardener?

Obviously, Haleya uses her time efficiently, and nowhere is that better illustrated than in the bluebird trail she has constructed. Most trail operators look for a piece of promising habitat — a rural roadside, a golf course, farmland — and then string up boxes throughout the habitat. The last step is to develop a route for monitoring the boxes.

Haleya started by designing an efficient route. Her trail starts in her backyard and traces a giant figure eight with her house at the center where the two loops meet. She can check half of the trail, be back at home base to take care of business if need be, and head out again. "I make a giant loop north and monitor half my boxes in an hour," she says. "Then I go south for another hour's worth of boxes."

Her trail runs through a variety of habitats. She has boxes in farmers' fields, on golf courses, near an old gravel pit, next to a horse farm, next to an office building, along the highway, and at a retirement community, to name a few.

Over time, Haleya has asked so many different property owners for permission to mount a box that she has the routine perfected. "I just go right up and introduce myself," she says. "I tell them what I'm doing, and I point out that it is for research purposes." (She sends her monitoring data to NABS, and her trail is part of the organization's Transcontinental Bluebird Trail.) "Most people like the idea of bluebird boxes anyway," Haleya notes, "and when they hear it's for research, they get really excited."

"I find my trail evolves and changes all the time," she says. "If I don't get any action in a box after a month or two, I move that box. Or if I have persistent house sparrow problems, I move the box. If I end up not liking the site for any reason, I move the box."

Haleya looks for nestbox sites that have open areas nearby, "because that is what will attract the bluebirds," she says. She recommends that anyone building a trail get familiar with potential sites before mounting any nestboxes. "Listen for house sparrows or house wrens," she advises. "Check to see if there's poison ivy. See if the grass is kept mowed in the area. Really get to know the site!"

Choosing a site with easy access is important too, Haleya learned. At one site, she had to wade through some tall grass to get to the box. "Tall grass when you've got the morning dew? Not fun!" she says. She took over another box that required a five-minute hike to monitor. "It's a pretty walk," she says "but it takes a lot of time, and it's near some wetlands. There are so many bugs!"

Start with a short trail, Haleya suggests. "Fewer boxes that are well monitored are much better than a whole bunch of boxes that someone feels stressed out about and can't monitor," she says. "You should really help each site become successful and *then* think about adding more boxes." She also notes that she's been able to tend to predator problems as they happen because she can monitor her small trail frequently.

Because Haleya's boxes are located in all kinds of surroundings, she encounters a variety of predators and nestbox competitors. "I have raccoons, house cats, snakes, house sparrows, house wrens, ants, wasps, and human vandals," she says, ticking down her list of adversaries.

"Mounting my boxes on half-inch electrical conduit solves a lot of predator problems," she says. Predators have a hard time climbing the slippery narrow poles.

If conduit alone doesn't do the job of preventing predators — and she knows it isn't working if she sees a raccoon's claw marks on a box — Haleya adds a predator guard to the pole. "What I've learned about raccoons is that even if they can't get in one night, they'll learn how to do it a little bit

Haleya Priest checks the Bolt sparrow trap in her backyard nestbox. Most of Haleya's boxes are mounted on conduit and predator-proofed with a hanging PVC baffle.

better the next night," she says.

She prefers baffles made from PVC pipe (p. 119). PVC baffles are inexpensive, about two dollars a baffles, and easy to make. "Sheet metal baffles are so hard to make," says Haleya. PVC baffles don't require any power tools except an electric drill. "They take me about 15 minutes," she says. "The other neat thing is that this kind of baffles swings back and forth," she adds. "When the raccoons go to climb up it, it wiggles. They really don't like that."

On only a few occasions has Haleya suspected a snake attack — when she has found eggs cleaned from an otherwise undisturbed box. So she does not guard against snakes.

To discourage house wrens, "I keep my boxes at least 150 to 200 feet from woods and bushes," Haleya says. If she can't solve a house wren problem by moving the box away from cover, she removes the box or plugs the hole until the following season.

Even at wren-prone sites, however, Haleya is able to fledge an early clutch of bluebirds. "In our area, house wrens don't arrive until after the first clutch of bluebird eggs has hatched," she explains. She says the wrens are more likely to poke holes in eggs than to attack nestlings, so the bluebirds that hatch early in spring are generally safe from wren attacks. After the early-spring clutch of bluebirds fledges, she advises, "you just plug up the hole and forget about your bluebirds having a second nesting."

Blowflies are another concern. Haleya checks for them and sweeps the fat gray larvae out of the box seven or eight days after the baby birds have hatched. Black ants occasionally show up but never stay long enough to require treatment, she says. Wasps can be a problem. "They make their nest on the ceiling of the box," she explains. "The birds will avoid using the box when it's occupied by wasps, so I always check the ceilings of my boxes."

To deter wasps, Haleya doesn't rub soap or Vaseline on the ceiling of the box. Instead, she takes the direct approach. "I carry a putty knife," she says. "And I always wear leather gloves when I open a box because I never know exactly what I am going to find." She scrapes out any wasp nest with the putty knife, and the wasps don't return. "That seems to work fine for me," she says.

When house sparrows become a problem at a site, Haleya's first ploy is to mount multiple boxes: a Gilbertson PVC box (p. 106) plus one or more of her wooden boxes of NABS or similar design. "Sparrows will go for the wooden boxes," she explains, "and bluebirds are perfectly content to go to the Gilbertson." She fits the wooden boxes with sparrow traps.

Haleya uses both the Huber-style sparrow trap (p. 120) and the Bolt trap (p. 121). When she uses them, she checks the boxes very frequently. She dispatches any sparrow she captures by putting it in a plastic bag and giving it a sharp blow against a hard surface.

"It was *very* difficult for me to decide to destroy house sparrows," she remembers. "When I first joined the online bluebird listserv and people started telling me that's what I needed to do, I thought, 'No, there must be some other way.' But I've learned the hard way how important it is to trap. And bluebirding has become much more enjoyable now that I've made my sites safer for my bluebirds."

Haleya says you can see to it that sacrificed sparrows ensure new life for other birds by delivering them to a wildlife rehabilitator. The sparrows will be used to feed injured raptors that cannot hunt for themselves. And you might like to adopt one other practice she has.

"Whenever I have to kill a house sparrow," Haleya says, "I give it a little wish that I hope it comes back as a bluebird next time."

Ann Wick
Black Earth, Wisconsin

Almost 200 years ago, the renowned bird artist John James Audubon found a nest of young phoebes in his orchard and tied silver threads around their legs.

The next spring he was delighted to see two of the marked birds return to the orchard where they had hatched. Audubon's experiment was one of the earliest examples of bird banding in North America.

Today banding is an essential tool for bird research, and in Black Earth, Wisconsin, 20 miles west of Madison, Ann Wick is putting this tool to work. She has been banding since 1996, shortly after she received the necessary permit from the USGS Bird Banding Lab in Pautuxent, Maryland.

Ann says it wasn't easy to get a permit. New banders must locate someone who holds a master banding permit and who is willing to supervise a subpermittee. "You have to connect with the right person," Ann says. "It took me seven years to locate someone who would take me on. I had just about given up." She works under the supervision of master bander Dr. Thomas H. Nicholls, who is based in St. Paul, Minnesota.

Ann feels especially fortunate to have her permit because these days they're not easy to obtain. Only 2,000 master banding permits and 2,000 subpermits are issued in the U.S. Governmental agencies, universities, and other organizations hold most of the master permits. Only about 500 are in the hands of what the Bird Banding Lab calls "avocational ornithologists."

To qualify as a subpermittee, Ann had to submit a detailed proposal through her master bander. She described her project, listed her qualifications for handling birds (she had worked as a volunteer with

Ann Wick attaches a small metal band with an identifying number to the leg of an eastern bluebird.

a bird rehabber), explained how she would publish the results of her research, and got three professionals (they can be lay banders or Ph.D. ornithologists) to vouch for her ability to identify all of the common birds in their different seasonal plumages.

"It was particularly important to show that I would recapture adults," Ann says. One limitation of early bluebird banding efforts was that, though many people banded nestlings in nestboxes, few people attempted to recapture the birds as adults. "And if you don't recapture the adults, you don't learn anything!" Ann explains.

These days most banding permits go to people who are doing raptor research, working with endangered species, or associated with a university or bird research center. But Ann says if you are determined to become a bander, it's worth a try. "Locate a banding station and offer to help," she suggests. "Many of the banding stations need volunteers and will train." A master bander may eventually take you on. Courses in banding and handling birds are offered by some universities and banding organizations.

Ann says even if you don't pursue a banding permit, you can assist with banding studies by keeping an eye out for banded birds. "Keep a pair of disposable latex gloves in your car or truck and watch for road-killed or other dead birds," she suggests. "It doesn't do us any good to band all those birds if none of them are ever recovered."

Ann does most of her banding on her own 177-box trail, "but if other people in the county call to say their bluebird nestlings are the right age, I'll hustle over and band them too," she says.

Although Audubon used colored thread, modern banding involves fixing a small metal band — it's like a miniature ankle bracelet — to the leg of a nestling or adult bird. Each band has a unique identifying number, as well as directions (in tiny letters) that tell you where to report the band number should you chance to find a dead banded bird.

Adult bluebirds don't sit still to be banded, so most banders capture them while they are in the nestbox. It's especially easy to capture the female when she is incubating because often she will hunker down on the eggs when approached rather than fly away. That makes it simple to lift her from the nest and put on a band. Unlike many other species, bluebirds rarely abandon a nest after being handled.

Ann waits to band adult bluebirds until the eggs have hatched. She tries to capture the adults on the nest in the first week after hatching. "When one of the parents is inside feeding the chicks, I race up to the box and press my hand over the hole," she says. Then she opens the box just enough to slide her other hand in and gently grasp the bird.

Banders who are not so fleet of foot can do the same job mechanically with a trap (p. 120). But

Ann wick returns banded nestlings to their nestbox. It takes her less than five minutes to band a clutch and get the babies back in their box, she says.

Ann's method is a lot quicker, and she uses it with great success. "I captured 46 females and 4 males on my 177-box trail in the year 2000," she says. Thirteen of the females were recaptures — birds that had been banded previously.

Bluebird nestlings are banded between 7 and 12 days after hatching. "I prefer to band on the 11th or 12th day," Ann says, "because then I can sex the nestlings by the color in the wing feathers." She slides a putty knife under the nest and removes it from the nestbox with the nestlings inside, puts it in a half-gallon ice cream container, and carries it back to her pickup for banding. Often Ann does a little light housekeeping before she returns the nestlings to their nestbox. "I replace the nest if it is wet or soiled or infested with blowflies," she notes.

In five years, Ann has banded a total of 2,650 bluebirds. "It just shows you what one person can do," she says enthusiastically. Or rather, two people. Ann manages to monitor all 177 of her boxes in a single day *and* band numerous bluebirds at the same time because she has an expert assistant: her mother, Helen Sarbacker, age 81, who taught Ann to appreciate nature as a small child

"Mom's in a power wheelchair now, so she wheels herself out to my little Chevy S-10 pickup truck, piles herself in, and rides along with me," Ann says. "I have a great big, thick ring binder with a data sheet for every box that we monitor. She keeps the binder on her lap and records the data. With her help, I can basically zoom from one box to another. I don't know what I'd do without her."

Linda Violett
Yorba Linda, California

You have to admit that California is different from the Midwest. And it's not just that Californians have

Just in case you can't read the fine print on the band, here's one way to report a banded bird: call toll-free, 1-800-327-BAND (2263). The operators will need to know the band number and how, when, and where the bird or band was found.

a reputation for choosing sushi over beef barbecue or riding surfboards instead of John Deere tractors. The fact is, even bluebirding is a world apart.

"I don't think people in the Midwest can really picture the places where our birds are nesting," says Linda Violett. "This is a city!" Linda monitors about 43 boxes in what she calls the "typical southern California suburb" of Yorba Linda. "We've got five homes per acre," she says. "It's a high-density area."

Some areas of open space do remain, but Linda points out that Yorba Linda is dry, rugged scrub-desert, and the large preserves are not irrigated. Without water, there is no grass, no insects…and no bluebirds. It is only the small, irrigated patches of greenbelt — walking trails, neighborhood parks, church lawns — that provide habitat for bluebirds in Yorba Linda. The largest parks, Linda explains, are only "about the size of a couple of ball fields, and you can't put a bluebird box out in the middle of a baseball field."

The first attempts to bring bluebirds to Yorba Linda were the work of Dick Purvis from nearby Anaheim (sidebar, p. 68). In 1997, when Linda was bitten by the bluebird bug, Dick let her take over his 17-box trail in Yorba Linda. What Dick, Linda, and other California urban bluebirders have discovered is that bluebirds don't require acres of open space; they just need greenbelt areas to feed from.

Only the lack of suitable nesting cavities had

Linda Violett displays the two-holed hanging "mansion" she provides for bluebirds on her trail. In the background is the lifter box and extension pole she uses to lift the boxes up to the tree limbs from which they will hang.

kept bluebirds from using these green spaces. Linda has made it her business to change that, and so have the other urban bluebirders in southern California. They have the passion of pioneers — and they need it. Urban bluebirding is different from rural bluebirding, and all the familiar rules — not just the one stating "bluebirds need large open spaces" — must be reexamined.

One of the questions that demanded a creative new answer was "How do you mount the box?" Rural bluebirders in the East and Midwest nearly always mount their boxes on posts or poles. In crowded southern California, the best place for a box is hanging from a high tree limb, "tucked up under the canopy," as Linda describes it.

You can travel Linda's trail and never notice a nestbox. And that's the point, or at least part of it. One of the predators that most concerns Linda is the two-footed kind. Even though many of her boxes are in high-traffic areas, they're so well hidden that only a few are vandalized each year. "Usually people who walk the trails will notice a box only if they see me monitoring it," Linda notes.

To lift her boxes to their perches up in the trees, Linda brings along that quintessential southern California backyard implement, the telescoping pole used to clean swimming pools. Attached to the end of the pole is a "lifter box" (see photo, left) developed by Dick Purvis. The bluebird nestbox fits securely in the lifter box while being raised or lowered. Linda's nestbox has a hook (made from galvanized wire or ¼-inch steel rod) poking up through its flat roof. "You just lift the box up and hook it over the tree branch," she explains.

Won't the box swing back and forth? "Sometimes we get 60-mile-an-hour winds through these canyons, and the boxes do swing," Linda agrees. But it's not a big problem, she says. The birds remain in the boxes, and the hooks are sturdy and don't fail. Linda says tucking her boxes up under a leafy umbrella also helps them to stay cool — an important consideration in southern California, where summer temperatures can reach the triple digits.

Compared to boxes on poles or posts, Linda says, "we find hanging boxes are actually less vulnerable to predation." Cats can't get to them, and raccoons and snakes are not common in high-traffic areas like small city parks. "I've never had a snake or raccoon bother a hanging box," she reports.

Although predators aren't a problem, Linda often has to deal with ants. "What I do," she says, "is take two or three pipe cleaners and wind them around the hanging wire, starting from the point where the wire hook will touch the tree limb. Then I put Tanglefoot on the pipe cleaners. If ants try to get into the box they'll get trapped on the sticky goo." Linda says it's a good idea to apply the

Tanglefoot before the nesting season starts. "I start in early spring and refresh it every other time that I monitor," she says, "about twice a month. That's kept most of the ants out."

But Linda's most difficult problem is not insects, reptiles, or mammals. It is that omnipresent urban bird, the house sparrow. Rural bluebirders can move a nestbox far enough away from buildings to avoid house sparrows; Linda can't. Rural bluebirders can trap house sparrows and eliminate them from the area; Linda can't. "House sparrows are never far from my boxes," she says. "They get a free ride here. I'd say at least one family in ten feeds them birdseed."

Linda found that she was constantly removing house sparrow nests from the bluebird boxes on her original inherited trail. "Often I knew the bluebirds wanted the box. I could see their unfinished nests. But the sparrows would keep taking the boxes over."

She happened to read of an eastern bluebirder who had lost not only a nest but also an incubating female to a sparrow attack. His response had been to put two holes in the box so the female bluebird could at least escape. "I thought that made sense," Linda says. At the same time, she was designing a new box, one that would be larger than the NABS-style box she had inherited, with its 4" x 4" floors. "The old box was too crowded for six baby bluebirds," she says, and the birds were badly stressed in hot weather. "So I built three large two-holed boxes and placed them at my worst sparrow sites."

Linda could see right away that bluebirds were investigating the boxes. "And I wasn't getting any sparrow nests," she says. "I got very excited." Soon bluebirds had built nests in all three boxes, and all three proved to be successful. She started replacing all of her nestboxes with the larger two-holed variety.

Toward the end of the first nesting, Linda noticed house sparrows lurking in the tree where one of her experimental nestboxes hung. "They want that box," Linda remembers thinking. The bluebirds did manage to start a second nest, incubate the eggs, and hatch their clutch. Then disaster struck. "The nestlings were probably around 10 to 12 days old when I checked the box and found them killed," Linda recalls.

Except for this one incident, Linda says no other bluebirds have lost a clutch to sparrows while nesting in one of her two-holed mansions. She also notes that when she removed the box with the ruined nest and hung out another two-holed mansion, the bluebirds that lost their clutch moved right back in. "I think that for some reason the sparrows couldn't hold the box," Linda conjectures.

She says she has seen house sparrows claim a two-holed mansion successfully, but under different circumstances. It was when she tried pairing the two-holed nestboxes, hoping the second box would attract a Bewick's wren or a titmouse. Bluebirds claimed one box in each pair, but "the only thing I got in the second box was house sparrows," Linda reports. She thinks sparrows were able to occupy the paired box only because the bluebirds, secure in their own box, didn't defend the second box. She says the experiment shows that house sparrows will use the two two-holed boxes if they can claim one. (She evicted the sparrows immediately.)

Other bluebird monitors have experimented with

Linda Violett extends her lifter box to catch a hanging nestbox. When the nestbox is in the lifter box, Linda will raise it from the tree limb and bring it to the ground.

two-holed boxes and large boxes in the past, of course. Linda admits she doesn't know why her boxes have succeeded in deterring sparrows so far or whether they will continue to work, but the experiment continues. "I am going to try to find out what feature of the box makes it work," she pledges.

Linda speculates that the two-holed boxes deter sparrows because western bluebirds can defend them for some reason. Perhaps bluebirds, with their longer wings, are at a disadvantage inside a small box when they have to fight with a stubby-winged house sparrow. The larger two-holed boxes may give bluebirds the roomy "boxing ring" they need to compete effectively.

Linda says her worst fear is that the sparrows will learn how to take over the boxes from the bluebirds. "I know sparrows are very clever," she says. "Some people have developed sparrow-resistant boxes in the past, and the sparrows have adapted to them." She urges anyone who wants to experiment with her box design to deal quickly with sparrows that move in. "Please don't let house sparrows get familiar with the two-holed mansions," she asks.

Dick Purvis, Urban Bluebird Monitor

Dick Purvis is a regional coordinator for the California Bluebird Recovery Program and a leader of the urban bluebirding movement. He got started in 1984 when, mostly as a shop project, he built a handful of bluebird boxes. When he nailed the boxes to tree trunks in a large park at the edge of Anaheim, western bluebirds found two of them and nested. "I was so delighted," Dick remembers.

Each year after that, Dick put up more boxes and attracted more bluebirds. Then, he says "I began to discover bluebirds closer in to town, in these little parks. So I put boxes on trees for them too." And when he saw bluebirds nesting in these more urban locations, he says, "I put boxes everywhere, even if I didn't see bluebirds — just in case." Eventually he was attracting bluebirds to downtown parks and urban yards.

Of course, house sparrows are common in these densely populated areas, and the aggressive little brown birds are an ongoing problem for Dick and the 25 or so urban bluebird monitors that he has recruited. Anytime he finds a sparrow using a box, he says, "I give up the site, because the house sparrow will never give up." It's no big deal to relocate a box, he assures us, because his boxes are no longer permanently attached to the trees. Instead, they hang high in the air, suspended from the branches.

Dick first heard about hanging boxes at the 1994 NABS convention. Nailing boxes to tree trunks, as he had been doing, was not as simple a mounting method as it sounds; Dick found that he had to hang his boxes high — out of reach of vandals and above the murderous jets of water produced by park sprinklers. "The water shoots out like it's from a fire hose," Dick exclaims. "A sprinkler can flood a box or blast it right off a tree." To put boxes high enough to avoid these two threats, Dick would take a 6-foot stepladder on his monitoring rounds. "It was hard work hauling that ladder around," he recalls.

Now that he uses hanging boxes, Dick says that monitoring them and moving them is easy — and they are in a safe place. "This hanging box trick has solved so many of my problems," he says.

In Linda's second year as a nestbox monitor she expanded her trail from the original 17 boxes to 30. The following year she increased her trail to 43 boxes, "and that covers all the green space I can find in central Yorba Linda," she says. It might be a good thing too, because those 43 boxes take 12 hours each weekend to monitor. Linda has to drive to each box site, unload and reload her equipment, and raise and lower the nestboxes for monitoring.

"What I need in a good site is an area that will have enough insects to support a bluebird family," Linda says. She tries to keep her boxes about 3 yards away from a busy street. "I know that sounds like nothing to people who are used to 15 acres of open space," she says, "but in our congested area, getting a box 3 yards from the street is sometimes a feat." A barking dog also helps, she says. "It keeps loiterers away."

"My favorite tree to put a nestbox in is the California pepper tree," Linda says. "It looks like a kind of scraggly weeping willow, with branches that come down in kind of a canopy. I can tuck a box up there, and it's absolutely invisible." Sycamore trees are another good choice; she finds they are less likely to be infested with ants and earwigs than are pine trees, the other common planting in her city parks.

Bluebirds can make a living in a row of yards as well as in a park, Linda discovered. "I have one box hanging in a tree in this tiny backyard that backs up to a cul-de-sac. The bluebirds use the short strip of front lawns on either side of the street for foraging." If a nestbox monitor provides mealworms, she finds that bluebirds can subsist on just a tiny patch of green and still raise a full-sized clutch.

Linda keeps the Yorba Linda city staff informed about the beginning and end of the nesting season, so the city's crew of tree pruners will know when the birds are using the boxes. At first, she also flagged her nestbox trees with ribbons to alert the pruners. Now that maintenance crews know the trail, she has removed the ribbons so the boxes stay inconspicuous. "I'm getting a lot of cooperation from the city," she says.

Since western bluebirds are resident in the area all year round, Linda cleans her boxes out at the end of the breeding season but leaves them in place. In winter, the bluebirds use them as roost boxes — and so do Nuttall's woodpeckers.

Reflecting on her city bluebirds, Linda says, "I think what we're doing here is very indicative of what we're going to be seeing on a lot of bluebird trails, say, 20 years from now. These are the trails of the future." She has heard bluebird monitors say that they have had to take down boxes because of encroaching development. "They don't have to," Linda is quick to say. "If you lose ground space, put the boxes up in the trees."

We Can Also ADVISE YOU

About...

by Cynthia Berger

Winterberry Fruits
Berries like the winter-
berry are a large part of
most bluebirds' diet in
winter and early spring.

Feeding Bluebirds —
Bringing Them Close

Bluebirds don't need you to feed them — wild food is everywhere, and these birds know how to find it. Experts do say a handout of food may help your backyard bluebirds through a difficult time — for example, the end of winter, when food is scarce, or early in the nesting season, when there might be a stretch of unusually wet or cold weather. You can also offer food to a bird that has lost its mate, to help it with the hard work of feeding a clutch of nestlings solo.

All of these are good reasons to feed bluebirds. But most bluebird monitors say they don't need an excuse to feed bluebirds. They do it because it is fun and because it brings the birds in close. Many of the monitors we talked to also said they follow a regular feeding schedule, offering food once or twice a day. The bluebirds seem to look forward to mealtime as much as the monitors do, and bird and human forge a relationship.

What's on the menu for bluebirds? Insects and berries, primarily. In the "insect" category, many bluebird enthusiasts keep mealworms on hand for bluebirds. "Mealies" are nutritious, and bluebirds relish them as treats. You can buy them, or you can easily culture them in your home. In the "berry" category, dogwood berries are the "beaks-down" favorite among bluebirds. You can grow dogwood berries in your yard, harvest them from the wild, or pick them in the yards of cooperative neighbors. The harvested berries will keep until spring and can be used throughout the winter. In this chapter, we'll tell you how to culture mealworms and preserve berries for your backyard birds.

You can also use homemade or purchased "bird puddings" to entice bluebirds to visit. Most puddings are mixtures of cornmeal and fat plus various additions. You'll find information about ingredients and a nutritionally balanced recipe in this chapter. And we also identify the nuts and seeds that bluebirds like. (Note that bluebirds eat very few of the seeds that are commonly set out at backyard bird-feeding stations.)

To dispense mealworms, berries, or puddings to bluebirds, you'll probably need to build or buy a special bluebird feeder. Bluebirds will eat from a simple tray or platform — but so will many other birds. Experienced bluebird hosts use special feeders to keep most of the avian competitors at bay. In this chapter, we'll tell you how to build various bluebird feeders and how to coax your bluebirds to use them.

"I don't generally recommend that beginners get involved with **feeding mealworms to bluebirds,**" says Arlene Ripley of Dunkirk, Maryland, "because they're expensive to buy and because I think it's unnecessary. But it sure is fun."

Despite their common name (and despite the fact that they look like small pale worms), mealworms are no relation to earthworms and other true worms. Mealworms are the larval stage of a beetle, *Tenebrio molitor,* sometimes called the darkling beetle or ground beetle.

You can purchase mealworms at most pet stores and also at bait shops. A number of companies specialize in bulk sales of mealworms and will take orders by phone or through the Internet (see Resources, p. 124). "I always buy mine on the Web," notes 14-year-old bluebird enthusiast Koby Prater of Seneca, Missouri. "You can get them pretty cheap!"

An eastern bluebird enjoys its mealworm treat. Some folks who feed bluebirds worry that the birds will come to rely on handouts and lose their ability to find wild foods. But the experts say there's no risk the birds will lose their self-reliance.

Whether mealworms are cheap to buy, as Koby says, or expensive, as Arlene claims, depends on how many you serve. A dozen or so mealworms, offered as treats each morning and evening, won't cost much, but experts at the North American Bluebird Society say you can expect a pair of bluebirds and their nestlings to eat several hundred mealworms a day if no other food is available.

At that rate, purchasing mealworms can get expensive. To save money, you might want to try your hand at **growing your own mealworms.** The idea of deliberately cultivating insects in your home might seem distasteful at first. But if stored and cultured correctly, mealworms don't smell, and they don't carry any diseases that are harmful to humans.

It will take about four months for your batch of "starter" worms to complete their life cycle and produce more mealworms. You start with larvae; the larvae feed and grow, then form pupae (a resting stage), which transform and hatch into adult beetles. The adults lay eggs, and the eggs hatch into new "worms."

To culture mealworms, you'll need a shallow plastic container with sides about 6 inches tall. A dishpan-sized Tupperware or Rubbermaid "kitchen storage bin" works well, but any plastic container with a 2- to 5-gallon capacity will do.

Fill the container about half full with wheat bran, cornmeal, or oatmeal. All of these grains are good sources of food for the developing larvae. (Note: If you use oatmeal, use old-fashioned oatmeal rather than the quick-cooking variety — and don't cook it first!) Arlene Ripley, who routinely grows her own mealworms, buys wheat bran in bulk from her local feed supply store. "It's really cheap that way," she says. "I get 20 pounds for seven dollars, and that lasts quite a long time." Another option is to feed your worms "chick starter," which is also available at feed stores.

When the container is ready, add some mealworms that you've purchased — about 100 or so to start. Add a lettuce leaf, which the mealies will eat for moisture. Instead of lettuce, some monitors cut a potato, apple, or carrot in half and push it down into the grain, skin side first, leaving the cut side poking up above the grain. You'll want to replace the apple or potato about once a week — whenever it starts to get moldy or it's been completely eaten. You will also need to replenish the grain as worms eat it up.

Finally, put a folded piece of cloth, paper towel, or newspaper on top of the grain (don't cover the entire surface); your larvae will eventually metamorphose into adults, and the adult beetles will lay their eggs between the folds of cloth or paper.

Some mealworm growers say there's no need to cover the bin (the worms won't crawl out), but depending on where you keep your worms, you may prefer to keep it covered. Jack Finch (p. 56)

And don't forget the water! Providing food isn't the only way to serve and attract bluebirds. Supply fresh water, and your bluebirds will be faithful visitors even in winter over much of the U.S.

says he discovered to his dismay that mice love mealworms — so if mice might be able to get into your bins of mealies, a cover is a good idea.

The worms will need air, so drill some holes in the plastic cover that comes with the storage bin. (If you notice condensation inside the lid, it means you need better ventilation, so drill more holes.) Alternatively, you can make a cover for the bin out of screening. Arlene uses old window screens to make inexpensive covers for her mealworm bins.

The basement is a popular place for storing bins of mealies. They develop fastest when the temperature is around 80 degrees, but will be active and grow in basements with temperatures in the 60s. "I keep the bins in a closet in the laundry room if I want the worms to develop faster," says Arlene.

The mealworms will eat and grow, shed — or "molt" — their external covering, and eat and grow some more. After a dozen or so molts, the larvae will start to transform into rounded white pupae, which bluebirds also like to eat. The adult beetles will emerge from the pupae. The whole cycle — from egg to larva to pupa to beetle — takes about six months, sometimes longer if you keep the bins in a cool place.

If you smell ammonia, that means it's time to clean the culture — waste products are building up. Sift the "worms" and adult beetles out of the grain and discard the grain. Wash the container and put in fresh food, then put the residents back in. Shelly Ducharme of Auburn, Alabama, puts the pupae and beetles in one container and the larvae in another. "If you start a new 'adult' container every few weeks, you will always have all life stages available and never run out of mealies," she says.

If you've got a lot of worms and you don't want them to keep reproducing, sieve them out of the bin and put them in another bin with more food. Then store them in a place that's quite cool — the refrigerator, for example. They'll keep in the refrigerator

When you have no mealworms, berries, or puddings to offer a bluebird in need of food, try putting out shredded cheese, scrambled eggs, or canned pet food.

for several months, but it's a good idea to let them warm up once a week so that they can spend some time eating. Provide cut fruit when the mealworms are feeding but not when they are refrigerated. Check the temperature in your fridge — the worms will die at temperatures colder than 40 degrees.

Now that you've raised a big crop of mealworms, you're ready to give your birds a treat. How do you separate the mealworms from the wheat bran or oatmeal in the bin? "I have a little sieve that I use," says Arlene Ripley. "It was a special lid you could put on a mayonnaise jar so you could grow bean sprouts."

But you don't have to get that fancy. Dixie Dickinson of Halifax, Massachusetts, says, "If I place an empty coffee can or something similar on top of the grain — bottom side down — the worms will congregate underneath it and can be scooped up by the handful." Arlene says, "If you put a piece of folded cloth in the box, then when the mealworms get big and are ready to pupate, they'll crawl under the cloth. You can get huge handfuls of them that way — they're not in the bran; they're between the layers of cloth." Or try putting a fresh slice of bread on top of the bran; the mealworms will come to the surface to feed on it.

Nancy Bocian of Newtown, Connecticut, who describes herself as a former "yucker" and "eeker," wants to assure you that mealworms aren't slimy. "They actually feel kind of good in your hands," she says.

If you raise a big crop of mealworms and don't want to keep the bins going, you can freeze some mealworms for later feedings. That's what Randy Jones of Allentown, Pennsylvania, does: he feeds his birds live mealworms during the nesting season, then freezes the remaining mealies for winter feeding. "The frozen condition doesn't seem to bother the birds at all," says Randy.

When Randy freezes his mealworms in fall, he sorts out the beetles and pupae and places them in bins to start the next generation. By mid-November, he has full boxes of squirming mealworms in his basement. "They have hatched from eggs laid by the beetles and are growing larger every day," Randy says. "Should be big enough to use in the spring."

If you don't want to get into mealworm culture, you still have many options for offering insect food to your bluebirds — if you're willing to do a little hunting and gathering. Co-author Keith Kridler has become an expert at rounding up free food for his birds. He says, go ahead and collect pretty much **any kind of insect** except the kinds that sting or the small gray isopods commonly called sow bugs or pill bugs. "Also avoid earthworms and any caterpillars that are spiny or hairy," he warns.

"During cool weather, hard-bodied insects such as grasshoppers or crickets are a good food source," says Keith. The trick is to lay sheets of old plywood out in a field; crickets will congregate underneath. "When I need bird food, I just flip over the sheets," Keith says.

Holly berries are a favorite winter food for bluebirds. Because some of the hollies don't ripen until very late (the fact that the berries turn red doesn't mean that they are ripe), this food source can last until spring.

Keith also uses a portable propane torch to flame paper wasp nests (he does this at night, when the air is cool and the wasps are torpid). With this technique, he says, you can collect hundreds of wasp larvae at a time.

Keith has another trick for fast insect collecting. Position a 5-gallon bucket under an outdoor light to collect night-flying insects. "The June bugs you gather this way can last for days!" he says. Note that June bugs, mealworms, and other insects with a hard (and indigestible) exoskeleton are too tough for very young nestlings to eat. You'll notice that, even when feeding older nestlings, parent birds will "tenderize" a mealworm first by pecking at it or whacking it against a hard surface.

During nesting season, **wild fruits and berries** serve mostly as emergency food for bluebirds, although adults routinely eat a small amount of plant material even when insects are available. Nestlings need the protein in insects, and they won't survive long on a diet of berries. When bad weather makes insects scarce during nesting season, mulberries become a popular insect supplement. Blueberries, blackberries, serviceberries, elderberries, small wild grapes, and chokecherries are other popular berries that are readily available in summer.

As the weather turns cold, bluebirds depend on wild fruits and berries to carry them through the late fall and winter. The list of berries that bluebirds will eat during their fall migration and in winter is practically endless (see sidebar, right). If you plant a variety of berry bushes in your yard, you'll notice that the favorites get stripped of their fruit first. Dogwood berries and fruit from the Chinese tallow are usually gone before winter weather arrives. Hollies and hackberries last longer. Some berries, such as deciduous holly, don't become edible until they have been repeatedly frozen and thawed. Mistletoe and juniper berries are often important bluebird foods that last on the trees throughout the winter. Finally, when everything else is gone, bluebirds may try to get by on the thin flesh of sumac berries.

The list in the sidebar is hardly complete; most red berries you see growing wild are good food for bluebirds. Note that with some of the plants listed, you can pick and store the berries for later use. Joe Huber, now a Florida resident, recalls how, when he lived in Ohio, he would pick rose hips and store them in paper sacks in his unheated garage. Joe notes that rose hips don't ripen until late fall, and you don't need to pick them right away. "I've cut rose stems as late as mid-December, and the rose hips were just turning red," he says. Joe adds that although his local bluebirds liked rose hips, other birds would ignore them when he set them out. "A cardinal might chew on one or two berries," Joe says, but in general, the bluebirds were able to enjoy rose hips without being harassed by larger birds.

Juniper berries are not red, and they aren't technically berries, but bluebirds love them and will survive on them throughout the winter.

"The best luck I've had feeding bluebirds," says Don Hutchings of Winfield, Texas, "is with dogwood berries." Jack Finch agrees. If you mix **dogwood berries** with other berries, he says, bluebirds will select the dogwood berries first.

Finch has planted a dogwood orchard on his farm just to provide berries for bluebirds in winter (p. 57). Some winters he has enough dogwood berries put aside to sell some to bluebird enthusiasts, but he recommends that you put aside your own stash

Some Berries for Bluebirds in Winter

- *Dogwood — flowering dogwood* (Cornus florida), *Pacific dogwood* (Cornus nuttallii), *and red-osier dogwood* (Cornus sericea)

- *Holly — including American holly* (Ilex opaca), *Foster holly* (Ilex attenuata 'Fosteri'), *deciduous holly* (Ilex decidua), *and yaupon* (Ilex vomitoria)

- *Juniper — including the widespread common juniper* (Juniperus communis), *one-seed juniper* (Juniperus monosperma), *western juniper* (Juniperus occidentalis), *Utah juniper* (Junierus osteosperma), *California juniper* (Juniperus californica), *Rocky Mountain juniper* (Juniperus scopulorum), *and eastern red cedar* (Juniperus virginiana)

- *Sumac — smooth sumac* (Rhus glabra), *staghorn sumac* (Rhus typhina), *and dwarf sumac* (Rhus copallina)

- *Mountain-ash — American mountain-ash* (Sorbus americana), *Sitka mountain-ash* (Sorbus sitchensis), *and European mountain-ash* (Sorbus aucuparia)

- *Mistletoe — mistletoe* (Phoradendron spp.) *and dwarf mistletoe* (Arceuthobium spp.)

- *Hackberry* (Celtis occidentalis)

- *Firethorn* (Pyracantha coccinea)

- *Poison ivy* (Toxicodendron radicans)

- *Multiflora rose* (Rosa multiflora)

- *Bradford pear* (Pyrus calleryana 'Bradford')

- *Chinese tallow* (Triadica sebifera)

rather than count on him. Fifteen to 30-year-old yard trees provide the best berries, Finch says. Don't pick the berries until they are ripe — when the flesh is easily removed from the seed. Finch says the berries that ripen latest will store best.

Finch stores his dogwood berries, mixed with sawdust for up to six months at temperatures just below freezing (29 to 32 degrees). Dogwood berries have a high oil content that prevents them from freezing and turning black at temperatures just below freezing. The berries you pick will probably hold for a few months if you store them in single layers between paper towels in the coldest part of your refrigerator. Check the berries every couple of weeks and remove any that have turned dark. Birds will not eat the spoiled berries, and one bad berry will cause others to spoil.

You can make a small quantity of dogwood berries last all winter by using them to draw the bluebirds to currants, raisins, or puddings. "Red berries are what attracts bluebirds," says Ron Kingston of Charlottesville, Virginia, who's been a bluebird monitor since 1978. "I mix dogwood berries with some raisins and currants. And if I've got a little extra money at the health food store, I buy freeze-dried blueberries — they go nuts over them!"

Don Hutchings also uses raisins as a convenient bluebird treat. "What I do," he says, "is take a box of raisins and put them in boiling water to swell them up a little bit. Some people cut the raisins, but bluebirds can swallow them whole."

In addition to mealworms and berries, bluebirds will take certain kinds of **seeds and nuts.** "I have a peanut feeder hanging from my suet feeder, and the bluebirds are on it all the time in winter," says Arlene Ripley. "They will also eat sunflower hearts once in a while." (Arlene notes that the feeder holds shelled peanuts; bluebirds can't peck open peanut shells the way chickadees do.)

The fruit of the flowering dogwood tree is the bluebird's berry of choice.

Laney Rigby's bluebirds even feed seeds to their nestlings. The Richmond, Virginia, resident says, "In winter, our bluebirds learned to like the peanut hearts, sunflower hearts, and safflower hearts we feed in a specialized mix." In spring, she says, Mom and Dad brought their fledglings to the seed feeder on her back porch to enjoy the shelled seeds.

Don Hutchings adds, "Bluebirds also go crazy for pecans. I have pecan trees in my yard, and one tree produces small pecans that we don't use, so I put them in the driveway and run over them with my truck. The birds love them." They also savor walnuts.

Cornmeal is another bluebird favorite, either served cooked as corn bread or, more frequently, as part of an uncooked **pudding mixture.** "I mix the cornmeal with peanut butter and lard," says Hutchings. He also throws in peanuts, currants or raisins, and several tablespoons of crushed eggshells. The eggshells provide calcium — which the female bluebirds need to produce sound eggs.

You can use any edible hard fat to make a bluebird pudding, including bacon drippings, lard, suet,

Bluebirds swallow dogwood berries whole and regurgitate the pits. Cardinals and most small birds peck the flesh of the berry off the pit.

or vegetable shortening. Peanut butter is often mixed in as part of the fat. Bluebirds enjoy peanut butter as much as a hungry kid does.

Cornmeal is the principal dry ingredient in a pudding, sometimes supplemented with oatmeal or wheat flour, either whole wheat or unbleached white. Mix one part fat with approximately two parts of dry ingredients. Vary the proportions until you get a crumbly texture. The most popular additions are the nutmeats, fruits, and berries previously mentioned, especially currants, raisins, and peanuts.

In the early 1990s, Linda Janilla Peterson developed a recipe (see sidebar, right) intended to appeal to bluebirds and to meet their nutritional needs. She tested various combinations of ingredients on a group of 20 or so bluebirds conditioned to come to her yard for food. By adding and subtracting ingredients and noting the birds' reactions, she determined their preferences. The nutritional goals of the birds were determined by the bird curator at the Minnesota Zoo.

Commercial bluebird treats available at this time often come in pellets that the birds seem to have trouble recognizing as food. Even when the pellets are crumbled, they aren't as popular with the birds as homemade puddings because the commercial products usually lack peanut butter.

Bluebirds must be conditioned to come to feeders for food, and the best time to condition them is when they are nesting. Start by placing food where your bluebirds can see it. Remember that the bluebirds must be able to recognize the items you offer as food. They'll probably pass on puddings, currants, or peanuts without even investigating them, but will quickly spot a wiggling mealworm in plain view.

"The best way to train your birds," says Anne Little of Woodbridge, Virginia, "is to find where the male bluebird perches and put a small saucer of mealworms underneath. He'll see them instantly. As he spots them, whistle. We did that two or three times, and he got used to us." If you never mastered the art of whistling, there are other ways to get the birds' attention; Anne says she sometimes uses a little handbell.

Put worms out at the same time each morning or evening, and before long, your bluebirds will be conditioned to show up for their treat when they hear your call. When they are conditioned, you can start moving their dish closer to where you would like their feeder to be permanently placed. Don Hutchings recommends that you place your bluebird feeder away from your other birdfeeders, perhaps in a different corner of the yard. "Bluebirds are kind of finicky and kind of shy, and they really don't do well around other birds," he says.

If you add other foods to their daily dish of mealworms, the bluebirds will sample them.

This bluebird recognizes the crumbly pudding mixture on the tray as nutritious food.

They will learn that currants taste great and that your bluebird pudding is fine dining. They might not even be disappointed the first day you put out the treat but leave out the mealworms.

After you have trained your backyard bluebirds to visit a permanent feeding station, you'll probably find that other, more dominant birds have learned to recognize your call. Mockingbirds, robins, jays, and other backyard birds like mealworms just as much as bluebirds do — and mockingbirds in particular can be very territorial, keeping other birds away from a feeder.

To deal with the crush at the feeder, some inventive bluebirders have designed **bluebird feeders** that exclude most other birds. Generally, bluebird feeders are designed so that a bird must enter the feeder through a hole — much like an entrance hole to a nestbox — to get to the food. Only small cavity-nesters are willing (and able) to pass through the small hole or slot.

Jack Finch has a favorite feeder for dispensing dogwood berries and other fruit. "It's a modified nestbox," he explains. "We lower the front panel of the box 2 inches to leave a rectangular opening." Inside, a plastic cup holds the berries. "We support it on some blocks so it's not way down at the bottom of the box," Jack notes. "Then we have a feed tray on top of the box, and we also put a perch across the top to take care of the pecking order."

One commercially available feeder that is widely used for feeding bluebirds is the Droll Yankees Seed Saver X-1. An adjustable plastic dome covers the round tray feeder; you can gradually lower the dome over the course of several days so that bluebirds can fit through the gap but bigger birds cannot.

Another popular bluebird feeder design that's available commercially in many variations is a wooden "hopper-style" feeder with clear plastic sides and wooden ends. The ends have a 1½- or 1⁹⁄₁₆-inch hole drilled through them. The bluebirds can see the

Bluebird Banquet

Mix:
1 cup peanut butter
4 cups yellow cornmeal
1 cup unbleached white
or whole-wheat flour

Add:
1 cup fine sunflower
seed chips
1 cup peanut hearts
(or finely ground nuts)
½ – 1 cup currants
(or raisins cut in half)

Drizzle and stir in:
1 cup melted rendered
suet

When the mixture cools, it should have a crumbly texture. Add more flour or melted suet if necessary to correct the texture. Refrigerate.

A male eastern bluebird feeds his family mealworms on top of a bluebird feeder. The entrance holes to the feeder deter many other birds.

mealworms though the plastic, and will go in through the holes to feed. Arlene Ripley notes that you don't have to buy a special feeder; you can easily imitate the design. "I use a cheapie hopper-style feeder with two Plexiglas sides," she says. "I just drilled a hole in each end."

Randy Jones, Lehigh County Coordinator for the Bluebird Society of Pennsylvania, notes that if you've been using a flat-tray feeder and you switch to a hopper-style feeder, the bluebirds may get anxious. He describes what happened in his yard after he made the switch: "The first in was the male," says Randy. "He scarfed up the mealworms and then had a panic attack because he couldn't figure out how to get back out. I opened the top, and he flew out — never to return to the feeder again."

Strolling with Bluebirds

You really feel a sense of connection when bluebirds start to recognize you, thanks to a feeding regimen. Anne Little recalls how one male bluebird learned to wait outside her house each morning. "I preferred to feed him down the street because we have so many hawks near our house," Anne explains. "So I'd go out and take my dogs for a walk, and the bluebird would fly along with me down the street. Then, when we got to a place that was safe, I'd feed him." After this bird's nestlings fledged, Anne says, they learned to follow the parade. "Pretty soon I felt like Saint Francis of Assisi, walking down the street with 12 birds flying over my head!" Anne says with delight.

Randy adds that the female bluebird was reluctant to use the feeder. To encourage her, he removed one of the Plexiglas sides. Once the female became conditioned to the feeder, Randy put the side back on it, and she started using the hole to enter and exit.

Ann Wick has had several bluebirds confused and "trapped" in a hopper-style bluebird feeder. But rather than opening the feeder to allow the birds to escape, Ann blocked the light coming in through the Plexiglas sides. "That way, the trapped bird sees only the light coming in through the entrance holes and can escape on its own," she explains. And, she says, the birds come back and continue to use the feeder without being afraid of it.

Steve Gilbertson of Aitkin, Minnesota, says he's concerned that birds sometimes are confused by the clear plastic walls of hopper-style feeders. He's designed a different feeder, one with no plastic walls. "It's simply two 10-inch-square pieces of lumber," Steve says. The bottom piece has a 1-by-2 railing around the edge, and the top piece has four legs that elevate it above the bottom. The gap between the top and the sides is wide enough for birds to go in and out.

Ron Kingston heartily recommends Steve's Gilworm feeder. "The top comes off and you put your berries or mealworms in," he explains; "then you leave the top off for a while till the bluebirds find them. When the birds are comfortable visiting the feeder, you put the top on.

"The top is adjustable,' Ron explains. "At first, you leave it so the entrance is really big. Then you gradually lower the top a little each day until the

An eastern bluebird picks a mealworm from the tray of a Droll Yankees Seed Saver X-1 feeder.

opening measures 1⅜ inch. The bluebirds will still go in, but a hermit thrush or robin won't be able to."

Don Hutchings made a special feeder for the bluebird puddings he likes to serve. "I've got a little log I drilled holes in," he says. "I just stuff the corn-meal mix in the holes; they like that." Don took a log that was 3 inches in diameter and about a foot long and used a flat wood bit to drill five 1-inch holes through it. "In about a week, the bluebirds found the feeder, and they would visit several times a day," he says. When bigger, more aggressive birds became a problem, Don built a cage out of 1½-by-2-inch wire mesh and hung the log feeder inside. "Only the bluebirds and smaller birds could go through the wire," he explains.

One last tip: You may have the best luck feeding bluebirds if you wait until late in the day, when most other birds have left to roost. After a while, the blue-birds will become conditioned. Michael Liebner of New Castle, Delaware, says, "I just wait for the birds to show up — which they do every night before dark. I put out five big worms, and they eat them. They're really something to see in the snow when they land on the big plate and grab the worms."

What the Law Says —
Possessing Birds and Their "Parts"

One thing to keep in mind as you make your rou-tine monitoring visits is a federal law called the **Migratory Bird Treaty Act of 1918.** This act protects migratory birds and their "parts" (that means eggs, nests, and feathers). The act applies to all U.S. bird species except introduced species, such as house sparrows and European starlings (plus certain game birds).

Specifically, the act prohibits "capturing, collect-ing, possessing, buying, selling, trading, shipping, importing, or exporting migratory birds or their feathers, parts, nests, or eggs," although special permits are often issued that allow scientific collec-tion and certain other practices. The Department of the Interior administers the act through the Fish and Wildlife Service.

The prohibition on collecting or possessing native birds and their parts has some important implications for you as a bluebird nestbox monitor. "You don't need a permit from the Fish and Wildlife Service to manage nestboxes with active nests when you are doing it for the welfare of the birds," says Susan Lawrence, the USFWS National Coordinator for Migratory Bird Permits. "But technically, if you are handling the birds or eggs, that is a violation of the regulations."

Let's get specific. You *are* allowed to remove and destroy old nests at the end of the nesting season because these nests are considered "inactive" — no longer used by the birds. However, you cannot remove an old nest from a box and keep it for

This male eastern bluebird doesn't mind squeezing through the narrow slots of Steve Gilbertson's Gilworm feeder to get a tasty mealworm.

show-and-tell at a bluebirding lecture unless you first get a permit from USFWS.

You are allowed to destroy house sparrow and starling nests (and their eggs and the birds them-selves) if you find them in your boxes because these species are not protected under the act. However, you may not destroy the active nests of native species, not even the nests of a species that some people consider to be a pest — the house wren. You may remove a male wren's "dummy" nests from your boxes because these are not actual nests. And you are also allowed to remove a wren's real nest from one of your boxes if the nest is still under construction and not complete. "How the law applies to wren nests can be confusing, so we're in the process of developing a policy to clarify the applicability of the MBTA with regard to inactive nests," Lawrence notes.

The prohibition on possessing eggs and birds means that, by the letter of the law, you should not transport orphaned eggs or nestlings to another box for adoption. Also, by the letter of the law, you shouldn't lift a sitting female to count the eggs or nestlings, and you shouldn't handle nestlings to remove blowflies. Certainly you shouldn't bring a cold or injured bluebird into your house to care for it — unless you have a permit to rehabilitate birds. "Technically, when you handle the birds or the eggs, that is a violation of the regulations and the act," says Sarah Lawrence. "If you were to break an egg or harm or injure a bird, it would be a mis-demeanor," adds Paul Chang, the USFWS Chief of Investigations. "The penalty could be up to six months in jail and a fine of up to $15,000."

"But obviously," Lawrence adds, "enforcement is a low priority in cases like these." She compares bluebirders to well-meaning Good Samaritans who help out at the scene of an accident. "When people are really acting for the welfare of the bird, we don't want to discourage them," she says, adding that it would be burdensome for USFWS to issue the hundreds of thousands of permits that would be needed for nestbox monitors over all of the country.

The bottom line: Know the law — both the federal law and any laws in your state that apply to migratory birds. And a proverbial ounce of prevention is well worthwhile. "I suggest that anyone who is managing bluebird boxes contact the local Fish and Wildlife Service law enforcement agent," says Lawrence. "Let them know what you're doing and make sure they don't have a problem with it."

It's also a good idea to contact your state game warden because states have their own laws protecting birds and other wildlife. For example, officials in some states may expect you to have a small game license or trapping license before you shoot or trap house sparrows. Also, try to get in touch with local law enforcement agencies. Let them know that you plan to monitor bluebird nestboxes and explain what that involves. Try to find out up front how law enforcement officials will view your activities.

Keith Kridler seconds this advice. When he was establishing his Texas bluebird trail, Keith says, he paid a visit to the local sheriff's office and the highway patrol office, equipped with brochures about bluebird nestbox monitoring and a prepared speech. "If you have a complaint filed against you in Texas, it is pretty much up to the field agent what action will be taken," Keith notes. "Believe me, it's easier to explain things in advance than it is to stand by the edge of the road and try telling a ticked-off patrolman what you are doing with all of those bird nests and eggs, not to mention that pellet gun."

War and Peace — With House Sparrows

Unless your nestbox trails are in remote rural areas, far from homes and farms where house sparrows hang out, chances are you'll have to find a way to deal with these birds.

We'll say it plainly: you can't keep house sparrows out of your bluebird nestboxes. Adjusting the size of the entrance hole doesn't help because house sparrows can squeeze through a smaller hole than bluebirds can (1¼ inches in diameter). So far, no one has come up with a nestbox design that works for bluebirds but reliably deters house sparrows.

You *can* keep house sparrows out of a nestbox intended for use by chickadees if you attach a 1⅛-inch hole restrictor (p. 118) over the entrance hole. Of course, bluebirds and tree swallows won't be able to squeeze into the box either. But as Gary Springer of Carnesville, Georgia, says, "Helping the smallest cavity-nesters can give you the same joy and personal satisfaction as helping bluebirds — without the negative aspects of house sparrow control," such as trapping and killing.

If there's no such thing as a sparrow-proof nestbox, it's not because no one's tried to build one.

> "If I find abandoned nestlings," says co-author Keith Kridler, "I assume it is a greater crime to allow the young birds to die than it is to move them to other foster parents." Doug LeVasseur, the NABS president adds, "I don't know any bluebirders who have been harassed or questioned for monitoring practices that most of us consider to be routine."

A male house sparrow is about to take off. Males bond to a nestbox rather than to a particular female.

Nestbox monitors have been tinkering for years trying to find **a box design that will deter house sparrows** but appeal to bluebirds. Dr. Wayne Davis in the mid-1980s and Andrew Troyer in the early 1990s experimented with slot boxes (p. 100) to discourage house sparrows.

Dr. Larry Zeleny experimented in the 1960s with nestboxes made from empty half-gallon bleach bottles. The results seemed promising: bluebirds readily accepted the unconventional nest sites, but house sparrows rarely chose them. Unfortunately, the slick-surfaced, thin-walled plastic bottles had some drawbacks: they provided no insulation in cold weather, and they overheated when temperatures got hot, frying the young birds inside.

In the early 1970s, Keith Kridler experimented some more with the idea of a slick, thin-walled plastic box, testing boxes made from 4- and 6-inch-diameter PVC pipe. Although the walls were only ¼ inch thick, these boxes didn't overheat like bleach bottles. In 1975, *Nature Society News* published the first record of a PVC-pipe nestbox used by cavity-nesting birds — Kridler's report of a pair of purple martins that fledged a family of four from a nestbox made of 6-inch-diameter pipe.

In 1979, NABS conducted a continent-wide search for sparrow-resistant boxes. Three different designs were accepted for testing, including a PVC model developed from Kridler's designs. The other two experimental boxes were made of wood. One had a raised roof over a ceiling made of wire, and the other had a roof with a large wire-covered hole in it.

Experts once thought — and some still argue — that house sparrows will avoid a box that is open to the light. In field tests, however, this did not prove

A female house sparrow sits on her nestbox roof.

to be true. After several years of tests, NABS experts concluded that only the PVC-pipe design was resistant to house sparrows yet attracted bluebirds and protected their nests safely from bad weather.

Steve Gilbertson is well known in the bluebirding community for his innovative nestbox designs. In the late 1980s, he developed a box made from 4-inch-diameter PVC pipe. Steve says the dimensions of this nestbox — its depth and diameter — are what deter sparrows from nesting. "Left to their own devices, sparrows make a bigger nest than bluebirds do — a huge glob with a tunnel route to the nest cup," Steve explains. Bluebirds make a neat little cup nest that will easily fit in a 4-inch-diameter PVC-pipe box, even though the floor space is only 12½ square inches. The slickness of PVC-pipe boxes and their thin walls are additional sparrow deterrents. House sparrows like an entrance hole with some depth to it — tunnel-like.

Steve has tested house sparrows' nestbox preferences by mounting PVC boxes side by side with conventional wooden boxes. "In all cases, if you pair a PVC box with a larger wooden box, sparrows will take the wooden box," he says — indicating the little brown birds don't care for the smaller, plastic alternative.

Dorene Scriven of the Minnesota Bluebird Recovery Program says, "In areas where house sparrows are found, we've found the PVC-pipe box very successful." But experts, including Gilbertson, agree that PVC-pipe boxes are house sparrow-resistant, *not* house-sparrow-proof. If a PVC-pipe nestbox is the best or only home that your backyard house sparrows can find, it's what they will use.

Those who have tried it say **monofilament fishing line** seems to repel house sparrows from nestboxes (or feeding platforms) — at least for a

while. The idea of monofilament as a sparrow deterrent keeps resurfacing in the bluebirding community, and anecdotal evidence suggests the trick works just long enough to get a new experimenter excited.

No one knows why house sparrows avoid monofilament, and there is no consensus on the best way to use it as a sparrow deterrent. Sometimes bluebird monitors hang filament in a "magic halo" around the nestbox or feeding station. Other times, they stretch it taut near the entrance hole. Barry Whitney of North Augusta, South Carolina, attaches screws at the front corners of the roof of his backyard Peterson nestbox. He stretches a piece of lightweight monofilament tight between them, and lets the ends hang straight down a foot or so. Large metal washers tied to each end of the line hold it taut. "House sparrows haven't bothered the box that is outfitted like this," says Barry. "And it doesn't bother the bluebirds at all!"

In a formal study in 1993, Patricia Pochop, Ron Johnson, and Kent Eskridge reported in the *Wilson Bulletin*: "Although lines did not repel house sparrows from nestboxes, they apparently cause an initial delay in use of newly erected boxes. Further study might develop this result as a method to help other cavity-nesters initiate and more successfully defend nests from house sparrows."

Haleya Priest of Amherst, Massachusetts, has tried monofilament around her backyard boxes, and she concurs that it delays but does not prevent house sparrows from occupying them. "The sparrows were deterred until June," she says. "Then, like a dam breaking, they seemed to ignore the monofilament and go into the houses."

A clutch of black-capped chickadee nestlings fits comfortably in the bottom of a Gilbertson PVC-pipe nestbox. Chickadee nestlings can be kept safe from house sparrows if the entrance hole is reduced to 1⅛ inch.

Bob Sitarski of south-central Indiana has had a similar experience. "I had a male house sparrow that treated the house with monofilament as though it had the plague," Bob reports. But after the sparrow spent three days closely scrutinizing the box and investigating the monofilament, it occupied the box.

Those who have tried monofilament agree that it deters house sparrows only if it is placed around the nestbox *before* a sparrow claims the box. If the nest has been built or if eggs have been laid, the sparrow will not abandon the box just because you put up some monofilament line.

Monofilament line seems to repel sparrows most effectively when you use line so thin it's hard for the sparrows to see. Extremely thin line should be avoided, however, because it might cut a bird's wings. Streamers made of mylar and other materials are sometimes used in place of monofilament with similar results.

Here's a bit of obvious but sometimes overlooked advice: **Don't feed house sparrows.** This is a very simple and effective way of reducing sparrow numbers. If everyone in your neighborhood would stop feeding sparrows, the birds might leave to find a place where food is more plentiful. Note that house sparrows prefer small seeds, such as millet, cracked corn, and milo — the stuff you find in many birdseed mixes.

"I have stopped filling my hopper and fly-through feeders with mixed seed," says Sherry Hunter of Byron Center, Michigan. She now offers only whole sunflower and thistle (niger) seeds in her seed feeders. "And I have noticed that my house sparrow population has been dramatically reduced," Sherry says with satisfaction.

The worst house sparrow problems that Bob Walshaw (Bluebird Bob) sees on his trail in northeast Oklahoma are at nestboxes located near homes where families put out cheap mixed seeds for their backyard birds. "I do not have sparrows in my own backyard," Bob says, "because I feed black-oil sunflower seeds exclusively. Either the sparrows cannot handle black-oil seeds easily or they do not like them."

Of course, if you live where spilled grain is readily available — for example, near a stable, a feedlot for cattle, or a poultry farm — house sparrows inevitably will be present. And they'll be interested in any nestbox you put up.

Another simple and effective way to control house sparrows is to **make sure house sparrows don't roost in nestboxes** over the winter. Leave the door of the box open, or plug the entrance hole with a block of wood or a bit of rag. In spring, don't get the box ready for bluebirds until just before you know they are due to return. If bluebirds are in your area all winter, wait for them to start investigating nestboxes before you unplug the hole or close the door. If the house sparrows don't have a chance to lay claim to a box before the bluebirds return, they will be less likely to interfere with the box after the bluebirds claim it.

No matter what passive measures you take — placing your boxes away from places where sparrows hang out, using sparrow-resistant boxes, or feeding only seeds that sparrows don't like — you must prepare yourself for the day when a male house sparrow claims one of your boxes.

What can you do then? You can run out and scare the sparrow off, but he's going to hold on to the box with the persistence of a terrier, and you can't guard the box 24 hours a day.

Dick Purvis of Anaheim, California, has a simple solution: he relocates a box if he sees it has attracted house sparrows. If the box is moved far enough, the sparrows won't follow. But you may not have a better place to put your box — or you may prefer to leave it where it is. In either case, you still have several options for dealing with intruding house sparrows.

Once the female starts to build her nest, you can **toss the nest out.** Julie Kutruff of Lorton, Virginia, says, "Most people have no problem taking the simplest sparrow-control step — removing the nesting material the sparrow has stuffed in the box." But be aware that this can turn into a daily battle and that house sparrows are remarkably persistent. "I cleaned out one nest 14 days in a row before the birds gave up," says Gerry Kopf of Fulton, Illinois. "The female got so desperate, she laid an egg on the bare wood on the bottom of the box."

Also be aware that when you remove the nest or toss out the eggs, your strategy may backfire. The sparrows may become agitated, and in some cases, the male house sparrow will go marauding. "If you

---

House Sparrows Made Homeless

In the "battle" between humans and house sparrows, sometimes you just have to take a step back and admire the tenacity and skill of your opponents. That's the case with Jim Walters of Iowa City, Iowa. Jim tells how he resolved to put a stop to all house sparrow nesting on his farm. "I closed every available cavity except our nestboxes, and I monitored the boxes with something approaching a religious passion," he says. Jim was determined that no sparrow would ever be allowed to complete a nest on his farm, let alone lay an egg.

Excluded from nooks and crannies in barns and buildings, the resident house sparrows proceeded to construct tightly woven nests in Jim's honeysuckle hedge. "These nests were truly something to behold," Jim exclaims. "They were so incredibly tight that they were never waterlogged, no matter how heavy the rainfall. Incubating parents, eggs, and nestlings always stayed dry. And the nests were so strongly attached in the forks of the honeysuckle that they never blew out — even though the ridge our farmstead was located on got frequent, punishing winds." Compared to those house sparrows' nests, bluebird nests are just "piles of grass," says Jim with respect.

This house sparrow nest and eggs have been removed from a nestbox.

pull the nest of a house sparrow, usually it will go into the nearest nestbox and kill whatever is inside," says Alicia Craig of Caramel, Indiana. Dean Sheldon of Huron County, Ohio, agrees. "Destroy a sparrow nest, and the male will move on down the line, wreaking death and destruction wherever he goes."

Even if a house sparrow does not go on a killing rampage when you take away the nest, you still have a problem: bluebirds will not be able to use the box as long as the sparrow continues to claim it.

Consider the experience of Cheryl Remington of Austin, Minnesota, who one day sent this appeal for help over Bluebird-L, the bluebird monitor's listserv run by Cornell Lab of Ornithology's Birdhouse Network in partnership with NABS. "I am removing sparrow nests every day. I can't seem to discourage them." Cheryl explained that she was removing the sparrow's nest one Friday when bluebirds showed up in her yard. "I had two pair around the yard for two days," she wrote. But each time either of the bluebird pairs showed interest in a box, the house sparrows would fight with them. "Once a sparrow went right into the house and did not leave until the bluebirds left," Cheryl wrote. By Sunday her bluebirds had moved on.

The solution to Cheryl's predicament may seem contradictory. In a case like this, it's actually preferable to let the house sparrows nest rather than try to prevent them. Usually, after the sparrows have built their nest, they will defend only the box that they are occupying. That means bluebirds can claim one of your other boxes, or if you have only one box in your yard, you can quickly put up a second, sparrow-resistant box for bluebirds. This strategy is often called **the decoy box method** of house sparrow control.

Bruce McDonald of Ontario, Canada, learned the hard way how to fool sparrows. After spending frustrating hours chasing house sparrows away from his boxes, Bruce tried waiting until the sparrows had completed their nests and laid eggs, and then he removed the nests. "Big mistake," he says. "The angry house sparrows raided every nestbox in the vicinity." Finally Bruce tried the decoy box strategy. He let the house sparrows have a box for themselves, but he didn't let the eggs hatch and produce another generation of house sparrows.

"After the house sparrow eggs were in place, I'd carefully remove two at a time," he says. "I would mark them with a black marker, refrigerate them overnight, and place them back in the nest. I'd repeat the procedure until all eggs had been marked, refrigerated, and replaced." The end result? The house sparrows were fruitlessly occupied for weeks incubating infertile eggs while bluebirds fledged from Bruce's other boxes.

As an alternative to chilling house sparrow eggs, you can also heat them briefly to stop their development. Some bluebird monitors put a pinhole in one end of the egg instead. Others coat the egg in vegetable oil, which stops air from reaching the embryo. Another idea is to substitute marbles for the eggs.

Bluebird monitors who use the decoy box strategy usually put up a pair of boxes of different design, one intended for the house sparrows and the other meant for bluebirds. For example, Ted Ossege of suburban Cincinnati, Ohio, uses a wooden NABS-style box as his "sparrow attractor"; the rest of his boxes are Gilbertson PVC boxes or Peterson boxes. "The house sparrows will always go to the wooden NABS-style box to nest," Ossege says.

Sometimes a male house sparrow will decide he wants a box that already has a clutch of bluebird eggs or nestlings inside. Keeping a decoy box in your yard reduces the risk that this will happen but does not eliminate the possibility. David Slager in southwest Michigan recalls the time he had bluebirds and tree swallows nesting in two boxes about 50 feet apart in his yard. One day while monitoring, Slager found a pair of house sparrows threatening the tree swallow box from a nearby tree. "They were doing their monotonous 'chirp-of-death' song," Slager recalls. He felt he had to take action — but what?

When an active box is threatened by sparrows and the nestlings inside the box are big enough and strong enough to reach up to the nestbox entrance hole to get food from their parents (about 10 days old), one good way to protect the nestlings from sparrows is to place a 1-inch-diameter **hole restrictor** (p. 118) on the box. "A sparrow can't get into a box with such a small hole and kill the babies," says Haleya Priest — but the parent bluebirds can still poke their heads through the hole to deliver food. The key is that the nestlings have to be far enough along in their development that they can go to the entrance hole and reach up for food.

Haleya has successfully used a hole restrictor to help a backyard box of bluebirds that were threatened by a persistent sparrow. "I went to the box several times a day and removed the hole restrictor so the parents could go in and clean out the nest," she says; meanwhile, she would stand guard against the sparrow, then replace the restrictor when the chores were done. "It worked great," Haleya exclaims. "The birds fledged right on time."

In David Slager's case, however, the tree swallows didn't yet have nestlings. They had just finished building their nest and the female was about to lay eggs. The female bluebird in David's yard had finished laying and was busy incubating her five eggs. So a hole restrictor wasn't a workable solution for David — it would have evicted the adults from the box.

How about quickly putting up a decoy box? David could have tried that, but there would have been no guarantee that the sparrows would accept it. They might have persisted in harassing the tree swallows, perhaps killing the female if she chose to defend her nest. Or they might have decided that the bluebirds would be less trouble to evict and attacked their nest and nestlings.

In a situation like David's, about the only sure-fire way to protect your swallows or bluebirds is to decide you are willing to destroy house sparrows. If you have made that decision, your first step is to catch the sparrows in a trap. **In-box sparrow traps** are designed to fit right inside a nestbox. When a sparrow enters the box, a mechanism triggers a plate that blocks the entrance hole, trapping the sparrow inside the box. Several different kinds of

The remains of a bluebird nestling lie on the ground outside a nestbox — victim of a house sparrow.

in-box sparrow traps (p. 120) are available through retailers, or you can build your own.

Don Hutchings of Winfield, Texas, warns that if you're going to trap sparrows, be prepared for a serious time commitment. "You've *got* to monitor that trap," he says, "because whatever bird goes in that box is going to be trapped in there until you let it out." You might not mind if a house sparrow expires from hunger or thirst. But what if you've trapped a bluebird or a titmouse — a species that is not only desirable but also federally protected?

Haleya Priest says she tries to keep a sparrow trap set up in one of her backyard nestboxes at all times (see picture, p. 63). "I keep an eye on the trap box, and if house sparrows come wandering by, they'll investigate that box and get trapped," she says. Haleya keeps a 1⅜-inch-diameter hole restrictor on the trap box. "That will allow house sparrows to go in, but not the bluebirds," she explains.

Of course, some nestbox monitors are not at home during the day to keep an eye on a sparrow trap. Keith Kridler sets his trap in the evening, after the birds have gone to roost. House sparrows will be up and about with the first light of dawn, so Keith doesn't need to watch his trap box. He simply checks it in the morning before going to work, removes any trapped sparrows, and disengages the trap.

You'll have to catch the male house sparrow if you hope to free up the nestbox for bluebirds to use. "If only the female is caught," says Joe Huber, "then the male simply stays and guards the box until another female is called in." A male sparrow can tie up a box for months if he is not trapped.

When it's time to remove a sparrow from a trap box, a common strategy is to cover the entire box with a plastic bag. Then you open the box door and release the sparrow into the bag. This way,

---

Killing House Sparrows to Protect Bluebirds

People will swat mosquitoes and flies or squish Japanese beetles, but insect pests are about the only critters that have anything to fear from many of us. Dorene Scriven, chair of the Minnesota Bluebird Recovery Program, understands those feelings but also knows that people's perspectives can change over time. "As soon as people have seen their first batch of bluebird babies dead in the box or find the bluebird female dead in the box with her eyes pecked out and her feathers off, they'll be able to take action," she says. "Controlling sparrows is not something that any of us enjoys doing," Dorene emphasizes. "We do it humanely if it is necessary."

Darlene Sillick notes, "It took me three years before I could get rid of my first house sparrow." She now recycles sparrows to a rehab center where she volunteers. They become food for injured sharp-shinned and Cooper's hawks that are undergoing rehabilitation. Dick Purvis puts the situation in perspective, pointing out that when bluebirds and house sparrows fight for a nestbox, it's not a fair fight in which the winner gets the box and the loser simply has to look somewhere else. "The house sparrow wins every time," Dick says. "And often he kills the female bluebird and destroys the bluebird eggs or nestlings."

it's less likely that the sparrow will slip past your hand and escape.

Another approach is to rig a string or fish line to the trap plate when you set the trap so that you can unblock the entrance hole by pulling on the string. When a bird is in the trap and you are ready to take it out, cover the entrance hole with a mesh sack or plastic bag before you open the trap by pulling on the string. Here's a handy way to keep the sack or bag in place over the entrance hole: cut both ends from a small can (like a soup can) and slip a bag through it, folding several inches of the open end of the bag over the outside of the can. Hold the can over the entrance hole and lift the trap plate. The sparrow will scurry out of the hole, through the can, and into the bag.

Most nestbox monitors say that once the sparrow is inside the bag, the simplest way to dispatch it is to grasp the sparrow with its back in the palm of your hand and apply pressure to the breastbone with your thumb. Doug LeVasseur explains that this stops both the heart and respiration of the sparrow and it is dead within a matter of seconds.

If you can't bring yourself to kill a bird, you can try clipping its wings. Don Hutchings trims the primary feathers (the outermost wing feathers) of the house sparrows he traps. Clipping the feathers doesn't cause the bird pain — it's like clipping your toenails — but with their wings clipped, sparrows can't fly well. "So most likely they're going to get caught by predators," Don says.

"It is much better to have your local predators searching for slow house sparrows than for 'blue sparrows,'" adds Keith Kridler. Keith trims several feathers on each wing, clipping off about two-thirds of the length. "If you trim only the first two feathers, the sparrows will continue to nest," he says. "If you trim three feathers on each wing, they normally will abandon their nest. I have never had any sparrow with four or five trimmed feathers return to a nestbox." Keith notes that the birds do remain in the area and continue to feed and drink.

Other monitors object to clipping the wing feathers of house sparrows and releasing them. As one nestbox monitor put it, "Letting the sparrow die out of sight by starvation, exposure, or the actions of one of its predators is not in my opinion a responsible way to deal with its demise."

Relocating trapped sparrows may seem like a humane alternative to killing the birds outright. But experts do *not* recommend this approach; you're just relocating the problem. If you simply must trap and relocate to be at peace with yourself, drop the birds off in urban centers where house sparrows are plentiful and native species are rare.

In-box sparrow traps capture only one house sparrow at a time, and only when the sparrow is actively trying to take over a nestbox. If you dispatch

Joe Huber demonstrates his in-box sparrow trap. The metal plate is in the tripped position, blocking the entrance hole.

one sparrow but other house sparrows remain in the vicinity, it is still risky for bluebirds to nest. To clear an entire farm or neighborhood of house sparrows, you'll need to trap the sparrows when they are feeding, using a **bait trap for house sparrows.**

Three types of bait traps (p. 122) on the market are small enough for the average nestbox monitor to carry: the funnel trap, the trio trap, and the repeating or elevator trap. Each type has users who swear by it and detractors who swear at it!

OK, you've just unpacked your new bait trap, checked it out, and you are ready to begin trapping, right? Wrong, says Keith Kridler. "The sparrows will be very wary of any of these bait traps at first. Start by placing the trap close to where sparrows congregate so that they can see it," he says. "The trap also must be where you can observe it from a window so that you can release any native birds that are caught." For their safety and well-being, you don't want native species to spend more than 30 minutes in a bait trap, Keith advises. Make sure the trap will be shaded during the heat of the day and that it sits on loose soil or grass, not concrete. Always keep food and water available for the trapped birds.

Keith says that in his yard, house sparrows like to land in a bush or tree — anywhere they can perch safely and search the area for danger before they head for the grain. "Normally, sparrows descend from their original landing site in a series of small drops until they reach the feeding station," Keith observes. He's discovered that he can direct the birds to his trap by taking advantage of their habit of "hopping down."

"Locate the house sparrows' favorite landing site in your yard," Keith suggests. "At the edge of their favorite tree or bush, build three small platforms. Make the highest one about 24 inches off the ground, the midlevel one about 16 inches high, and the lowest one at the same height as the entrance to your trap." Make the platforms out of anything that looks right for your yard — sections of log, slabs of flagstone, railroad ties. The sparrows won't care.

"Sprinkle some millet, cracked corn, or other food that sparrows like — white bread is a favorite — on the platforms and in the trap," Keith continues. "If you use either the trio or elevator trap and you hope to catch a large number of sparrows quickly, you must first condition the birds to the trap. If you skip this step and catch the very first sparrow that enters a trio or elevator trap, you will spook the others into staying away. Soon you will be cursing your worthless new trap!"

To get the sparrows accustomed to the trap, wire the trap doors or elevator arms in the "ready" position so they cannot operate. Let the sparrows come and go as they please. After a week or so, you will probably see a large number of house sparrows using the trap as a feeder. When that happens, says Keith, "you are ready to begin trapping.

"The night before 'trapping day,' you need to remove all the sparrows' favorite seeds from any other feeders you might have in your backyard," Keith continues. "Serve your other birds only niger (thistle), sunflower, or safflower seeds, which house sparrows will eat only as a last resort."

Keith also puts some of the less-preferred seeds on the top two platforms. "On the third platform, I sprinkle a small amount of the 'preferred' sparrow food right next to the trap opening, and I also make an enticing pile of this food inside the trap," he says. "After a quick search of my other feeders, the sparrows approach the series of platforms. They go hop, hop, and drop right into the trap!" With this

All of the bait traps work best after the first sparrow is trapped. The live decoy will call out to other house sparrows, helping to entice them into the trap. During nesting season, you can use sparrows that you remove from your in-box traps as the first decoys in your bait traps. Note that decoy sparrows must be given food and water. "These are the only house sparrows that you pamper," says Joe Huber. "They do the work for you."

system, Keith is able to keep his yard free of house sparrows by trapping only a couple of hours a week.

Be aware that captured sparrows can attract the attention of hawks, cats, raccoons, and other predators. The door to the holding compartment should be wired securely shut to prevent these predators from opening the cage and getting to the decoys. At night, the trap and decoys should be moved into a garage to keep them safe from nocturnal predators.

Beating Blowflies — Parasites on the Nestlings

Adult bird blowflies look a bit like houseflies with iridescent blue or green bodies. Their wormlike larvae (the juvenile stage) are parasites that get all their nourishment by drinking young birds' blood. In North America, scientists have identified about 26 different species of blowflies that parasitize birds (there are many other kinds of blowflies). All bird blowflies are in the genus *Protocalliphora*, and new species are still being discovered. You may have heard that the species *Protocalliphora sialia* infest bluebirds exclusively, but entomologists say that at least five other species infest eastern bluebirds and three other species infest western bluebirds; meanwhile, *P. sialia* infests not just bluebirds but many other bird species. In general, cavity-nesting birds tend to experience heavier blowfly infestations than birds that nest in open-cup nests.

Free-flying adult blowflies typically enter nestboxes in order to lay their eggs either in nest material or directly on nestlings' bodies. After just a day or two, the pale gray, wormlike larvae — also called maggots — hatch out, attach themselves to the nestlings, and begin to feed. A feeding bout lasts about an hour; then the maggots return to the nest. They feed most actively at night; during the day they usually stay in the nest material. But if the interior of the box remains quite dark during the day or if the nest is badly infested, you may see maggots clinging to the heads, legs, or abdomens of nestlings during your daytime nestbox checks.

The idea of bloodsucking parasites that feed at night may seem horrifying. But you have to remember that it's not to a parasite's advantage to kill its host — which would be the end of the free meal. The presence of just a few blowfly larvae probably does a chick no harm, says Dr. Kevin Berner of Richmondville, New York, a State University of New York (Cobleskill) wildlife professor and the NABS research chairman. "I've noticed that mortality in nests is more often related to severe weather than it is to blowflies killing the nestlings during good weather," Berner says.

"Baby birds are incredible 'blood factories,'" adds Dr. Terry Whitworth, who has been studying bird blowflies from his home base of Puyallup, Washington, for more than 30 years. Dr. Whitworth

A trapped house sparrow inside an elevator trap helps lure more house sparrows inside the trap.

An adult blowfly and numerous pupae infest an empty bluebird nest.

says, "The birds can replace the blood they've lost to blowfly larvae at an amazing rate. As fast as the blowflies suck blood out, the birds produce new blood. So they stay ahead of the parasites."

Over the years, Dr. Whitworth has systematically evaluated **the effects of blowfly larvae** on nestling birds and published his results in research journals. In one study, he compared blood samples from parasitized birds and parasite-free birds. "When there were more than 10 blowfly larvae per nestling," he says, "I did start to see lowered hematocrit and hemoglobin levels, indicating the birds were becoming anemic." But he notes that anemia, in and of itself, isn't necessarily a problem for the birds. Dr. Whitworth agrees with Berner that environmental conditions probably play a bigger role in the birds' well-being. "Anemic birds are sick and weakened," he explains, "but they often survive if they experience no other adverse conditions."

Experimental evidence supports the idea that bird blowflies seldom kill nestlings outright. In a study published in the ornithology journal *Wilson Bulletin* in 1992, scientists compared the survival of eastern bluebird and tree swallow nestlings in infested nests, nests where blowfly larvae had been removed, and nests where extra larvae had been added. They found no significant difference among the nestlings, either in regard to the number that survived to fledge or in regard to the average age at which the young birds fledged.

Despite these reassuring findings, nestbox monitors regularly report loses to blowflies in boxes that are severely infested. Most **monitors control blowflies aggressively** when they find them in their nestboxes. "If you see blowflies, get rid of them promptly," advises veteran nestbox monitor Bruce Burdett, who deals with a few infested boxes each summer along his 58-box New Hampshire trail. Some nestbox monitors sweep the larvae out of the bottom of an infested box. Others also pull the nest out of the box, temporarily remove the nestlings to a safe place, such as a shoebox, and tap the nest gently to shake the larvae out.

Bruce's approach is to get rid of the infested nest entirely when the chicks are about 7 to 10 days old, and to this end, he keeps dried grass on hand as a replacement nesting material. "I simply put the babies in a box, throw away the old nest with all the blowflies in it, and clean the house out thoroughly," he explains. Remember to dispose of the smelly old nest well away from the box so that it doesn't attract predators.

You can make a replacement nest by pulling some tall, dead, dry grass and wrapping it around the closed fingers of one hand. Form a cup with the grass and place your completed nest in the cleaned-out nestbox. Don't worry if your creation isn't as finely woven as the original nest, Bruce advises. "As soon as the female returns, she'll rework it and make it more to her liking."

Before placing the chicks back in the nest, Bruce inspects each one and carefully removes any larvae. "I just pull them off with my fingers," he says. "They're not very firmly attached, and they come off very easily. It's not pleasant, but you gotta do it."

Keith Kridler suggests a modification that you can make to the floor of many nestboxes that he feels helps to control blowflies — make the corner cuts on a slant (drawing, below). "Any blowfly larvae unlucky enough to crawl close to the corners of the bottom will free-fall out of the box," he says.

Keith's angled corner cuts make a lot of sense for top-opening boxes, which prevent you from checking for blowflies without removing the nestlings and dumping the nest out of the box — not something you want to do as part of routine monitoring.

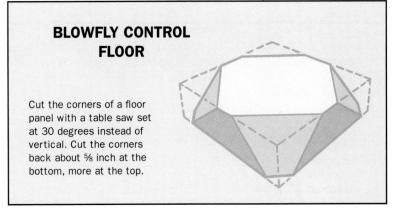

BLOWFLY CONTROL FLOOR

Cut the corners of a floor panel with a table saw set at 30 degrees instead of vertical. Cut the corners back about ⅝ inch at the bottom, more at the top.

Some monitors have tried placing inverted wire mesh cups in the bottom of their boxes for blowfly protection. In theory, any larvae that drop through the wire will be unable to climb back up to feed on the nestlings. At least one study has shown the cups to be effective, but monitors who have experimented with them note that bluebirds push their nesting material through the wire mesh, making it easy for the blowflies to climb back up to the nest. Another complaint about wire mesh cups is that they sometimes bring the top of the nest too close to the entrance hole.

If you use Peterson boxes (p. 101), notes Dorene Scriven of Minneapolis, Minnesota, blowfly control is a little easier because of its unique slanted-floor design, which causes the larvae to roll to the front. "You just open the door and brush the larvae out," Dorene says.

Dr. Whitworth doubts the effectiveness of corner cuts, slanted floors, or wire cups in controlling bird blowflies. "Larvae are not inclined to fall from nests until they are ready to pupate," he says. And when they are ready to pupate, they are finished feeding. "Remember, they live happily in open bird nests with no box surrounding them, and if they fall, they die," says Dr. Whitworth.

Insecticides approved for caged birds (see sidebar, p. 25) can also be used to kill bird blowflies. Carefully spray on nests and the inside of boxes after the nestlings are removed.

Some sources say that blowflies do not infest bluebird nests made of pine straw. Not so, says Diane Barbin of Harrisburg, Pennsylvania. "My bluebirds build almost all their nests exclusively of pine straw," she says. "Every year I find a significant number of blowfly larvae in these nests." She reports that Dr. Whitworth found 50 to 100 blowfly larvae in pine straw nests she sent him that were used in mid-summer.

What if you don't remove larvae from your nest or nestlings? After 7 to 9 days, *P. sialia* larvae stop feeding and begin to develop into pupae. If you check the nest after the birds fledge, you may see the pupal cases in the nest material — they're oval-shaped, brown or black, and about a quarter of an inch long. ("They look like rat droppings," notes Keith Kridler.) Adult blowflies emerge from these cases after 7 to 10 days and fly off to locate another active nest where they can lay their eggs.

As much as nestbox monitors like to help nestling birds, Dr. Whitworth says, it's important that they consider the big picture. "A researcher in France who did a lot of nest replacement found that the nests were rapidly reinfested," he says. "I think that removing larvae from a nest just opens things up for new larvae. More eggs hatch and replace the population.

"Here's the rest of the story," he continues. "When you pull baby birds out of a nest to change the nest material or pick off larvae, you also create stress for the birds. To my mind, unless you have a very severe infestation, it may be more distressing to the babies if you remove the larvae than it would be if you left them alone."

What constitutes a severe infection? One rule of thumb is 10 or more actively feeding larvae per nestling. Since it's not exactly easy to get a blowfly head count, look for other signs. "It's like when your dog has fleas," says Dr. Whitworth. "You'll see scabs, scratching, signs of irritation. The young birds' abdomens are bare, so you'll see a lot of scabs all over their breasts, or fresh blood, or even larvae still clinging." If an infestation is this bad, he concedes, it may be helpful to change the nest material and pick larvae off the nestlings. To minimize stress, wait till the nestlings are seven or eight days old before you check for blowflies.

"I know telling bluebirders that they should let their nestlings be parasitized isn't going to be a popular message," Dr. Whitworth concludes. "It's natural for us not to want baby birds to suffer. But remember, birds and blowflies have coexisted for millions of years."

If you really want to reduce the effects of blowflies on nesting birds, Dr. Whitworth suggests an alternative course of action: work to reduce the overall population of blowflies. "Right after the nestlings fledge," he suggests, "put the nest in a sealed plastic baggie. That will ensure that no adult flies emerge to infest other nests. To my mind, this step would really make a difference."

The young birds have flown, and now the debate begins: should you remove the dirty old nest and **clean out the box or not?** On first thought, it might seem obvious that it's better for birds to build a nest in a clean box rather than on top of an old, soiled nest. But left to their own devices, blue-

Send Your Nests for a Test

If you want to send a nest to Dr. Whitworth to be evaluated for blowflies, here's what to do: Wait until the nestlings fledge, then remove the nest. It's important to select a nest that was used for most or all of the nestling period so that there will be a good chance blowflies are present; incomplete nests, replacement nests, or nests that were abandoned early in the nesting season will not be helpful.

Place the nest in a gallon plastic baggie. Seal carefully, because small insects such as mites will crawl out of a poorly sealed bag. ("That's a problem for the U.S. Postal Service," Dr. Whitworth notes.) Keep the bag in a cool, dry location until you are ready to mail it; do not freeze it or leave it in the sun, as that will kill the larvae and pupae.

With a waterproof marker, write on the bag the nest number (if you're sending more than one nest) and bird species. On a sheet of paper, using pencil or waterproof ink, write your name, your home and e-mail addresses, the nest number, the species of bird, and the location of the nest (state, county, and nearest town), plus any other relevant data. Place the nest and data sheet in a mailing envelope (don't worry about padding) and send to Dr. Terry Whitworth (see Resources, p. 124).

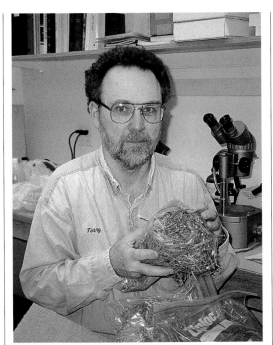

Dr. Whitworth unpacks one of the 1,600 nests sent to him in the year 2000 for blowfly evaluation. He has a special permit from the U.S. Fish and Wildlife Service that allows anyone to send him bird nests.

birds don't remove old nests; some other birds clean out a cavity before nesting, but bluebirds don't. Maybe they gain some advantage by leaving an old nest undisturbed.

The nestbox monitors we talked to overwhelmingly favored cleaning out boxes. The thought behind the practice is that old nests are probably infested with bird blowflies, not to mention mites, lice, and other parasites. By emptying the boxes, the reasoning goes, you reduce the risk of infestation for the next pair of birds that nests in the box.

The trouble is, scientists haven't had much luck gathering evidence that birds uniformly prefer clean boxes to dirty ones. In one study, tree swallows clearly preferred clean boxes, but in another study, eastern bluebirds overwhelmingly preferred boxes with old nests. In a third study, house wrens chose empty boxes and boxes with old nests at about equal rates.

Nor have scientists been able to demonstrate that clean boxes offer any clear advantages, such as lower rates of blowfly parasitism. The citizen scientists who take part in Cornell's Birdhouse Network have collected preliminary data showing that new nests are about equally likely to be infested with blowflies whether or not the previous nest has been removed. And though you might expect that infested nests would fledge fewer birds because the parasites would be harmful to nestlings, research reveals the opposite. In a study of purple martins, birds nesting on old nests raised more young than birds nesting in clean, empty boxes.

The most surprising finding is that by cleaning out old nests, you may actually be helping to increase — not reduce — the blowfly population. That's because blowflies are themselves parasitized by another insect, **the jewel wasp.** Destroy the old nest, and you may be destroying a helpful insect that naturally controls blowfly numbers.

Jewel wasps are members of the wasp genus *Nasonia.* Adult female wasps lay their eggs in blowfly pupae; when the eggs hatch, the larval wasps eat the blowfly pupa. Then the wasps themselves become pupae and, after a period of time, emerge as adults — ready to seek out and destroy more blowflies. If cold weather sets in before metamorphosis is complete, the wasp larvae suspend their development and hibernate inside the pupal cases till spring.

So when you seal an old nest in a plastic baggie or destroy it in some manner, you are destroying helpful wasps as well as blowflies. Keith Kridler carefully gathers all the old nesting material from boxes on his trails and carries it home in a bucket or bag. At home, he dumps the material into a storage barrel covered tightly with wire mesh (⅛-inch window screen works well). "Blowflies that hatch out are trapped by the screen and die, while any jewel wasps can pass through ordinary window screens to attack more blowflies!" Keith says.

Keep your container of old nests in a covered location, such as an open carport or a barn, so rain doesn't drown the developing wasps. Before you open the screen on the container to add more nests, make sure you won't be letting any blowflies out. Keith advises you shine a bright light over the screen and rap the container sharply. "Any flies old enough to fly will try to head to the light," Keith says. "If adult flies are present, start a new container."

Packing Your Bag — Tools for Monitors

Whether you're just checking a couple of backyard nestboxes or monitoring a lengthy bluebird trail with hundreds of boxes, your job will be easier if you put together a "monitor's tool kit" containing essential equipment and supplies needed for data collection, box maintenance, and bird rescue operations.

If you're a backyard bluebirder, you don't need an elaborate kit — especially if you have a well-organized workshop close at hand. Your monitoring "kit" may be as simple as a clipboard with data sheets, a pencil, and a pair of gloves. On the other hand, the trail monitors we talked to are, like Boy Scouts, prepared for any emergency; many of them seem to pack everything but the kitchen sink. "The whole back end of my truck is my monitoring tool kit!" says Dick Walker of Loogootee, Indiana. (His blue Chevy S-10 pickup truck even has a sign on the front that reads "Bluebird Express.")

Nests sent to Dr. Whitworth by New York state members of Cornell's Birdhouse Network in 1999 contained a previously unknown species of bird blowfly. It has since been found in several northeastern states, Canada, and Alaska.

Don't be discouraged; you don't have to fill up an entire truck to be prepared. An old toolbox or tackle box should be big enough to hold most of the essential items for monitoring — and the compartments are handy for storing small items. Or use a sturdy plastic bucket to carry your supplies — you can also turn the bucket upside down and stand on it to get a better view inside a nestbox. (If you do this, please be careful!) If you must hike to get to some of your boxes, you may prefer to carry your monitoring tools in a backpack, fanny pack, or the pockets of a fishing vest.

What goes in your kit? An annotated list is provided below. Note that not all the items listed here are essential; what you'll pack depends on your situation and the season. For example, if the birds are still building their nests or incubating eggs, you won't need any "rescue" supplies for transporting orphaned nestlings.

We asked expert trail monitor Dean Sheldon of Greenwich, Ohio, who monitors 120 nestboxes, to take us on a "tour" of his monitoring kit. Dean keeps his kit in the back of his Ford Ranger pickup truck. The kit itself is a large Plano tackle box with his "items of first response" in the removable upper tray and large tools in the bottom of the box. "It would take some time to tell you all the things I carry with me," he says, "but here are a few of the 'must-haves.'

"I always take a pair of vise grips for opening nestboxes — to get hold of the nail and pull it out. I also have a beekeeper's hive tool, which is flat on one end, like a hefty putty knife, and hooked on the other end, with a sharpened blade. It's indispensable for scraping and cleaning the walls and floor of a nestbox.

"I finish the cleanup job with a parts cleaning brush," Dean says. "You can get one at any auto supply store." This stiff-bristled, round brush works well when you need to scrape debris out of a box. "I remove part of the handle to save space," Dean notes.

Also purchased at the auto supply store is a Bondo spatula — a flexible plastic spatula designed for applying auto body cement. What's that for? "Some bluebirds, especially first-time nesters, will build an incomplete nest, with no bottom," Dean notes, "so if you reach in to pull out the nest for monitoring, the eggs or nestlings will fall right out the bottom of the nest. I use the Bondo spatula the way you turn eggs over easy — I shove it under the nest and pull the whole nest out on the spatula. Since I've been doing that, I haven't lost any eggs at all."

Other items in Dean's monitoring kit include some *big* felt markers, used to mark identifying numbers on the boxes, insect repellent, paper towels, hand cleaner, and a stock of bluebird information brochures to hand out to interested onlookers. "Perhaps the most important," he concludes, "is that plastic bread bag containing clean, dry, abandoned nesting materials or dried grasses collected at the roadside. I use them to rebuild or replace nests that are wet or infested with insects."

> "I discovered early on in my nestbox monitoring days that it was most helpful to have both hands free, as many unexpected circumstances arise when you monitor nestboxes," says Ann Wick. "As a result, I wear an inexpensive, washable, carpenter's cloth apron around my waist. In it are the items that I use most often."

TOOLS OF THE TRADE

DATA COLLECTION

Notebook or data sheets

Pencil or waterproof pen

Binoculars

Maps of box locations

Roll of surveyor's tape — for marking potential locations for new boxes

Stepladder if needed

Bondo spatula or pancake turner — for pulling nests out of a box

Mechanic's mirror — to help you see inside boxes

Magnifying glass — to help you read those tiny numbers on banded birds

Camera

CLEANING SUPPLIES

Gloves (rubber and leather)

Trowel, spatula, or putty knife

— for squashing wasps and scraping out debris

Whisk broom, paintbrush, or toothbrush — to get the box really clean!

Plastic or paper bags — to carry away abandoned nests or dead birds

Spray bottle with dilute bleach solution — to spray on mice nests before removal

NESTBOX MAINTENANCE

Screwdriver and screws

Hammer and nails

Pliers

Cordless drill and drill bits

Wire cutters and wire

Weather stripping — to seal box vents in cold weather

Duct tape — can serve as emergency weather stripping or door hinge

Extra box-mounting clamps

Vise grips

Spare nestboxes or box parts

Pocketknife or multipurpose tool

Sandpaper

Pruning tool or handsaw — for cutting back vegetation around mounting posts

PREDATOR CONTROL

Baffles and hole guards

Hole restrictors

Tanglefoot — to deter ants

Bar of soap — to deter wasps

In-box sparrow trap

Grease — to deter climbing predators

RESCUE GEAR

Mealworms — to feed hungry orphaned nestlings

Shoebox or small bucket — for carrying orphaned nestlings to new nest

Hot-water bottle — to keep orphaned nestlings warm during transfer

Bag of dry grass — to replace wet or blowfly-infested nests

Name and phone number of your local bird rehabilitator

PERSONAL ITEMS

Sun hat

Snack

Drinking water

Sunscreen

Insect repellent

Baby wipes — for quick hand cleaning

Paper towels

Cell phone

Spare key to your vehicle

Homes and HARDWARE
for Bluebirds
by Keith Kridler

Nestbox with Baffles
A cylindrical baffle protects this nestbox from climbing predators, and a barbed wire baffle protects it from livestock. A hole guard protects the entrance hole.

Building Boxes for Bluebirds — Design Concepts, Materials, and Tools

It wasn't that long ago that "nestboxes" for blue-birds were created exclusively by woodpeckers and Mother Nature. Neither one showed any noticeable concern for a bluebird's well-being in the designs of the cavities they offered. An open knothole leading to a hollow tree trunk might be any size or shape, often large enough to admit competitors that could take over a bluebird's cavity or predators that would devour the eggs or young.

Although Mother Nature seemed as interested in feeding snakes and raccoons as in fledging a new generation of bluebirds, over the ages, the birds managed to reproduce and maintain their numbers. Eastern bluebirds started losing their constant battle for survival when the dead and diseased trees that contained their nesting cavities were largely cleared by early white settlers. They were further endangered when European starlings — another invader from Europe — proliferated and dominated the nesting cavities that remained.

A colorful male western bluebird finds a home in the rotted, hollow limb of a tree.

But the bluebirds didn't give up. Instead, they struggled to coexist with encroaching civilization by using makeshift cavities that people inadvertently provided. **Bluebirds are adaptable.** If a particular location and habitat suits their feeding needs, they will do their best to find something to nest in that resembles a cavity. A bluebird returning in spring to nest in the same area it did in previous years is probably thinking more about the bounty of insects available than about any preference in housing.

The late John Grivich of Huntsville, Texas, experimented with all different kinds of objects for nestboxes. He had eastern bluebirds nesting in old cowboy boots and hats, as well as his many different wooden nestboxes. He found that bluebirds would readily nest in almost any object if it contained a cavity large enough for them to build a nest in. It didn't need an entrance hole; an entire side could be open.

Farms and farm machinery offer a variety of compartments that interest bluebirds. Ruth O'Briant relates the story of bluebirds in central Missouri that chose to nest in a space between the radiator and grill of a tractor. No problem — until the tractor was needed for farmwork. "The tractor was taken to the hay field until noon," Ruth explains. "After lunch, the tractor and baby birds returned from the hay field." Each time the tractor returned, "the parent birds, each with an insect in its bill, were waiting to start feeding," she remembers. The birds seemed to find the arrangement convenient. After the first successful nesting, they did it a second time!

Bluebirds have been found nesting in holes in buildings, in the metal box designed to hold an electricity meter (before the meter is installed), in the ends of football goalposts and other pipes, in abandoned barn swallow nests, and in concrete blocks — the cavities of which just happen to be very close to the dimensions of an ideal bluebird nestbox. Bluebirds will also nest repeatedly in tiny wood boxes only 2¾ inches square at the bottom, 4 inches deep, and with the entrance hole just 2 inches above the base.

At the Northeast Texas Gun Club's skeet shooting range just south of my home in Mt. Pleasant, Texas, shooters toss empty shotgun shells and shell boxes into 55-gallon metal drums to be burned. One year I found active bluebird nests among the spent shells in two of the three barrels about 100 feet apart. In a panic, I implored the man in charge, "Don't burn the barrels or shoot the bluebirds!" The shooters were aware of the birds, he told me, and all were proud of the fact that they broke only clay birds and not bluebirds at their range. Hundreds of shotgun shells were fired every week, and between rounds of skeet shooting, the bluebirds calmly perched on the high and low trap houses, hawking for insects to feed their young!

The most common alternative cavities used by bluebirds in my area of Texas are rural mailboxes and the 4-inch-diameter PVC-pipe tubes that often hang from the same posts and are used for newspapers. Some of my nestboxes happen to be located along roadsides near these mailboxes and newspaper tubes. In the year 2000, there were five bluebird nests in newspaper tubes along a 15-mile section of my bluebird trail and another nest in a mailbox missing its door. Even with my carefully designed and constructed nestboxes readily available, six pairs of bluebirds chose to nest in these alternative cavities.

Some of the first "nestboxes" to be deliberately set out for bluebirds in the mid-1900s were plastic milk jugs, bleach bottles, and metal coffee cans with plastic lids. The coffee cans (other cans, up to gallon-sized paint buckets, were also used) were very popular with schoolchildren. They were nailed through their bottoms to posts or trees. Then the kids would cut a bluebird-sized hole in the plastic lid and snap it over the end of the can. Usually the lid disappeared quickly, but the birds would continue to use the can.

In the early 1980s, several lumber companies designed and distributed hundreds of thousands of pieces of waxed cardboard that could be folded into a nestbox by the youngest of schoolchildren. Thousands of bluebirds fledged from these early nestboxes, but thousands more didn't survive because of the poor protection from weather and predators the boxes provided.

We humans aren't as impartial as Mother Nature about the nesting success of bluebirds, especially in the nestboxes that we provide. We tend to be passionate about making sure that Mom and Pop bluebird don't have their kids gobbled up by a predator or washed away by a storm. We want young birds to fledge from our nestboxes. And for that to happen, I recommend some guidelines for building nestboxes.

Use only durable materials. **The lumber used for constructing a box** should be ¾ inch thick and untreated. The best lumber is "flat" cut — the growth rings visible at the ends of the pieces resemble the flat lines of plywood. The closer together the growth rings are, the stronger the board will be. Nestboxes made of redwood are the most durable in my experience here in northeast Texas, followed in order by those made of white pine, yellow pine, pine plywood, and western cedar. Cedar is decay resistant but very soft. Squirrels and woodpeckers can't seem to resist enlarging the entrance holes on cedar boxes. When used for a roof, cedar splits in just a year or two in my area.

The roof of a nestbox deteriorates faster than the other panels. Choose a board with tight, flat growth rings for the roof panel. And place the roof panel so that the growth rings bend down in a

A male eastern bluebird feeds his young. Note how the grain in the roof of the box has caused it to warp up at the edge, creating an opening between the roof and the side panel through which rain can enter.

"frown" rather than up in a "smile." Solid pieces of lumber always warp in the same direction as the curvature of the growth rings. If the edges of the roof were to warp up, the roof would not cover the sides of the box tightly, and rain could easily enter.

Exterior grade plywood with five or more plies makes a longer-lasting roof than any of the solid boards do, and it is very resistant to warping. Avoid interior grade plywood, including that made with exterior glue. Wafer board, sometimes referred to as chipboard, lasts only a few years unpainted.

Painting or staining wooden nestboxes is controversial because nobody can say whether or not residual fumes from the chemicals harm the birds. And it isn't likely that conclusive tests will be made anytime soon. Consequently, most monitors paint only the exterior of a box if they paint it at all. I don't paint my trail boxes, but not because I fear that paint on the outside of a box will hurt birds. My boxes are made from scrap, and it takes me longer to brush paint on a box than to build a new one.

Whether harmful or not, the longest-lasting boxes are those submerged in a thinned solution of either latex paint or oil-based stain. The paint or stain seals all the surfaces, including the porous end cuts of the wood. Nestboxes should be painted or stained in the fall and allowed to dry over the winter to minimize any fumes. The paint should be a light color. Boxes painted a dark color may get deadly hot inside when the sun shines directly on them.

Screws or nails can be used to join the panels. Screws hold a box together tighter and more securely than nails do. Screws are also simple to remove, so a damaged panel can be replaced easily. For ¾-inch lumber, I recommend 1⅝-inch-long deck screws with either a Phillips head or square head. Deck screws are coated with paint for exterior use. If deck screws aren't available, use sheet rock screws.

If you don't have a variable speed drill to drive screws, you can use a hammer and nails to put a nestbox together. To join softwoods, use 6-penny (6d) box nails. Avoid 6d common nails, which are larger in diameter than box nails and are more likely to split small pieces of wood. I prefer to use a nail designed for residential house flooring, called a "cement coated" nail. It is coated with glue that "cements" the nail to the wood so that the nail can't back out and allow panels to separate, creating cracks that let water or cold drafts enter your nestbox. There are also siding nails with "ring shanks" or a "spiral twist" that will not back out.

To join hardwoods, you should use the nails made for installing hardwood flooring in houses. These 7d "hardened" nails have a spiral shank and will not bend but are a little longer and more expensive than siding nails. Although these nails are not galvanized, they will outlast the life of the wood used in nestboxes.

Electrogalvanized and stainless steel nails will not rust, but they have smooth shanks and don't hold tight to the wood — so they will back out over time. If you decide to use galvanized nails, choose "hot-dipped" ones. They have rough shanks and will join wood panels together securely.

You can avoid problems created by nails backing out by applying a thin bead of flexible latex or silicone rubber caulking to each joint before you fasten the panels together. The caulk will waterproof the joints for the life of the box, helping to keep it dry inside. Of course, on side- or front-opening boxes, the doors cannot be sealed with caulk.

A nestbox must open — either at the top or at the side or front — so that any nest it contains can be monitored. There are several ways to **fasten a box shut** when it is not being monitored. For rapid monitoring, top-opening boxes can be fastened with a simple hook and eye. Side- or front-opening boxes can be fastened with a duplex-headed concrete nail used as a "lock pin." The nail is slipped into a hole drilled down at a slight angle through the box front and into the edge of the side-opening door (see NABS box illustration, p. 97). Better yet, use an aluminum pop rivet instead of a nail to "lock" the door in the closed position.

In public areas, boxes with a hook and eye or lock pin closure invite vandalism. To prevent curious humans from easily opening a nestbox, fasten the door shut with a Phillips or square head screw (see chalet nestbox illustration, p. 101). Eventually a screw fastener will strip the threads from its hole and have to be replaced with a longer screw, or the hole will need to be repaired. A drop of waterproof glue and a wooden kitchen match pushed into a stripped hole will repair it for another few years.

The amount of **floor space** in a nestbox for bluebirds can vary considerably. Bluebirds will build a nest in a corner of a wood duck nestbox if that is what is available. Eastern bluebirds need only enough room to build a nest 4 inches in diameter. A square box 4 inches on each side or a PVC-pipe box 4 inches in diameter is sufficient. If the floor shape is rectangular, an eastern bluebird can get by with a 3-by-5-inch space.

Western bluebirds could get by with the same size nestboxes as their eastern cousins, but they usually lay one more egg than eastern bluebirds. Also, in much of the West, the larger mountain bluebirds share range with western bluebirds. So most western trail operators provide a large box — typically 5 or even 5½ inches square — that can be used by either species. PVC boxes in the West are usually made of 6-inch-diameter pipe rather than 4-inch-diameter.

Box depth can be as varied as floor size. It is usually measured from the bottom of the entrance hole to the floor. The deeper a box is, the harder it will be for a starling or jay to stick its head in the entrance hole and snatch an egg or nestling. Six or 8 inches is a convenient depth, and there is no useful purpose in making a box more than 10 inches deep. Bluebirds generally build up their nests in deep boxes to bring the cup within several inches of the hole. Especially in deep boxes, it is important that the inside surface below the entrance hole be rough so that tree swallows can climb to the hole.

The minimum box depth I would recommend is about 4½ inches. This does not provide protection from predatory birds, but it usually keeps the nestlings below the hole — and house sparrows don't like shallow boxes with a small floor size.

One of the critical design considerations is the size of the **entrance hole.** Any size greater than 1⁹⁄₁₆ inches in diameter is at risk of admitting starlings. Eastern and western bluebirds don't need an entrance larger than 1½ inches. Mountain bluebirds should have a 1⁹⁄₁₆-inch-diameter hole. Ash-throated flycatchers also need a 1⁹⁄₁₆-inch hole to enter a box easily. Entrance holes don't necessarily need to be round, and other shapes — slots, ovals, and "mouse holes" — are described later in this chapter as part of specific box designs.

Chickadees and house wrens need only a 1⅛-inch entrance hole; titmice use a 1¼-inch hole. House sparrows can also fit through a 1¼-inch

The size of the entrance hole determines who gets in a nestbox. Ash-throated flycatchers (far left) need a 1⅜-inch-diameter hole. House wrens (center left) can enter a 1-inch hole. The tufted titmouse (center right) has had the hole in its box enlarged by a squirrel or wood-pecker. The big-eyed critter (far right) is a flying squirrel. It will enter a 1¼-inch hole if it can get to the box without touching the ground.

hole, which is smaller than a bluebird, tree swallow, white-breasted nuthatch, or Carolina wren can squeeze through. The only common cavity-nesters that can use an entrance hole smaller than a house sparrow can enter are chickadees and house wrens.

The entrance hole needs to be near the top of the box. The closer the entrance hole is to the top, the better the roof overhang will shield it from sun and rain. If the entrance hole is within 1 inch of the top, however, you will not be able to use the popular Huber sparrow trap (p. 120).

A peg placed below the entrance hole to serve as a perch is not necessary for native cavity-nesters. Pegs should not be placed on nestboxes because house sparrows will use them to defend boxes from bluebirds. House sparrows like to perch on the peg and block the entrance hole with their body. It is easier for bluebirds and swallows to drive a sparrow away from a nestbox when the sparrow is standing on the roof or hanging precariously onto the front.

A good nestbox is designed to keep water out. For this, the **roof has to overhang** the front and both sides of the box by 2 inches or more, and it should overlap at least the top of the back panel. In the absence of adequate roof overhang, rain can easily pass through the entrance hole, ventilation openings, or top seams of a box.

Flat roofs — those that aren't mounted at an angle so that rain will flow off — should have grooves cut on the underside of the roof, ¼ inch from each edge (see Tuttle box drawing, p. 98). The grooves force water to drip at the edge of the roof rather than migrate under the roof and drip inside the box. They need to be only ⅛ inch deep to do the job. (In the past, builders used this trick on houses for humans. Grooves cut under the outside edge of windowsills and handrails would prolong the life of the wood.)

Roof overhang also keeps the sides of a box and the entrance hole in shade for much of the day, helping to keep the box from overheating. You can effectively shade an entire box by adding a large second roof on ¾-inch spacers over the nestbox roof. In hot areas like my part of Texas, adding a second roof is a useful way to keep exposed boxes from overheating. The second roof also prolongs the life of a nestbox by protecting it from rain. The second roof can be metal or wood. If it is wood, be sure to cut rain grooves on the bottom. An excellent material for a second roof is a cement board material called Hardipanel, made by the James Hardie Company. It is a very durable product made from cement and cellulose fiber.

Water that gets inside a box will be absorbed by the nest even if there are **drainage holes.** And a cold, wet nest can be lethal to nestlings. That's why it is so important to keep water out of a box. When water does enter a nest (from a lawn sprinkler, perhaps), it is critical that it be able to drain out so that the nest doesn't sit in standing water.

A ¼-inch hole drilled near each corner of the floor will provide ample drainage even if some of the holes become clogged. An easier way for most people to create drain holes is by cutting about ⅜ to ⅝ inch off all four corners of the floor with a table saw. The cut corners are large and less likely to become plugged with nesting material than are small drilled holes. The corners can also be cut at an angle to provide a measure of blowfly control (p. 85).

Instead of drilling round holes or cutting the corners off the bottom for drainage, you can leave a thin slot down one side. Drilled holes have the advantage of being easily plugged in winter with dowel rods so that the box can serve as a draft-free roosting box. One hole should always be left open for drainage. Boxes that are side- or front-opening

A male eastern bluebird prepares for a landing at his nestbox. Note how the entrance hole is shaded by the roof overhang, helping to keep the inside of the box from overheating. Roof repairs keep the old box in service.

typically have a slight gap between the door panel and the bottom board, which helps provide drainage.

The size of **air vents** and their location in a nestbox can vary considerably. Ideally, each box would be fitted with adjustable shutters that could be closed on cold days and opened wide during hot afternoons. On some small trails, monitors actually do adjust simple shutters on every nestbox!

I have found that a ½-inch vent across the top of each side — giving about 4½ square inches of ventilation in addition to the entrance hole — is good for the hot and humid area of northeast Texas. In more northern areas such as central Ohio, you'll probably want about half this amount of additional ventilation. Some monitors in northern Minnesota and Canada will not need to provide extra ventilation if their boxes are placed in shaded locations.

The Edison of the Nestbox

The late T. E. Musselman of Quincy, Illinois, is generally credited with coining the term "bluebird trail." He was one of the first people to establish a trail, back in the 1930s and '40s, and he needed something to call it. Musselman is less well known as the inventor of the precursors to many modern nestboxes. Many, if not most, of the nestbox designs in this chapter owe a debt to him.

Most of Musselman's boxes were made from six or seven pieces of board and were boxes in the traditional sense. He experimented with different depths, floor sizes, and roof styles. Some of his boxes were 12 inches deep; others had only an inch or two between the bottom of the entrance hole and the top of the floorboard. He also experimented with gourds, boxes made from logs, and boxes made from cylinders.

Musselman investigated entrance holes as thoroughly as he did nestbox shapes. He tested many different styles — square holes, mouse-type holes (with an oval top and flat bottom), inverted mouse holes, and rectangular slots. He also experimented with round and oval holes of many different sizes.

You need only simple **tools to build a nestbox.** Later in this chapter, I'll describe boxes that you can construct with just a handsaw and a hammer. If you have a power saw, you can easily build enough boxes to supply a trail!

If you want to have a round entrance hole for your nestbox, you'll need a drill. A handheld power drill will do, one with a large enough chuck to hold a 1½- or 1⁹⁄₁₆-inch bit. Three different styles of bits will drill entrance holes through ¾-inch-thick wood: a Forstner bit, a hole saw bit, or the common spade or paddle bit.

The spade bit is cheapest; you might already own one the right size. Spade bits, however, have a tendency to rip through the back of a board, leaving rough edges and splinters that can snag a bird's feathers. You can avoid this problem by stacking the board you are drilling on top of another. Use sandpaper or a half-round steel file to smooth the sharp edges of the entrance hole. Feel the entrance hole with your finger. Sand it if it isn't smooth.

I prefer Forstner bits, especially the style with the sawtooth rim, but the solid-rimmed style also drills a fine entrance hole. Forstner bits cut a precise and smooth entrance hole, and it is possible to stack up to five panels and drill them at one time.

A hole saw bit also cuts a smooth, precise hole. It has a sawtooth-rimmed circular blade with a ¼-inch-diameter pilot-hole drill bit in the center. Each hole drilled produces a plug of wood that has to be removed from the bit. I drill most of the way through the front board from one side and then flip the board and finish drilling from the other side. With this procedure, enough of the plug sticks out of the bit that I can grasp and remove it. Only one panel can be drilled at a time with a hole saw bit.

If you have a drill press and a table saw with a premium carbide saw blade made for "ripping," you can cut out boxes by the hundreds. Some of the boxes for which I give plans have angles that are best cut by a table saw, but since the angles don't have to be precise, a hand saw will do.

Wooden Nestboxes —
A Floor, Four Sides, and a Roof

The first nestbox to become widely popular in North America was **the Duncan box,** which was featured in most of the government publications about nestboxes that were published prior to about 1960. William Duncan, who was born in 1897 and lived most of his life in Louisville, Kentucky, gets credit for designing this box. He corresponded with T. E. Musselman (see sidebar, p. 94) in the early 1930s, and the box was a favorite of both gentlemen.

The Duncan box opens at the top, and when the top is lifted, the nest is well lit and easy to monitor. Top-opening boxes are a favorite with bluebird monitors who like to take photographs, because the nest is so well illuminated. The 5-by-5-inch floor area is ample for mountain and western bluebirds, as well as eastern bluebirds.

A weakness of the Duncan box is that the roof does not overhang the sides. This can be a problem in hot southern climates where extra shade is desirable. And in regions that experience driving rains, water can enter through the top ventilation slots. If the Duncan box is not located where it is protected from hot sun or driving rains, the top should be modified so that it overhangs the front and sides by at least 2 inches.

Mounting a Duncan box can be a challenge. Since the top is flush with the back of the box and hinged to it, the box cannot be opened easily if the mounting post or pole extends above the top of the box. Also, the only way the back of the box can be nailed or otherwise fastened to a mount is through the nesting compartment or below it.

The Duncan box is simple to build. Each cut is straight except for two that allow for the sloping roof, which are cut at a 12-degree angle. Duncan designed the box with the sides 1 inch longer in back than in front, which causes the roof to slant so that water flows off. The roof overhang in the front helps to shade the entrance hole and keep rain out of the box.

In parts of Canada and the U.S., a popular variation of the Duncan box reverses the slope of the roof so that water flows off the back of the box, away from the entrance hole. As a result, birds are

William Duncan was active in bluebird conservation from the beginning of the movement, and he continued working on behalf of bluebirds well into his 80s. He published a free newsletter several times a year, and his mailing list approached 1,800 in 1979, when he was 82 years old.

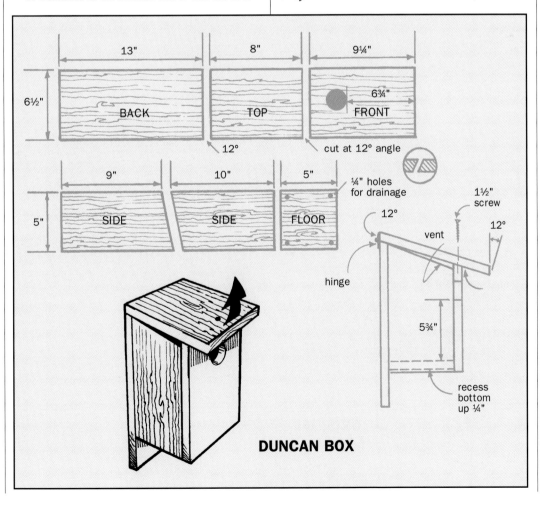

DUNCAN BOX

little less likely to get drenched when they go in or out. To reverse the roof, simply drill the entrance hole in the longer "back" piece and hinge the top on the "front" piece. With this configuration, the normal roof overhang won't shield the hole sufficiently, so the roof should be cut about 3 inches longer than usual.

Dr. Lawrence Zeleny, the founder of the North American Bluebird Society, created **the Original NABS box.** It was an adaptation of one of T. E. Musselman's designs and became known as the NABS box because plans for it were included with all information packets from the North American Bluebird Society (NABS) from 1978 until well into the 1990s. NABS now has approved many variations of the original design, most of which have a larger floor area and more roof overhang than the original.

Zeleny believed that the average family of five eastern bluebirds needed a box with no less than 15 square inches of floor space if they were to keep the nest clean and have adequate room for the growing young. So his boxes had 4-by-4-inch bottoms — a floor plan that's a little small for the mountain bluebird, which is larger than its eastern and western relatives and also has bigger clutches. A variation of the Original NABS box that provides more floor space is described on p. 99 under the topic "larger floor sizes."

The Original NABS box is a bit more difficult to build than the Duncan box but is less expensive and can be completed more quickly. The removable top saves the expense of hinges and the time to install them, and the compact size keeps lumber expenses down. Original NABS boxes also weigh less than most other "standard-sized" wooden nestboxes. For a trail operator, the compact size means that more boxes can be stuffed in the trunk of the car or in the back of the garage. The back of this box extends both above the roof and below the floor, making it very easy to fasten the box securely to a mounting pole.

Besides being inexpensive, the Original NABS box has a removable top that provides a practical advantage for bluebird monitors who have to deal with paper wasps. These stinging pests often build their nests on the underside of the roof. So it is a simple matter to carefully remove the top of the box and crush the wasps and their nest against the front of the nestbox.

The removable top has some drawbacks, however. A roof with more overhang would provide better shade and more rain protection. Furthermore, the

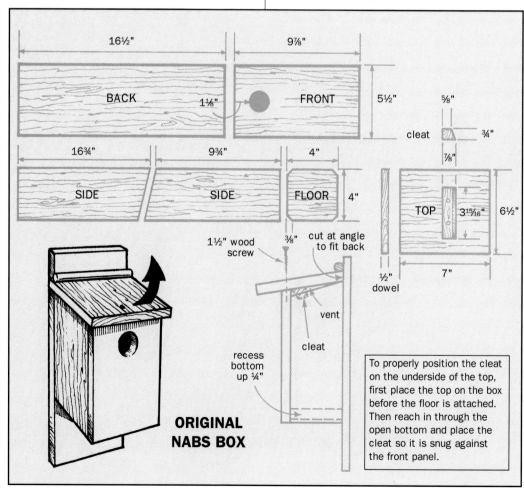

BACK 16½" 1⅛"

FRONT 9⅞" 5½"

⅝" cleat ¾" ⅞"

SIDE 16¾" SIDE 9¾"

FLOOR 4" 4" cut at angle to fit back ⅜"

TOP 3¹⁵⁄₁₆" 6½" 7"

1½" wood screw

½" dowel

vent

cleat

recess bottom up ¼"

ORIGINAL NABS BOX

To properly position the cleat on the underside of the top, first place the top on the box before the floor is attached. Then reach in through the open bottom and place the cleat so it is snug against the front panel.

joint between the roof and the back can leak if the cleat is not kept sealed with caulk. Also, the back cleat does not secure the top as reliably as hinges do. The top is easily torn loose if livestock rub against it or when vandals try to pry it open. In such circumstances, the top may fall off altogether, leaving the nest exposed to the elements and predators. Hinges would keep the top in place even if the screw or other fastener that holds it shut were torn loose.

In regions with hot summer weather, consider increasing the size of the ventilation gaps to ½ inch.

Dick Irwin of Anchorage, Kentucky, pioneered a major innovation in nestbox construction in the early 1960s. He popularized **the front-opening box.** Irwin made his door by recessing the front panel inside the side panels. He then drove a nail through each side panel and into the front panel near the top. The nails serve as pivots. Lift up on the bottom of the door, and it swings open to reveal the box's contents.

With a front-opening box, you can get at the nest easily for whatever reason. You can inspect for blowfly larvae in active nests and easily clean out old nests at the end of the season. The pivoting front door is typically secured at the bottom with a pin or screw fitted through one of the stationary side panels into the door. Even if the pin or screw is removed or falls out, the door will hang in the closed position.

About the only drawback to Irwin's front-opening door is that it makes it difficult to take good pictures of a nest without removing the nest from the box.

Because of its advantages, Irwin's door design has been used in many different nestboxes, and we show two of them here, the NABS box and the Tuttle box. **The NABS box** is a design copyrighted by NABS and has replaced the Original NABS box in the society's recommendations. It is a side-opening variation on Irwin's front-opening box. A side-opening box is much like a front-opening box, except it makes the Huber sparrow trap (p. 120) more difficult to install.

The NABS box is easy to build from 1-by-6 and 1-by-10 boards. All the cuts except the entrance hole can be made with a handsaw. Even the drain "holes" are made by cutting off the corners of the floor — another of Dick Irwin's innovations.

It can be difficult to mount the NABS box for the same reason it can be difficult to mount the Duncan box — the back of the box does not extend above the top. Both boxes must be attached to the mounting structure through the nesting compartment or below it.

Dick Irwin started his first bluebird trail in 1961. He was able to enjoy using his innovations for only three seasons before his death, but in the years since, hundreds of thousands of bluebirds have fledged from the front-opening boxes that he helped popularize.

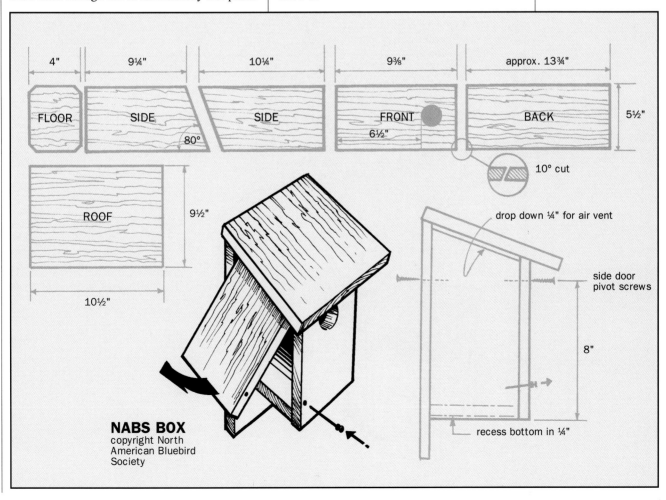

NABS BOX
copyright North
American Bluebird
Society

Although the NABS box is a particular design with specific dimensions, nearly every similar design that opens from the front or side is popularly called a "NABS-style" box, including **the Tuttle nestbox.**

In the late 1970s, Richard M. Tuttle of Delaware, Ohio, developed this box — one of the best bluebird nestboxes ever created. Tuttle's box was first publicized by the Ohio Division of Wildlife in their brochure *Hit the Trail for Bluebirds.*

As a schoolteacher, Dick Tuttle wanted to design a nestbox that schoolchildren could build using only a handsaw and a drill. It had to be as simple as possible to construct — and inexpensive. The box Tuttle developed is made from a single board, a 1-by-10, which is actually ¾ inch thick and 9¼ inches wide. Three nestboxes can be built from one 10-foot-long board. All the cuts are straight — no odd angles. Simple. And it has everything a small cavity-nesting bird needs.

Though it may seem surprising, the flat roof on this box is actually an improvement on most sloping-roof designs. During a rainstorm, sloped roofs can drop a sheet of water a few inches in front of the entrance hole. Not only do birds get wet when they enter or exit the box, but wind can blow the cold dripping water right through the entrance hole into the box. To keep water from puddling on the flat top or dripping off its front edge, tilt the box very slightly to one side when mounting it.

A tilt of ¼ inch or so will do the trick. The Tuttle design also calls for rain grooves to be cut on the underside of the roof, ¼ inch from each edge.

Although it is designed to open from the front, the Tuttle box is easily converted to side-opening: just drill the entrance hole in a different panel and reposition the top. Nestbox monitors who prefer top-opening boxes can hinge the top to one of the side panels. The top may be held shut with a hook and eye or with a screw threaded through the top and into one of the side panels.

The Tuttle box is intended to be mounted on a metal pole and must be attached through the inside of the box. While this can be difficult to do with a top- or side-opening box, it is easy with the front-opening style.

Tuttle used the small block of wood that is left over after the nestbox panels are cut as a predator guard. You may prefer to drill a 1⅛-inch-diameter hole in the leftover block and use it as a hole restrictor (p. 118) to be added to the box if it is claimed by chickadees.

Instead of cutting the corners of the floor to provide drainage, as is done in the NABS box, Tuttle drilled four ¼-inch holes in the floor. He wanted to be able to plug three of them in winter with round dowel rods to create a draft-free roosting box for his overwintering birds. He filled the vent slots at the top of the box with foam insulation.

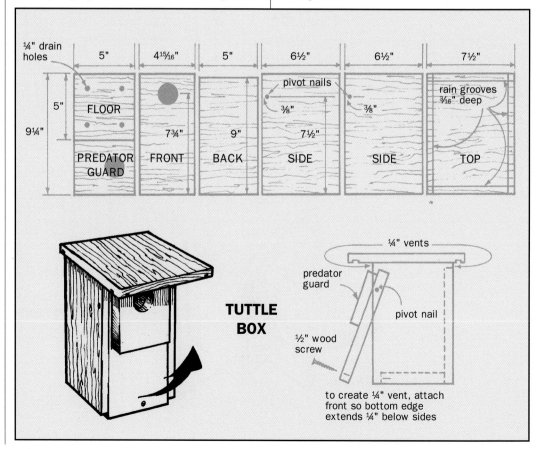

TUTTLE BOX

The box that Jack Finch of Bailey, North Carolina, developed in the late1970s is the same size and basic design as the Tuttle box. But several innovative improvements in **the Jack Finch nestbox** make it extremely durable and easy to monitor.

To prevent the entrance hole from being enlarged by woodpeckers or squirrels (a circumstance that often results in the box being entered by starlings), Finch nails a 3-inch-square aluminum entrance hole protector on the box. The protector has a 1⅝-inch hole, slightly larger than the 1⁹⁄₁₆-inch hole in the wooden nestbox. The aluminum is not shiny, but brown — the same color as the rest of the box, which is dipped in a thin solution of brown acrylic latex paint. The paint protects the wood, and the brown color makes the box less conspicuous to vandals. (Jack also makes boxes that are unpainted, for people who prefer the look of natural wood.)

Finch's roof design provides better protection from rain than the groove in the Tuttle box roof. To begin with, Finch constructs his roof panel from two layers of wood nailed together from both sides. The bottom layer fits inside the box, while the top one overhangs the sides. The rooftop and edges are covered with the same brown aluminum sheeting that surrounds the entrance hole. The metal protects the most vulnerable panel in the nestbox from the destructive effects of successive drenching and drying.

The door pivots on the Tuttle box are points of wear and eventual failure. Finch has remedied this problem. Instead of using a pair of nails or screws for pivots, Finch drills one small, continuous hole all the way through the front and sides of the box and runs a plastic-coated 12-gauge copper wire through it. This is the same wire used for routing electricity to the wall plugs in your house — it never rusts or breaks! The door is fastened with a piece of plastic-covered 10-gauge copper wire in a simple arrangement that allows the box to be monitored in seconds.

"But there's more!" as late-night TV infomercials invariably announce. Finch's box comes with two valuable accessories. The first is a simple metal strap (p. 58) bolted to the back of the box and fashioned so that the box can easily be mounted on poles, posts, or tree trunks.

The second accessory is inside the nestbox — it's a 5-inch-diameter flowerpot, 4 inches deep, made of recycled cardboard (see picture, p. 30). Finch trims the sides of the pot so that it fits into his 4½-inch-square box. This pot serves several functions. The birds will build their nest in the pot, making it easy to remove the nest from the box for monitoring. Instead of maneuvering the nest out with a spatula or some other tool, you can grab the flowerpot with your hand. After the young birds fledge, the old nest and its debris can easily be

cleaned from the box. The pot keeps the box bottom from getting soiled, so the bottom doesn't rot prematurely. The pot also reduces the amount of nesting material the birds must gather to build a nest.

All of the box designs described so far can be made with **larger floor sizes** using a single 1-by-6 or 1-by-8 board. When cut from a single board, each panel is the width of the board. When the panels are assembled, the boxes will have rectangular floors.

The Jack Finch box on the left is manufactured by the nonprofit Homes for Bluebirds. It is mounted on 1-inch conduit and is protected by a stovepipe baffle. On the right is a **Grivich-style nestbox** cut from a single 1-by-8 board. The box is mounted on ½-inch conduit over a rebar stake. A wobbly baffle of 4-inch PVC pipe deters climbing predators.

A female eastern bluebird prepares to feed her young through the entrance slot of her nestbox.

Panels cut from a 1-by-6 board (actually ¾ inch by 5½ inches) will be 5½ inches wide. A nestbox constructed from them will be 4 inches by 5½ inches on the inside and have 22 square inches of floor area. This is ample room for eastern or western bluebirds — and for mountain bluebirds as well, many would agree.

Panels cut from a 1-by-8 board (actually ¾ inch by 7¼ inches) will produce a box with a floor space of 41 square inches (5¾ by 7¼ inches). This is more than twice the size of the floor space in the original NABS box. Even the largest broods of mountain bluebirds will have more than enough room in a box this spacious.

Building a box from a single 1-by-6 or 1-by-8 does have one drawback: the roof panel can be no wider than the rest of the panels, so there can be no side overhang. The late John Grivich of Huntsville, Texas, solved the problem by sloping the side panels of the box inward 1 inch at the top. That way they are recessed under the edge of the roof.

A Grivich-style box constructed from a 1-by-6 board tapers at the top to an inside measurement of 2 by 5½ inches. The shape of the box — small at the top and large at the bottom — resembles that of a typical woodpecker cavity. Although that shape may seem natural to a bluebird, it limits the kind of house sparrow traps (p. 120) that can be used. Only the Gilbertson or Van Ert styles designed for PVC boxes will work in a Grivich-style box.

All of the boxes discussed thus far have entrance holes, but you can build a perfectly serviceable box without the bother of drilling a hole.

Birds enter **the slot box** through a rectangular gap — usually located between the top of the front board and the roof. A slot entrance can be incorporated in any of the boxes previously discussed.

The slot concept has been around at least since Musselman (see sidebar, p. 94), but this design feature has never been as popular as the circular hole. Many years ago, Rita Efta of Iowa popularized a model that is a cross between the Duncan and Tuttle nestboxes. It has a 4-inch-square floor and a slightly sloping roof. The slot is created by fitting the top of the front panel 1³⁄₁₆ inches short of the roof.

In the 1980s, Dr. Wayne Davis of Lexington, Kentucky, developed a nestbox he called the Kentucky slot box. More recently Andrew Troyer developed a slot box with a slanted front panel. Both the Kentucky slot box and the Troyer slot box are somewhat resistant to house sparrows, but probably because they are both small, shallow boxes, not because they are slot boxes.

Boxes with a slot entrance are thought to deter house sparrows...to various degrees...by some monitors...in certain situations. Dr. Davis had good success discouraging sparrows with his Kentucky slot boxes at first — enough to prompt testing across the country. In many areas where the slot boxes were tried, however, house sparrows quickly adapted to them. Even in Kentucky, where the first successful tests occurred, house sparrows learned to use the Kentucky slot box.

The slot on a slot box is typically 1³⁄₁₆ inches high. Research by purple martin landlords has shown that many starlings can enter a slot that big (see sidebar, p. 103), but starlings prefer deep, roomy cavities, which are seldom found in a slot box. For a slot box with a deep cavity and over 25 square inches of floor space, the gap might need to be reduced to 1⅛ inches to help keep starlings out.

The slot entrance is advantageous in areas with hot summers because it provides good ventilation. Also, because the slot is so much wider than a conventional hole, a nesting bluebird has a better chance of escaping if a snake or house sparrow tries to enter the box.

On the negative side, the roof has to warp only an eighth of an inch or so to create problems — and pieces of solid lumber often warp that much. If the roof warps up, making the slot wider, starlings will have easy access to the box. If the roof warps down, bluebirds can find it difficult or impossible to enter. To prevent the roof from warping, make it from exterior grade plywood that is a full ¾ inch thick and made with either five or seven plies. Also, measure the gap of any slot box regularly as part of your normal monitoring routine.

If it seems as though we've already presented a variety of nestboxes, there are undoubtedly even more variations on steeply pitched **"gable roof"**

nestboxes than on any other type. People like the way these boxes look. Many are designed as wood-working projects and are elaborately painted and decorated. Very few are created with the birds' well-being in mind.

A gable roof nestbox that does serve its occupants' needs especially well is designed and produced by Gary Springer of Carnesville, Georgia. The gable roof of his Chalet nestbox slopes at a 45-degree angle and has generous overhang on all four sides, which makes it virtually impossible for water to enter the box. Half-inch vent slots run the entire width of the box at the top of the two sides, providing excellent ventilation.

The Chalet nestbox is especially suited for the Deep South in places where a box needs to be mounted in full sun. The wide roof overhang on all sides acts as an air scoop if there is any breeze, keeping the interior temperature of the box very near the outside temperature. Even on windless days, there is a natural convection because the vent slots are not at the top of the box but well below it. Nestlings can stretch up and feel the cooling air being drawn in through the vents.

Springer constructs his nestbox from unplaned 1-inch thick yellow pine lumber, and he increases the thickness of the entrance hole to more than

2 inches by attaching a small block of wood over the entrance. The block is predrilled and attached with wood screws. Springer also includes a coupler on the bottom of the box that will connect to 1-inch conduit

Since the Chalet box is held together entirely by screws, any panel can easily be removed and replaced. The box, which has a side-opening door, can be opened from the top if desired by removing the four screws that secure the roof to the sides.

**More Wooden Nestboxes —
Built to the Beat of a Different Hammer**

In the mid-1970s, Dick Peterson of Clarissa, Minnesota, created what is today one of the most popular and most widely used bluebird nestboxes. With the amount of research and experimentation Peterson invested in the design, he felt justified in calling it the Peterson System. Most bluebird monitors know it fondly as **the Peterson box.** The design is complex by nestbox standards, and it incorporates numerous original ideas. This is one box that can't be traced back to Musselman's pioneering work (see sidebar, p. 94).

Every innovative feature of the Peterson box has a clearly conceived purpose. The roof slopes steeply (27 degrees) toward the front, which deters raccoons and other four-legged predators from sitting

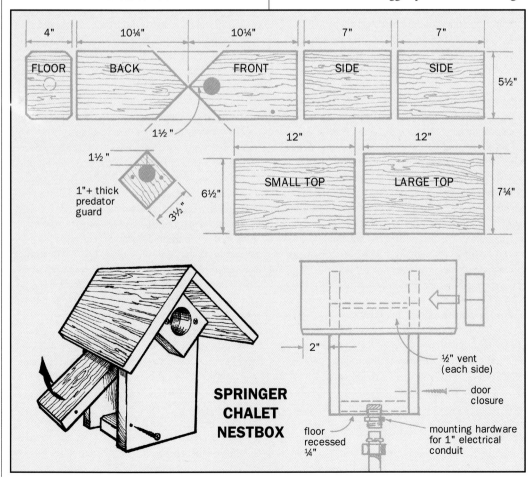

A male eastern bluebird stands guard on his Peterson nestbox. The entrance hole is protected by a Noel guard made of hardware cloth.

In 1978, Dick Peterson and his wife, Vi, asked the Minneapolis chapter of the National Audubon Society for help coordinating the box-monitoring efforts of all the people who had contacted Dick for information. As a result of their request, the Minnesota Bluebird Recovery Program was created in 1979. Now more than 900 people strong, the organization serves bluebirds by distributing information, making research grants, offering seminars, and providing individual help to bluebird monitors.

on it and reaching into the box through the entrance hole. The front overhang of the roof is angled down and does an excellent job of shielding the entrance hole from rain or from the late afternoon sun.

The floor of the Peterson box also slopes at the same angle as the roof. Any water that does enter the box seeps out through the joint where the floor meets the door. The sloping floor also tends to concentrate blowfly larvae toward the front of the box, where they can easily be removed.

Even though the floor area in a Peterson box is small and sloping, that doesn't mean that the parent bluebirds have to sit on a tiny, tilted nest or that the nestlings will be crowded. When the bluebirds finish building their nest, its cup is well above the floor, at a level where there is about 16 or 17 square inches of room for the nest. And the bluebirds are smart enough to construct their nest so that the cup is level even though the floor slants.

Unlike most front-opening boxes, which open from the bottom and swing up, the Peterson box opens from the top and swings down. This is an important feature. Without it, a nest might fall out of the Peterson box because of the slanted floor and door panel. The Peterson door can — and should! — be opened carefully to make sure that the contents aren't about to slide out. This is rarely a problem with bluebird nests, but the nests, eggs, and nestlings of chickadees and titmice may well tumble out if the door is carelessly thrown open wide.

At the top of the front panel is a ½-inch vent space. Two ¾-inch-diameter vent holes in the top of each side panel work with the front panel vent to create some natural convection.

The Peterson box is the only one we describe that uses 2-by-4 lumber in its construction. As a result, it is heavy. The original plans call for the remaining panels to be ¾ inch thick, but $\frac{7}{16}$-inch-thick hardboard siding is now more commonly used. Even when constructed with the thinner siding, the Peterson box is heavier than any of the other boxes we describe.

Despite this drawback, the Peterson box is designed to last and will resist rough handling. And it can be built inexpensively by anyone who has the shop equipment to do so. Siding and 2-by-4s are common scrap at construction sites; Dick Peterson built and gave away more than 5,000 of his boxes, and he never bought a board!

Bluebird monitors who don't have the table saw and power miter needed to cut lumber for the Peterson box can order the panels precut as a kit from Ahlgren Construction Company (see Resources, p. 124). Dave Ahlgren, who runs the operation, also makes fully assembled boxes and has sold more than 70,000 kits and boxes since he began in the early 1980s.

The oval entrance hole is the most controversial of Dick Peterson's design innovations. Peterson felt that bluebirds preferred an oval hole over a round hole. They don't have to go all the way inside the box to feed the nestlings or remove their fecal sacs, as they must do with a round hole. Instead, the parents can perch right on the oval hole and simply tip in to feed or take care of sanitation.

Controversy arises because starlings can squeeze through the oval hole to occupy a box or attack the occupants. Peterson's tests showed that the width of the oval hole had to be reduced to 1⅛ inches to keep starlings out, but he felt that a 1⅜-inch-wide hole was more attractive to bluebirds. Only three starlings ever claimed a box in his tests, but in other parts of the continent, nestbox monitors report that starlings seem ready and willing to thread themselves through the oval hole. Perhaps the different results have something to do with the local prevalence of starlings and the relative scarcity of nesting cavities.

If the Peterson box is not starling-proof, it is certainly starling-resistant. Not only is the hole a tight squeeze for the average starling, but the inside dimensions of the box are a tight squeeze for its nest. A Peterson box is probably a starling's last resort. If one does lay claim to a box, it can be evicted because, as a non-native species, starlings are not protected by federal law. You can prevent the problem from recurring by placing a block drilled with a round hole over the oval hole.

A Gilwood box attracts the attention of a male eastern bluebird and his companion — a house finch! Nestbox monitors regularly report seeing house finches "hanging out" with bluebirds.

Only certain sparrow traps and entrance hole guards will work with the Peterson box because of the oval hole and narrow shape. Peterson designed a sparrow trap (p. 121) that covers the large oval entrance hole. It is mounted on a separate front panel that can replace the regular door. Predator guards (p. 117) and entrance hole reducers that accommodate smaller cavity-nesters can also be mounted on separate fronts, so the Peterson box "system" can be quickly adapted to the changing situations a monitor might encounter.

Steve Gilbertson of Aitkin, Minnesota, best known for his popular PVC nestbox (p. 106), also developed a wooden nestbox known as **the Gilwood box** in the late 1990s. It has two interesting features that set it apart from the other nestboxes described: (1) the front panel is recessed, and (2) the entrance hole is an upside-down mouse hole. Because of these innovations, the entrance hole gets good protection from wind, rain, and sun. Rain would have to be blowing nearly head-on and horizontally to enter this box.

The unusual entrance hole is quite large, approximately 4 square inches in area. Gilbertson feels that bluebirds are attracted to a large hole, and some early tests indicate that bluebirds do like the Gilwood box, although who is to say exactly why? Starlings can easily enter a 4-square-inch

hole, however, so Gilbertson reduces the functional entrance size by running a steel wire across the hole. The wire, which also serves as the pivot for the door, reduces the actual entrance height to between 1¼ and 1⅜ inches — large enough to admit starlings, as tests by Kevin Berner, the NABS research chairman, demonstrated in 2000. However, any starling that negotiates the entrance hole will likely be discouraged by the tight quarters inside the box (3½ by 4¼ inches).

Precut panels for the Gilwood box are available from Gilbertson as a kit (see Resources, p. 124).

Most sparrow traps will not work on the Gilwood box because of the large entrance hole, but the Van Ert trap (p. 121) is the exception and does a good job. Removing a captured house sparrow from the Gilbertson box is particularly easy. Because the front panel is recessed, there is no gap along the sides of the door when it is opened the first 2 inches. The gap is only at the bottom, so a house sparrow cannot escape out the sides when the monitor reaches in from the bottom.

Ventilation is provided by the entrance hole. Thanks to the large opening at the very top of the box, hot air rises and escapes rather than being trapped inside. There are no other ventilation holes, and Gilbertson feels they are not needed — at least, not in Minnesota, where he lives, or in the other northern areas where the box has been tested. In cold climates, the concern is that water might enter through the ventilation holes — cold spring rains are a much greater threat to bluebirds in the North than are scorching-hot summers. If the Gilwood box is used in the South or if the upside-down mouse hole is replaced by a circular or oval hole, additional ventilation might be needed. A gap ⅜ inch high between the roof and backboard will provide cross ventilation.

The late Laurance Sawyer of Ringgold, Georgia, created **nestboxes from logs.** In 1975, he designed and built a machine that could bore a 4-inch-diameter hole into the end of a log. His daughter and son-in-law, Elaine and Edward Whittemore (see Resources, p. 124), are still using

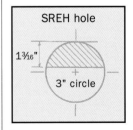

SREH hole

1³⁄₁₆"

3" circle

Starling-Resistant Entrance Holes

Gilbertson's upside-down mouse hole is very similar to the Starling-Resistant Entrance Hole developed in the late 1980s by Charles McEwen of Moncton, New Brunswick, Canada, for purple martin houses. The SREH entrance is a "right side up" mouse hole that is wider than Gilbertson's but not as high — only 1³⁄₁₆ inches. Extensive testing of the SREH entrance throughout the 1990s showed that it successfully blocks nearly all starlings but that higher entrances admitted progressively more starlings.

Because the Gilwood mouse hole is ³⁄₁₆ inch higher than the SREH entrance, the Gilwood box is at risk of being taken over by starlings. The narrow radius of the Gilbertson mouse hole (1⅛ inches instead of the 1½ inches of the SREH entrance) may help to compensate for its additional height.

Attractive log boxes can be made by cutting a log in half with a large band saw and drilling each piece separately from the center. Join the two halves with a 3-inch-long strap hinge and use a hook and eye to latch the box. Drilling an entrance hole and drain holes completes the job.

Sawyer's "woodpecker lathe" to bore out logs. The hole in the top of the log is plugged with a block of wood. A metal cone roof is attached to the block. An entrance hole is drilled through the log's side, and drainage holes are drilled through the bottom.

While log boxes are no more attractive to bluebirds than are smooth-planed board boxes, most people consider their natural, bark-covered appearance much more beautiful. Sawyer made his boxes from tulip poplar, and they will retain the bark on the outside for 20 years or more.

It isn't necessary to design your own log-drilling machine, as Sawyer did, to build these boxes. The largest Forstner drill bit, measuring 4⅝ inches in diameter, will do the job. But it can be dangerous if the bit hits a nail or tree knot while drilling. It is important to clamp the log section securely to a very heavy lathe or milling machine for safety.

Logs cut in winter when a tree is dormant will keep their bark for the longest time. Bark will come loose in a year or so from logs cut when the sap is flowing. If the bark starts to peel away from your log box, use small brads or staples to tack it back in place.

Few people have access to the shop equipment needed to create a log box, but naturally occurring hollow logs can be collected from tree trimmers and turned into fine-looking nestboxes. And there is one other way to create a nestbox with a natural look: use slab lumber, with the bark still attached, in place of planed lumber. Many of the wooden nestboxes we describe can be built with slab lumber.

People have experimented with horizontal nestboxes since Musselman (see sidebar, p. 94). They are intended to mimic a hollow horizontal tree limb and are usually called **"tree branch birdhouses."**

The early designs were all wood, but PVC boxes are now sometimes hung horizontally with a hole drilled in one end cap.

Tree branch birdhouses are harder to mount, often harder to monitor, and are popular with house sparrows, among other problems. Dick Purvis of Anaheim, California, is experimenting with a tree branch birdhouse that may have overcome some of the problems characteristic of the horizontal design. He calls his design the "baffle box." It is a wooden box with a hole in each end. The extra hole is an exit for the birds in case of attack by a predator or house sparrow.

The entrance holes are at the side of each end panel, not in the center. When a bird enters the baffle box, it immediately encounters a vertical wood baffle that runs from floor to ceiling but is only half the width of the nestbox. The bird must turn and walk around the baffle to reach the larger nesting area. The baffle thwarts raccoons and cats from reaching the nest. It also prevents direct sunlight from entering the box — which may be good or bad, depending on whether cold or heat is your enemy.

Most tree branch birdhouses have a baffle placed deep inside the box, and birds often nest in front of the baffle rather than in the safe compartment behind it. Purvis makes sure that birds don't have room to nest in front of the baffle. To make monitoring easy, an entire side of his baffle box pivots up, exposing the nesting compartment.

A male eastern bluebird perches on the attractive slab front of his nestbox to feed his nestlings.

Nestbox designers other than Purvis have experimented with **multiple entrance holes** in nestboxes. Often the alternate entrances are intended to be emergency exits, but sometimes they are added to attract bluebirds; the idea is that extra holes will catch the birds' attention, just as "attraction spots" (p. 17) are thought to do. If attraction spots painted on all sides of a box help attract bluebirds, the reasoning goes, real multiple entrance holes should work even better.

In at least one case, the multiple entrance holes were not an intended design feature. Robert McKinney of Mt. Vernon, Texas, recounts how he helped a Boy Scout troop build 50 nestboxes back in the early 1980s. In one room, McKinney and some of the boys nailed together the nestboxes. In a second room, other Scouts drilled the entrance holes, installed latches, and painted the boxes. Well, drilling the entrance holes was fun, so the boys drilled holes in each side as well as in the front. McKinney ended up with three entrance holes in each of the 50 boxes.

"Let's try them and see what happens" was his attitude. He found that eastern bluebirds used the three-holers as often as they used nestboxes with a single entrance hole. Birds would often enter one hole and exit another. Although the multiple holes did have the advantage of allowing both parents to feed the young at the same time, McKinney noted that the birds seldom took advantage of the opportunity. Usually one bird preferred to stand guard while the other did the feeding.

Linda Violett, who works with western bluebirds in Yorba Linda, California, has begun experimenting with a box that has two holes in the front panel (see picture, p. 66) and a large floor area. She believes that this combination of features may make it easier for western bluebirds to defend their nestbox from house sparrows. Time will tell.

Multiple entrance holes might be a useful feature in boxes used in areas of the South that have snakes. An extra hole could be a lifesaver when a rat snake enters a box. On hot days, an extra hole would increase the ventilation, but in colder parts of the continent, an extra hole would just make a box drafty and chilly. If you decide to experiment with extra entrance holes, be sure to provide plenty of overhang over each entrance, and monitor the box closely to note any advantages or problems that might occur in your area.

Alternate Nestbox Materials — PVC, Pottery, Gourds, and...Cement?

Why use PVC pipe for nestboxes? Let me count the reasons. It doesn't decay. It is light. It is easy to work with. Woodpeckers can't enlarge the entrance hole, and squirrels seldom try. It is readily available. It is cheap. And bluebirds like it! What's more,

house sparrows tend to reject 4-inch-diameter PVC nestboxes — the size most commonly made to attract bluebirds.

Don Hutchings of Winfield, Texas, makes his **PVC nestboxes** out of 4-inch PVC pipe. They are especially quick and easy to build because Hutchings doesn't try to cut roof and floor pieces out of wood to fit the round pipe; he uses factory-made PVC end caps.

The bottom cap can be glued to the pipe, but Hutchings prefers to fasten it with a short steel wood screw. By removing a single screw and twisting off the bottom cap, he can quickly clean his nestbox. The roof cap can just slip over the pipe. It's a snug fit, so the pieces don't need to be screwed together except to protect the nest from vandals and predators.

The section of pipe used for a nestbox can be anywhere from about 8 to 11 inches long. There should be at least 4½ inches from the bottom of the entrance hole to the floor. Shallow boxes are best where house sparrows are a problem. Deeper boxes tend to be cooler and keep the nestlings a safer distance from the entrance hole, where starlings or other predatory birds might easily reach them.

Hutchings drills several small drain holes in the bottom cap and some ¾-inch vent holes near the top of the pipe. To protect the box from rain and direct sun, he attaches a square of PVC board or

Several nestboxes made from 4-inch PVC pipe by Don Hutchings. (The pipe is available in several colors as well as white.) The box on the left has a hanger strap (p. 110) bolted onto its back for mounting. The middle box is attached to the barbed wire by wires that are threaded through two pairs of small holes drilled in the back of the box. The box on the right is bolted to a conduit pole.

wood to the PVC roof cap with screws and glue. The finished box is compact and easy to monitor.

Some swallows need help getting out of a 4-inch-diameter PVC box if it is deeper than about 4½ inches from the bottom of the hole to the floor. The slick PVC surface below the hole needs to have toeholds added to produce a ladder that swallows can climb. Bluebirds, chickadees, and titmice have no trouble exiting even 8-inch-deep PVC boxes, but the boxes can be death traps to swallows if ladders aren't provided.

The silicone rubber developed by General Electric and supplied in tubes for caulking guns makes the longest-lasting toeholds. Lay several thin horizontal beads of this caulk between the entrance hole and the box bottom so that they resemble the rungs of a ladder.

PVC pipe can be cut to length easily with power miter saws, fine-toothed push handsaws, or hacksaws. It can also be cut on a table saw but will probably need to be rotated by hand to be cut completely in two.

Forstner or hole saw bits (p. 94) can be used with either drill presses or handheld drills to drill PVC pipe. The hole saw bit is the best choice with a handheld drill. Paddle-style bits will not work with PVC. There is also a drill bit called a "single wing" or "fly cutter" that will do a good job cutting entrance holes in PVC pipe, but it cannot be used in a handheld drill. A single-wing bit can be adjusted to cut holes from 1 inch to about 2 inches in diameter, but the pipe must be securely clamped so that it will not shift while it is being drilled.

Schedule 40 PVC pipe in the 4- to 6-inch size will have a wall thickness of ¼ inch. If the pipe is left white or painted a very light color, it will have the same heat resistance as ¾-inch-thick unpainted wood. But painting the box a dark color can raise the temperature inside by 10 degrees or more over the ambient temperature.

The Gilbertson PVC nestbox is made from white 4-inch-diameter PVC sewer and drain (S&D) pipe. The walls are barely more than ¹⁄₁₆ inch thick and will be slightly less heat resistant than the heavier walls of Schedule 40 PVC pipe. Steve Gilbertson uses the thinner-walled PVC because it is more flexible, and flexibility is what makes his unique box-opening method work.

Two small holes opposite each other at the top of the PVC box fit over two pins attached to the wooden roof. To open the box, the monitor squeezes the box at its top until it comes free from the pins. The box — looking like an open tin can — is then free to be moved wherever needed. The roof remains attached to the conduit/rebar mount (p. 108) that Gilbertson designed with this box in mind.

Having the box detach from the roof is very handy. It is easy to look inside the box or position it so that the lighting is perfect for photography. A lot of times, the parent will stay on the nest when you open the box. Old nests can be dumped with a flick of the wrist. The entire box can easily be exchanged if desired.

The disadvantage of Gilbertson's box-opening system is the same as that of top-opening wooden boxes — because you have to reach in from the top, you can't get at the bottom of the nest when there are eggs or nestlings in it. So you can't monitor for blowflies or easily change a wet or soiled nest.

The roof and floor of the Gilbertson PVC box are both made of wood. The 7¼-by-9-inch roof has enough overhang to provide good protection from rain and sun. The box is only 4½ inches deep from the bottom of the entrance hole to the floor. This lack of depth helps to discourage house sparrows.

Gilbertson finishes his box by streaking dark stain on the white PVC to give it an attractive birch-tree look. Inside, he stains the white walls brown so the incubating female will find it comfortably dark. The small amount of stain on the outside will not cause the box to overheat. Ventilation holes are provided along the top edge of the pipe.

An experimental front-opening box made of PVC pipe was developed in the late 1990s by Frank Navratil, Sr., of North Riverside, Illinois. His **Bluebird Buoy PVC nestbox** has another clever innovation. A long section of the pipe remains below the nestbox cavity to serve as a predator guard. The guard and box slide over the mounting

The Gilbertson PVC box can trace its origin back to the Gilbertson cardboard nestbox. It was created on a bet in 1989 and never produced for sale. Gilbertson made the box out of a 4-inch-diameter heavy cardboard tube used as the core for a roll of carpeting. Wood preservative and varnish kept the cardboard from rotting. "And I had bluebirds nesting in them," says Steve, proud winner of the bet. "Then I did the same thing but with PVC," he says.

A Gilbertson PVC-pipe nestbox is home for an attentive male bluebird. When is a cylinder a box? When it is a nestbox.

conduit or pipe, which couples into a hole on the underside of the box floor.

But the best feature of the Bluebird Buoy is its innovative (for a PVC-pipe box) front-opening door that lets you get at the nest and the nestlings if need be. The door is not hinged and doesn't pivot. It is a removable section of 4-inch-diameter sewer and drain PVC pipe — 10 inches long and cut in half vertically. It fits over a cutout in the wall of the nestbox that extends 8 inches from floor to roof and is over 3 inches wide.

The entrance hole is drilled into the door. Changing the hole size — to fit chickadees, for instance — is just a matter of popping on a different door. Narrow slots at the top and bottom of the door fit under screw heads on the box, which clamp the door in place securely. At this time, Navratil is developing a sparrow trap that will fit the door.

The top and floor of the box are squares of 2-by-4 board, 3½ inches on the side, with the corners rounded so that they will fit the pipe. They provide good ventilation and drainage. A 12-inch-square plywood roof wrapped in aluminum sheeting shades the box from the sun and protects the entrance hole from rain.

Navratil is experimenting with numerous variations of his front-opening PVC design, including ones made from 5-inch-diameter pipe and ones designed to hang from trees. The lightweight, durable PVC pipe is ideal for use in tree-mounted boxes — which are much easier to lift at the end of a 15-foot pole than most wooden boxes.

Bob Wilson of Grand Junction, Colorado, is testing another form of PVC nestbox that has exciting possibilities. In 1966, he began using **PVC fencing material for nestboxes.** This material comes in planks that look like 1-by-6 boards — except they have a hollow center and they measure a true 1 inch by 6 inches. The planks are white and have two reinforcing ribs across the hollow center that form three 1-by-2-inch cells. The box that Bob constructs is a front-opening model very much like the Tuttle box (p. 98).

PVC fencing can be substituted for wood in any of the boxes described at the start of this chapter. To make planks wider than 6 inches, glue the edges of planks (or portions of planks) together with PVC cement (it's made for gluing PVC water lines). For an 8-inch-wide plank, rip one cell width from a plank and glue it onto the edge of a 6-inch plank.

PVC panels can be glued or screwed together to form a box. The hollow PVC material won't hold a screw in place, so Bob inserts scrap pieces of wood at places in the cells where screws will be used. An alternate and perhaps easier method is to make the floor of the box from wood and screw the sides onto it. Some experimenters have had success simply gluing all the panels — except the door — together.

A box made of PVC fencing, Number 321 on Bob Wilson's trail in Colorado, makes a cool and spacious home for a pair of mountain bluebirds.

PVC fencing has a lot of advantages as a nestbox material. The inch of dead air inside each plank provides outstanding insulation from the heat of direct sunlight, keeping the interior of the box very nearly the same temperature as the outside air — which is the best you can hope for until the day someone invents miniature air conditioners for nestboxes.

PVC fencing is light, easy to work with, and rugged. It is guaranteed for 20 years when used as fencing and will likely last for 20 generations (of bluebirds, of course) when used to build nestboxes. But the feature that attracted Bob was the price. PVC fencing can be had for free. Fencing contractors often have barrels of scrap material that usually ends up in landfills. It is yours for the asking.

Pipes and 1-by-6 fencing are not the only forms of PVC that might be used for nestboxes. There are many forms to be explored, including hollow PVC posts 5 inches on a side that will make excellent nestboxes. The experiments are just beginning.

Gourds have been used as nestboxes for hundreds of years, but they have a lot of drawbacks. They are thin, fragile, and have a short life. Predators and squirrels can easily tear them apart. They are almost impossible to clean out. The newer "super gourds," made from injection-molded plastic for purple martins, have fewer problems.

Cement nestboxes are not a practical option for the do-it-yourselfer, but one manufactured model is safe for bluebirds, and it carries a 25-year

A hollow gourd with a large entrance hole is accepted as a nesting cavity by an eastern bluebird. Gourds provide little protection for the birds that nest in them.

Although it is hard for me to recommend gourd nestboxes, I might never have become involved with bluebirds without them. As a kid, I was not allowed to use a power saw, but I could use a drill — which is all that is required to turn a gourd into a nestbox. I would grow gourds by the hundreds each year. And because they are very light, I could carry about 50 at a time when I set out to hang them. Mile after mile, I'd hike along country roads and remote pastures, hanging my gourds from the outstretched limbs of solitary oak trees.

warranty. This box is made in Europe by the Schwegler Company and can be obtained in the U.S. from Thomas Wildbird Feeders (see Resources, p. 124). The box is made of 75 percent sawdust and 25 percent cement and weighs almost 5 pounds! Actually a cylinder, it has an inside floor area of just over 13 square inches. The door is a front panel that slips into place and is held very securely by a quick-opening tab.

The cement box has no ventilation other than the entrance hole, so in southern areas, the light-colored model should be used rather than the dark brown one. Since the cement compound is very dense, it probably conducts heat into the interior of the nestbox, so the box may need to be kept out of direct sun in southern locales.

The entrance hole is a circle a bit smaller than 1½ inches in diameter. It may be a little tight for mountain bluebirds but should work satisfactorily for eastern and western bluebirds.

Nestboxes are sometimes made of **clay pottery**. The designs can be attractive, but I have never seen one that would make an acceptable nestbox.

Mounting Nestboxes — Poles, Posts, and Tree Limbs

A good nestbox mount serves two purposes — it places the box at a convenient height for monitoring and, more important, it helps protect nesting birds and their babies from predators. If cats can leap to a nestbox or raccoons can climb the mount and get to the box, you may not be raising bluebirds but helping to feed predators.

Poles are the most convenient mounts in most areas. Many climbing predators can be kept from

a nestbox by a smooth, small-diameter mounting pole. A simple telescoping pole system can raise the nestbox too high for even the strongest leaping feline while allowing it to be lowered for convenient monitoring. Care must be taken when mounting nestboxes on poles in public places, however. The boxes and mounts are inviting to vandals and can easily be destroyed or removed.

Electrical metallic tubing, also known as EMT conduit, is thin-walled metal pipe that has been electrogalvanized with zinc for an extremely smooth and rust-resistant finish. While designed for use inside buildings — to route electrical wires and protect them from wear — it also makes an excellent outdoor mounting pole for nestboxes.

New conduit comes in 10-foot lengths of various diameters. It is lightweight, easy to cut, and easy to drill. However, it is not very strong or durable — the ½-inch size isn't likely to last for long if it is buried directly in the ground. A single encounter with a riding lawn mower can flatten it, and in acidic soil, rust will quickly eat through the thin wall at ground level.

Steve Gilbertson discovered that a good way to reinforce EMT conduit is with ½-inch-diameter concrete reinforcing rod — known as "rebar" to builders. Rebar comes in 20-foot lengths. Gilbertson cuts it into four 5-foot pieces with a hacksaw or metal-cutting chop saw. He also cuts a 10-foot length of ½-inch conduit into two 5-foot pieces (a hacksaw, pipe cutter, or tubing cutter will do the job). Some lumber stores will cut rebar and conduit to length at no extra cost.

To assemble the mounting pole, drive a piece of rebar about 2 feet into the ground with a metal fence post driver or sledgehammer. This provides an anchor for the conduit pole, which slides over it. (Half-inch conduit is actually nearly ⅝-inch inside diameter, so it fits snugly over ½-inch rebar.) When a nestbox is attached to the top of the 5-foot-tall conduit pole, it will be at the perfect height for monitoring.

The mounting system can easily be modified to a telescoping mount (see picture, p. 110) by the addition of a conduit connector. A conduit connector is designed to join two pieces of conduit, but in this case, Steve uses the connector — and a long screw — to clamp the end of the conduit to a rebar stake. Only one screw needs to be loosened to raise or lower the box.

Even if you don't want to make a telescoping system, a conduit connector is useful to keep the conduit and nestbox from rotating around the rebar with the wind. Although the movement does not seem to bother the birds, it can leave the entrance hole facing the sun or bad weather. A few wraps of duct tape around the rebar can also be used to stop rotation — it will act as a brake shoe.

Steve Gilbertson monitors one of his PVC-pipe nestboxes mounted on ½-inch-diameter conduit over a rebar stake.

The Gilbertson mounting pole is durable, predator resistant, and easy to construct. Rebar is inexpensive, and conduit can be had for free at demolition sites or scrap yards because it is not reused in construction.

In most soils, the Gilbertson pole will be very sturdy, but in extremely sandy soils, it may lean or fall over during wet periods. For added stability, substitute ¾-inch-diameter water pipe for the rebar. The outside diameter of ½-inch EMT conduit is such that it will just fit inside ¾-inch water pipe.

Three-quarter-inch water pipe can also be used with ½-inch conduit to make a telescoping pole. Drill a 5⁄16-inch bolt hole through the water pipe about 2 feet above the ground. When a ¼-by-2-inch-long bolt is inserted in the hole, it will stop the conduit from sliding any lower, and the nestbox will be 7 feet above the ground.

To lower the pole for monitoring, hold onto the conduit and pull the bolt out. Slowly lower the 5-foot-long piece of conduit until the bottom rests

on the ground. The nestbox will then be at the right height for monitoring.

Raising the conduit and reinserting the bolt can be tricky. If you raise the conduit too high and it comes out of the water pipe, you may be unable to balance the heavy nestbox, which will then come crashing to the ground. To avoid this calamity, it is helpful to mark the conduit with paint 1 foot from the bottom.

One-inch conduit is more expensive than the smaller sizes, but it is durable enough to be buried in the ground and used for very heavy nestboxes. Some nestboxes are made with a 1-inch conduit connector attached to the bottom so that they can easily be screwed onto a 1-inch conduit pole.

The most durable pole mount for all types of nestboxes is metal pipe — **schedule 40 zinc-galvanized steel water pipe.** It will outlast almost any nestbox and deter most climbing predators by itself, although some pipes require a little sanding for a smooth, predator-resistant finish. To test the smoothness, rub a washcloth along the length of the pipe. If the pipe tends to pull threads from the cloth, it needs to be sanded. Snakes and determined raccoons may still be able to make their way up a pipe that has been sanded smooth, so nestboxes may need to be protected by baffles where these predators abound (p. 114).

Water pipe does have some drawbacks. It can be fairly expensive to outfit a large trail with it. It is hard to cut with a hacksaw, and few people other than plumbers have the heavy-duty pipe cutters, threaders, and pipe vise needed to work with it.

If the pipe is to be set directly into the ground, it should be cut into three 7-foot-long pieces. Each piece can then be driven into the ground 2 feet, and the nestbox, when mounted at the top of the piece of pipe, will be at a convenient height for monitoring. Top-opening boxes need to be mounted slightly lower than front- or side-opening boxes.

In hard or rocky soil, it may be easier to drive a piece of rebar partway into the ground and slide a section of water pipe over it than to drive the pipe itself into the ground. In this case, the water pipe should be cut into four 63-inch-long pieces to have the nestbox at a convenient mounting height.

Rebar is also used to create a telescoping water-pipe pole. Drill a 5⁄16-inch hole about a foot from the bottom of a 5-foot section of ½-inch water pipe. Slide a ¼-by-2-inch-long bolt through the hole and slip the pipe down over a rebar stake driven into the ground. The bolt will rest on top of the rebar, leaving the box towering over the ground.

Don't try drilling a bolt hole through ½-inch EMT conduit to make a telescoping pole. A bolt hole drilled through the thin walls of ½-inch conduit will weaken the conduit so much that it might buckle in a high wind.

Water pipe comes in 21-foot lengths of various diameters. The ½-inch (interior diameter) water pipe is the smallest size suitable for using as a mounting pole. Although it is called ½-inch pipe, the interior diameter measures nearly 5⁄8 inch and the outside diameter is almost 7⁄8 inch.

In soft, sandy soils that won't support ½-inch rebar, 1-inch-diameter water pipe can be substituted. The ½-inch pipe slides inside the 1-inch pipe to create a rigid mount for the softest of soils and the heaviest of nestboxes. The two pipes can be drilled and bolted together to reduce theft in public locations.

At permanent nestbox locations, pipe or rebar can be set in concrete. Fill a gallon can or plastic jug with wet concrete mix. Place the pipe or rebar in the mix and brace it so that as the cement dries, it will be straight and plumb. Planting this cement bucket 18 inches deep will make the pole almost theft-proof while creating a very sturdy nestbox mount.

A telescoping mounting system (left) of ½-inch EMT conduit over rebar is raised to keep the nestbox safe from leaping felines. The conduit connector (inset) permits the box to be lowered (right) to a convenient height for monitoring.

There are several ways **to connect a nestbox to a mounting pole.** If the pole is conduit, it is easiest to flatten the top couple of inches with a hammer, drill a hole through the flattened piece and the back of the nestbox, and bolt the two together.

Water pipe can also be drilled and bolted to the back of a nestbox, although it can't be flattened. The box will pivot on the bolt unless you clamp or wire it to the pole at the bottom, as some bluebird monitors do. A top-opening nestbox secured to a water pipe with a single bolt on the back can be cleaned quickly by swiveling it upside down and dumping the used contents into a bucket or bag.

Water pipe can be coupled to the bottom of a nestbox with a plate called a pipe flange. The pipe flange is screwed or bolted securely to the bottom of the nestbox. The center of the flange has a threaded hole that the water pipe screws into. If you grease the threads of the pipe, you can change boxes easily by unscrewing one box and installing another.

A pipe flange can also be used to attach a nestbox to a conduit pole. However, both the conduit pole and the pipe flange are female, so a male conduit connector is needed for joining the two.

Jack Finch of Bailey, North Carolina, has developed a versatile hanger strap that will couple a nestbox to 1-inch conduit or water pipe or to any kind of wood post or tree. He attaches the hanger strap to the boxes he manufactures (p. 58), and you can use his method with most other nestboxes.

The hanger strap is a strip of 16-gauge steel — 12 inches long and $^{15}\!/_{16}$ inch wide. Finch centers the strap on the back of the box, with one end of the strip even with the bottom of the box and the other extending about 1½ inches above the box top. Then he bolts the strap to the box about 2 inches from the bottom and again several inches above the bottom bolt.

To attach the box to 1-inch-diameter conduit or water pipe poles, bend the upper part of the hanger strap by hand so that the top end points down and can be inserted into the conduit or water pipe. Then bend the 2 inches of strap below the bottom bolt at an angle, creating a standoff between the back of the box and the water pipe. You can easily adjust the bends in the strap so that the box will hang perfectly vertical.

If attached to a wood post, utility pole, or tree trunk, the hanger strap can simply be nailed in place. Finch provides two small holes at the top of the strap for this purpose. To provide protection from fire ants, I like to bend the hanger as if I were mounting it on conduit before I nail it to a post (see picture, p. 105). That way I can grease the strap and keep ants away from the box.

Finch's custom-made straps can be replaced with ¾-inch-wide flat steel bar. It is available at companies dealing in structural steel and comes in

20-foot pieces in thicknesses as thin as ⅛ inch, which is ideal for a hanger strap. It can be cut with a hacksaw or a metal-cutting chop saw. It is easiest to have it cut to length where you buy it.

Chain-link security fences, 6 feet or higher, have been used by some bluebird monitors very successfully. Many companies maintain miles of this fence around their property, and bluebirds often perch on and hunt along it. Although most predators can climb the chain links, predators are often scarce near security fencing. That's because the area around the security fence is often kept mowed, which reduces the rodent population and thus discourages predators.

Instead of mounting nestboxes at the posts, place them along the top of the wire, between posts. Mount the boxes facing east, and on the opposite side of the fence, attach a large board to provide shade. The shade and the air gap between the board and nestbox will permit young birds to fledge in the hottest weather.

Although **T- or U-shaped metal fence posts** are very heavy and durable, they are not a good choice for a nestbox mount, either as part of a fence or standing alone. Neither are the lightweight versions often sold as garden stakes. The ribs and bumps on these posts or stakes are like steps on a ladder for climbing predators. And effective predator guards are not easy to fit around them.

Metal fence posts can be used as the base of a predator-proof telescoping mount, however. It is easy to convert a nestbox presently mounted on a metal fence post to one mounted on a telescoping section of conduit attached to the fence post.

The procedure is to attach a short length of ¾-inch EMT conduit to the metal post with a U-bolt. It serves as a sleeve through which a ½-inch EMT conduit mounting pole can be raised and lowered. The sleeve needs to be only 10 or 12 inches long, with a bolt hole drilled near the bottom. When a bolt is inserted in the hole, the ½-inch conduit pole rests on the bolt, raising the nestbox well above the metal post.

Heavy nestboxes may require larger conduit. Just make the sleeve one size larger than the pole. The 1⅜-inch top rail used for chain link fences makes an excellent sleeve for 1-inch conduit.

Wood fence posts are especially easy for predators to climb, and it is very hard to successfully install predator guards on a post that is part of a fence. However, a telescoping conduit pole can be attached to a wood post with a sleeve much the same way it is attached to a metal fence post — except the conduit sleeve can be screwed to the wood post.

Wood posts or landscape timbers, such as railroad ties, that are not part of a fence can be fitted with some guards. Flashing metal wrapped tightly

around an entire post, for instance, makes it harder for snakes and raccoons to climb the post.

One other problem with using posts, whether wooden or metal, that are part of a fence: the fence often encloses livestock. Horses and cows are a real threat to nestboxes mounted within their reach. They can destroy nestboxes by chewing them, rubbing against the mounting poles, or just trampling them for no apparent reason.

If horses are present, nestboxes must be mounted more than 8 feet high on heavy poles. Cattle guards made of barbed wire (see picture, p. 112, left) will keep livestock from rubbing against a mounting pole. Beware of applying grease to a mounting pole that cattle can reach; they will lick it up and may topple the pole in the process.

There are some circumstances in which **fence lines of barbed wire** can make a good bluebird

A nestbox is raised above a fence post with conduit that slides into a metal sleeve attached to the post. By cutting the ends of the sleeve at a 45-degree angle, two surfaces are exposed that can easily be drilled for screw holes.

Susan Lousberg of Texas rides horseback to monitor a heavily guarded nestbox mounted in a pasture with livestock. Susan's box is protected by a barbed wire cattle guard and a stovepipe baffle. The box is mounted on a heavy mounting pole, out of reach of livestock.

box mount if livestock is not present. One of my personal favorite mounting locations is between the top two strands of a barbed wire fence, midway between two fence posts.

My most dreaded predator is the fire ant, and while fire ants will climb a post, they do not then crawl 10 or 15 feet horizontally out on barbed wire in search of a meal. This nonpoisonous, passive, ant-resistant mounting method works well for me. Raccoons, opossums, and snakes will rarely venture out along barbed wire either.

Cats are predators that are not be deterred by barbed wire fencing. Nestboxes mounted on this kind of fencing will be low enough to be within their leap. Fortunately, feral cats are seldom a problem in my area.

A barbed wire fence that is electrified and remains so all summer can be an ideal place to mount nestboxes — on the posts, not the wire. Any snake or raccoon that tries to climb to the box will get any thoughts of dinner knocked clean from its mind when it touches the hot wire. Insects will still be a problem, however. They have no need to touch the hot wire when they climb the post.

Just perching on the hot wire will not be a problem for a bluebird, as the electric current has to run to a ground contact to be dangerous. If a bluebird happens to alight on the hot wire right next to a post and then touches the post, it can complete a

ground circuit and be electrocuted. This area of the post can be wrapped with electrical tape to prevent any mishap to the birds. And be careful yourself working with nestboxes on electrified fences, or at least have a friend come along to capture the excitement on videotape.

Because they require no investment and are common in rural and remote areas, **utility poles** have long been a favorite place for trail operators to hang their nestboxes. In many areas of the country, utility companies have cooperated with trail monitors in allowing their poles to be used for the benefit of bluebirds. Main utility lines have poles spaced 300 feet apart or more, so boxes can be mounted on every pole and not be too close to one another.

One significant advantage of utility poles is that they are wide enough to provide excellent shade during hot afternoons if the box is located on the east side of the pole. Whether you are in the northern or southern states will determine if you need to shift the box a little north or south of due east for optimum protection.

Trees and brush are usually kept clear of utility lines, even when they run through heavily wooded areas. Bluebirds can hunt in these open spaces, and the lines overhead provide excellent hunting perches. In some areas, however, weeds and brush are now controlled with herbicides instead of mowing.

The downside of using utility poles as box mounts is that permission must be obtained from several utility companies (poles are often shared by power, phone, and cable companies), and there is no predator control that is safe to use because linemen must have unimpaired access to the poles. All climbing predators and insects can and will climb utility poles. Pests such as mice can take over boxes. Trail operators using utility pole mounts for their nestboxes often find that predation rises each year as predators learn and remember box locations.

A lightweight PVC nestbox mounts easily on two strands of a barbed wire fence. It is hard to find fence wire stretched tight enough to support the weight of a wooden nestbox.

Since repairmen must climb utility poles, the utility companies may ask you to attach boxes so that they can easily and quickly be removed without tools. A good way of doing this is to drill a ³⁄₁₆-inch hole on a 45-degree angle down through the box back and into the pole. An 8-penny (8d) or 16d nail can then be slipped through the box (or through the hanger strap if you are using that coupling method) and into the pole so that the box hangs on the nail. Being able to remove the box quickly makes it safe for linemen to climb the pole, but it also makes it easy for people and predators to make off with the box.

The trunks of living trees should be avoided as mounts for nestboxes in most parts of the country. Predators and insects climb trees easily, and it is difficult to provide any sort of protection against them. Living trees should not be wrapped with metal for predator protection, as this stunts their growth. Squirrels and porcupines are more likely to chew on boxes mounted on tree trunks than those mounted on other poles, even wooden ones; snakes are more likely to climb trees in search of food.

In parts of the West and Southwest, tree trunks are used as mounting poles with fair success. These are areas where large predators keep the population of feral cats, raccoons, and opossums in check. Most of the trees used are less than 12 inches in diameter, are located in open areas, and have no low limbs near the box. In some ways, they resemble a utility pole more than the trees seen in the East.

On living trees, a nestbox can be attached with wire protected by a piece of rubber hose to prevent the tree from growing around the wire. The wire should be loosened each year. Attaching a box to a living tree with a nail requires regular maintenance, or the nail will disappear into the tree, and the nestbox will end up on the ground.

If you are nailing a hanger strap to a tree, use an 8d duplex head (double-headed) nail. The inner nail head will hold the mount to the tree, and the outer head will make it easy for you to pull the nail out a little each year so that the strap and nail don't become embedded.

Nestboxes can also be attached directly to a tree with 16d (3¼-inch-long) casing or finish nails driven through the back of the box. If the nails are driven flush with the back of the box, the tree will likely draw the nails through the wooden back as it grows. But if the nails are left sticking out an inch or so inside the box, the tree can grow for several years before the box will need to be reattached.

Historically, nestboxes were not mounted on poles, posts, or tree trunks; they were **hung from tree limbs.** And they weren't nestboxes exactly; they were hollow gourds.

Compared to pole-mounted boxes, hanging boxes are much more difficult to monitor and cannot be

A cat calculates how to reach the nestlings inside a nestbox mounted on a utility pole. A disadvantage of mounting nestboxes on utility poles is that they can't be placed out of the reach of cats and other climbing predators.

protected from predators. That's enough to discourage most bluebird monitors from using them, but Dick Purvis (see sidebar, p. 68) in southern California has hung nestboxes in trees very successfully and has inspired many others to do the same.

Purvis's predator problem is minimized because his boxes are placed in public areas such as city parks and golf courses, which have high human traffic, crowding out most predators. The boxes are also placed far out on limbs so that climbers are less likely to reach them.

In heavily developed areas, vandals are a bigger problem than predators, and that's where boxes hanging high out of human reach become especially useful. They permit bluebirds to remain in (or return to) areas overwhelmed by urban sprawl. Boxes hung in trees are also well shaded, which is an important consideration in hot climates.

Heavy-gauge wire, steel rods, or steel straps can be bent into hooks and used to hang a nestbox. If wire is used, it should be at least 9-gauge (almost ³⁄₁₆-inch-diameter) high-carbon wire, which resists bending. When the wire is hooked over a tree limb, it must be strong enough so that the weight of the nestbox won't slowly straighten out the hook. Zinc-coated or galvanized steel wire will resist rusting as well. Connect the wire to the center of the nestbox roof.

The same flat steel strap used to make a hanger strap for pole- and post-mounted boxes (p. 110)

Nails and screws present a safety hazard and costly expense to sawmills when a tree is harvested for lumber. I saw $8,000 damage done to a sawmill because someone had laid a wrench in the crotch of a tree 80 years earlier and the tree had swallowed it up. Nails can be just as devastating.

can be used for hanging boxes. On one end of a strap about 14 inches long, bend a short tab at a right angle and fasten it to the center of the nest-box roof with a single bolt. Bend the other end into a deep hook large enough to fit the limbs you expect to encounter.

A dab of good caulking compound placed around the bolt and under the strap just before tightening the nut will make the roof waterproof. Using a fender washer (they are larger than normal flat washers) on the inside of the box between the nut and the roof will help preserve the box.

In order to get the boxes high in a tree (up to 16 feet or more), Purvis uses **a telescoping extension lifter pole.** The pole itself is a fiberglass pole that painters use when painting high ceilings and walls. Swimming pool poles are another good choice (see picture, p. 67).

Most lifters have a catch basket rigged to one end of the pole — a bucket or rim that is able to pivot easily so that the box will remain upright on its trip to the ground. Purvis screwed a yoke made from PVC pipe to the end of his pole and uses a lightweight 1½-gallon plastic bucket that pivots freely in the yoke to catch his boxes and cradle them to the ground. Barry Whitney of South Carolina built a frame (or rim) that catches under the roof of his nestboxes.

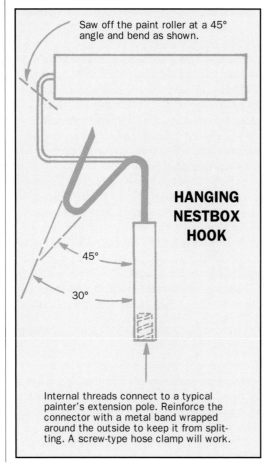

Saw off the paint roller at a 45° angle and bend as shown.

HANGING NESTBOX HOOK

45°

30°

Internal threads connect to a typical painter's extension pole. Reinforce the connector with a metal band wrapped around the outside to keep it from splitting. A screw-type hose clamp will work.

John Skatch designed a lifter (see illustration, below) that catches the hook of the hanging box rather than the box itself. Made from a common wire paint roller, Skatch's lifter is the lightest of the box lifters.

Using a lifter pole requires care. A mistake can ruin the day for you and your birds. Do not hang nestboxes anywhere near power lines! The farther away from the trunk of the tree, the less likely a nestbox is to be found by a predator, but the limb it is hung on must be substantial and not likely to break. You may need to install a hole guard (p. 117) on hanging boxes to prevent squirrels from chewing on the entrance hole and enlarging it.

**Pole-Mounted Baffles —
Keeping Climbers Away from the Box**

Some baffles will reliably defeat snakes, raccoons, and other climbing predators; others are **bad ideas we don't recommend** — for example, wrapping a pole in barbed wire. Carpet tack strips, razor blades, sharpened spikes, and fishhooks are other dangerous baffles that have been suggested or tried in the past. They are cruel to animals and a threat to humans — especially kids.

Some other designs aren't dangerous or cruel, but they aren't very effective either. One idea that gets published from time to time is to sandwich two sheets of thin metal around a mounting pole. Typically, the sheets are bolted together at the top and bottom of each side with short, smooth-headed bolts and a small nut. Supposedly, a raccoon can't get a foothold to get over the slick baffle, which is usually suggested to be 18 inches wide and 30 inches tall. But raccoons soon learn how to climb the edge of the baffle. And most snakes can get past it without a problem.

Bluebird monitors using T-posts or galvanized water pipe as mounts frequently try covering them with a small tube of PVC pipe for protection against raccoons. With its slick surface, PVC pipe would seem to foil most climbers, and it works at first. But over the first year or two, the surface of the pipe oxidizes and gets scratched. When the surface is no longer slick, raccoons can climb it.

Greasing the PVC guard may help but won't necessarily stop a raccoon. To some degree, it is a matter of how determined a raccoon is. A PVC pipe that stops a raccoon on a particular night may not defeat it on another night when the 'coon happens to be hungrier, more determined, and a little wiser.

PVC pipe is a smooth path to a nestbox for a snake. Jack Finch (p. 56) found that a black rat snake could grip smooth new PVC pipe and climb 6 feet or more. Even greasing the pipe won't stop a snake with a bluebird dinner on its mind.

One baffle that does perform well and that I can recommend is **the stovepipe baffle** developed by

Ron Kingston displays the stovepipe baffle he developed. Ron is the longtime chairman of the speakers bureau for the North American Bluebird Society.

Ron Kingston of Charlottesville, Virginia. Kingston's baffle is simple, lightweight, and low cost. It can be used on all types of small-diameter poles, including ones that telescope.

Metal air-conditioning duct can be substituted for the stovepipe. It comes in flat pieces, 60 inches long. The long edges are grooved to snap together and lock tight. If you fudge the numbers a little, you can cut three baffles, each 20 inches long, from one piece.

Tin snips (offset snips work best) are needed to construct and mount the baffles. Be careful to fold over any sharp corners that might be dangerous. The baffle isn't fastened to the mounting pole; it simply rests on a metal strap that Ron attaches to the mounting pole.

One reason this baffle is so effective against raccoons is because it is not bolted tightly to the mounting pole — it wobbles. The motion makes it impossible for a raccoon to hold a grip on the pipe.

The hardware-cloth plug used in Kingston's baffle is more effective against snakes than a solid top. The snake can see the nestbox and smell the scent of the birds from inside the baffle, but the hardware cloth stops it. It is likely to remain in

the baffle, the victim of its own limited reasoning power, rather than climb around the baffle on the outside — which a large snake can do. For added safety, a Krueger snake trap (p. 117) can be added above the stovepipe baffle to capture any snake that makes it that far.

Be careful to place the baffle high enough that cats can't leap to the top and use it as a platform for raiding the nestbox. Consider using a telescoping pole to raise the baffle and the nestbox out of a cat's leaping range.

A coat of paint will make the baffle a little more presentable for use with a backyard nestbox. And the paint won't lessen the baffle's effectiveness.

A telescoping pole baffled with a stovepipe should deter any four-legged predator other than a bear. If you apply a thin ring of fresh grease on the mounting pipe under the baffle, climbing insects will be excluded as well. The grease will also reveal if snakes are trying to reach the box. When they slither over the grease, they'll smear it around.

A commercial snake guard similar to Kingston's is available but is only about 8 inches tall. This is not high enough to deter snakes, which can easily get over it.

Large versions of Ron Kingston's baffle can be made to fit over large-diameter poles, wooden posts, and even utility poles. Just snap together two or three sections of metal duct pipe. If the baffle can't be lifted over the top of the mounting pole, it can be built on the pole. Baffles 12 inches in diameter or more don't need to wobble; they can be attached rigidly. Raccoons can't hug a cylinder that large.

A wobbly section of large-diameter PVC pipe baffles raccoons as well as stovepipe does. Many nestbox monitors are now experimenting with

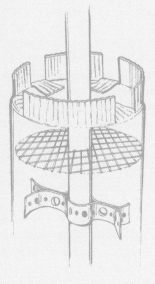

STOVEPIPE BAFFLE

Make the baffle by cutting ½-inch hardware cloth into a 9-inch circle. Make a small hole in the center so that the circle will slip over the mounting pole. Bend the edges of the circle down so that the hardware cloth fits snugly into a 24-inch-long section of 8-inch diameter stovepipe. Cut four tabs on the top end of the stovepipe and bend them over the hardware cloth.

To hang the baffle, bolt metal straps (plumber's tape) around the mounting pole for support. (Several wraps of duct tape around the pole below the metal straps will help keep them in place.) Slide the baffle down over the top of the mounting pole until it rests on the metal straps.

PVC-pipe baffles, often gluing a solid PVC cap to the top end. A hole drilled in the center of the cap fits over the mounting pole, and the baffle rests on any sort of clamp placed around the pole — the stainless steel screw clamps used on car radiator hoses work well.

PVC pipe is more expensive than stovepipe or metal air-conditioning duct, but it comes in a variety of colors besides the white most commonly seen. The colored PVC pipe might be the most attractive choice for a backyard.

Small-diameter PVC pipe is much less expensive than the larger sizes and is often used for this reason. But PVC baffles 4 inches or less in diameter will probably not stop as many predators as 8-inch-diameter baffles. Raccoons have mastered climbing solidly mounted poles of 4-inch PVC pipe in many areas.

Before Kingston designed the stovepipe baffle, **conical sheet metal baffles** were the only reliable raccoon guards. They are harder to make and more expensive than stovepipe baffles. To be effective against raccoons, they need to be 3 feet or more in diameter. Their sharp edge could be dangerous to kids and makes weekly monitoring a little more difficult.

Conical baffles do not stop large snakes. Jack Finch (p. 56) discovered that a snake will first wrap itself tightly under the solid metal sheet. Then it uncoils the front of its body and extends its head out and over the edge of the cone. It continues to uncoil slowly as it climbs the top of the cone to the

An eastern kingsnake coils up inside a bluebird box. The expanded spaces between the scales are evidence of the bluebird nestlings that it consumed.

pole. Upon reaching the pole above the cone, the snake wraps around it and then releases its coils below. The whole process takes less than a minute!

Testing revealed that a snake can cross a conical baffle if it is 24 inches longer than the diameter of the baffle. Any snake longer than 5 feet can make it around a 3-foot-diameter sheet metal baffle. Anyone using a paint-bucket lid, a metal pie plate, or a worn-out plow disk as a baffle can do the math and determine what size a snake has to be to make it to the nestbox.

A flat square of hardware cloth makes a good baffle if it is 4 feet or larger on each side and is mounted horizontally directly under the nestbox. It confuses snakes, which can see the box but can't reach it. Raccoons have difficulty climbing upside down on the hardware cloth. As with conical sheet metal baffles, drawbacks include cost, sharp edges, and the inconvenience of reaching over the guard to monitor the box.

The Krueger snake trap is not a baffle; it is a trap. It acts like a gill net, entangling the scales of any snake that tries to cross it. The snake seldom if ever escapes.

Any snake left in a trap and exposed to the sun will die in a few hours. Although the snake is then no longer a danger to the eggs or nestlings it was hunting, bluebirds often abandon a nestful of eggs at the sight of a dead snake just below the nestbox. If the nest contains young more than a few days

---

Snakes Along a Bluebird Trail

In May of 1989, a reporter from the Dallas Morning News *accompanied me one evening as I monitored one of my roadside trails. I had gotten up early before work and checked the trail to make sure there wouldn't be any unpleasant surprises hanging in a snake trap — I wanted this interview to be about bluebirds, not snakes. I found one snake dead in a trap near the end of the trail and decided to leave it to show how well the trap worked.*

Well, that evening the reporter and I encounter a very angry snake trapped under one of the first nestboxes on my trail. I quickly find out that the reporter is deathly afraid of snakes. Two miles farther down the trail — another snake. The interview starts to change. Four more miles, and the reporter sees the next snake first! Now he wants to know if I have talked to anyone at the News. *I can tell he's thinking that his co-workers might have cooked this up with me. As we near the dead snake that I know is caught in a trap, I try to distract the reporter by pointing out an interesting view on the other side of the road. "I already saw the snake!" he says. So we stop.*

Not only is the dead snake there, but another one is in the trap trying to mate with the dead one! And then I see a big snake lying in the grass by the pole just inches from my foot. Instinctively, I catch it on the toe of my shoe and pitch it about 20 feet — nearly the same distance the reporter jumps when he sees the snake go flying. By the time the snake hits the ground, the reporter is sliding across the hood of the car, 50 feet away. That was the end of the interview. It was a very quiet drive back into town.

old, however, the bluebird parents may continue feeding them in spite of the dead snake. In my experience, about half the parents will keep up their feeding routine, sometimes even when the snake in the trap is still alive.

When the Krueger snake trap is used in a backyard, it can be monitored frequently, and a snake can be removed before bluebirds abandon their nest. By their frantic behavior, bluebirds will let you know immediately if they spot a snake near their nestbox.

On a trail, snakes will often be dead when they are found in a trap, and the eggs or nestlings the snake was after may also be dead or abandoned. This is not a happy result, although without the trap, the eggs or nestlings would also be destroyed — and perhaps the incubating female as well.

To reduce the chance that bluebirds will abandon their nests because of a dead snake, the Krueger snake trap should always be placed above a baffle, as a last line of defense. A stovepipe or PVC-pipe baffle will deter many snakes before they reach the lethal mesh of the Krueger snake trap.

You can easily remove a nonpoisonous snake caught in a trap by using scissors to cut the strands of mesh that hold it. But you will need heavy leather welding gloves and a long-sleeved heavy jacket to ensure that the now angry snake doesn't take a bite out of you! Grasp the snake firmly behind the head with one hand and cut the strands of the mesh that entrap it with the other.

A captured snake can be placed in a 5-gallon bucket and transported away from the nestbox to be released if local laws permit. If an old towel or piece of clothing is placed in the bottom of the bucket, the snake will try to hide under it rather than climb the sides of the bucket. Make sure the lid fits tight, and if you are transporting the snake in a car, make sure the bucket is placed where it won't fall over or roll around. The only thing worse than finding that a snake has escaped into your car when you go to release it is having it find you while you are driving!

After you trap a snake, monitor the nestbox closely for several days. Male snakes will follow scent trails left by the females of their species, and often you will catch two or three more snakes at the same nestbox if the first one caught was a female.

I have caught snakes over 84 inches long and as short as 24 inches. Shorter snakes can be thin enough to work their way through the ¾-inch netting. I have also found the skins of small snakes — shed and abandoned — in the mesh netting.

Entrance Hole Devices —
Protectors, Restrictors, and Guards

Squirrels and woodpeckers can enlarge a nestbox entrance hole until it is large enough for a starling

A Krueger snake trap protects the nestbox above it from snakes. Halfway between the upper edge of the netting and the wire loop at the bottom, the material is gathered and clamped to the mounting pole with a wire. The netting above the clamp hangs down loosely over the netting below the clamp.

to enter and take over the box. **A hole protector** prevents this or overcomes the damage without your having to replace the front panel of the box.

Dusty Bleher of San Jose, California, uses Lexan hole protectors on his nestboxes when woodpeckers or squirrels become a problem. Lexan is a brand name for polycarbonate, the same squirrel-resistant plastic used in high-quality birdfeeders. The cheaper and softer acrylic, or Plexiglas, is lunch for squirrels.

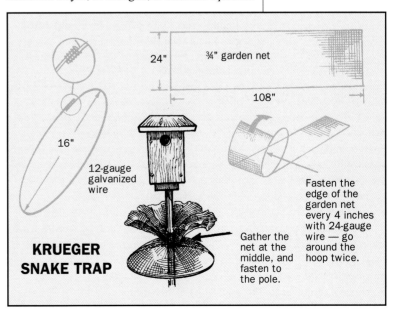

24" ¾" garden net 108"
16" 12-gauge galvanized wire
Fasten the edge of the garden net every 4 inches with 24-gauge wire — go around the hoop twice.
Gather the net at the middle, and fasten to the pole.
KRUEGER SNAKE TRAP

Lexan is sold in large sheets, but scraps can be found at many commercial glass shops. It is ¼ inch thick and can be cut into pieces 3 inches square with a fine-toothed carbide blade in a table saw. The entrance hole can be drilled with either a Forstner-style drill bit or a hole saw bit; the Lexan must be securely clamped before it is drilled.

Lexan will have dangerously sharp edges where it is cut or drilled, and these need to be dulled. A router fitted with a ⅛-inch quarter-round carbide bit can be set to relieve this sharp corner, or a half-round steel bastard file could be used. Machinists have a handheld de-burring tool that works well on Lexan.

To install the hole protector, drill screw holes in the corners, fit it over the damaged hole, and watch the woodpeckers get a headache hammering it.

Sheet metal can be used in place of Lexan (p. 99), but it is too dangerous to drill, and few people have access to a 1⅝-inch metal hole press. Trail operators might find it worth their while to locate a supplier if they have a serious problem with entrance holes being enlarged on their trails.

If you do use sheet metal hole protectors, note that a 1⅝-inch hole in the metal was specified, just a little larger than the standard 1⁹⁄₁₆-inch nestbox entrance hole. The sheet metal is sharp and could cut a bird or damage the feathers if it were flush with the nestbox hole. Center the protector around the entrance hole carefully.

The most practical protector for most backyard bluebird monitors is a wooden one — a thick wooden one that discourages gnawing rodents and hammering birds. A 1½-inch-thick block — the actual thickness of a so-called 2-by-4 — is perfect. Bluebirds don't mind the added depth of the entrance hole, although they will hesitate to accept a deeper one. And scrap 2-by-4 is usually easy to come by.

Cut the 2-by-4 into 5-inch lengths and drill the entrance hole about ¾ inch from one end. The other end will serve as a tail brace for the birds when they land at the hole.

A PVC-pipe entrance hole guard protects the bluebird eggs inside this box from the long, prying arms of raccoons and cats.

Trail operators often carry wood block hole protectors with them on their rounds so they can repair boxes without removing them from the trail. Some blocks are drilled with the standard 1⁹⁄₁₆-inch entrance hole; others are often made with 1⅛-inch holes. The smaller ones are **hole restrictors** and are used when chickadees are found nesting in a box. The restrictor is big enough for the 'dees and helps protects them from house sparrows and bluebirds. Yes, bluebirds! Like house sparrows, bluebirds will remove chickadee eggs or young to take over a nestbox.

In years past, wood block hole protectors were often added to a box as a **hole guard against predators.** The 1½-inch depth was thought to deter raccoons and cats from reaching into the nest and snaring eggs or birds. In reality, it takes a far deeper entrance hole to stop a four-legged predator, and bluebirds don't like going through long, narrow tunnels.

The nestbox entrance hole is the final obstacle that a predator must overcome before it claims its meal. If a snake has gotten that far, the battle is lost. Four-legged predators can be stopped at the hole by some guards but can often claw or rip a box apart. Even if the box is sturdy, imagine the stress to a female bluebird sitting on eggs and having a raccoon or cat trying to break into her house every night!

You should try to stop predators before they reach the nestbox, but sometimes you can't — for example, when boxes are hung on utility poles. In that case, a well-designed hole guard can help.

How Deep Can a Raccoon Reach?

To test the reach of my local raccoons, I filled five nestboxes of different styles with dry dog food. The raccoons quickly learned to strip all of the food from the shallow nestboxes. They seemed to find shallow slot boxes and oval-holed nestboxes the easiest to raid, as these were emptied first. The 8-inch-deep box (from the floor to the bottom of the round entrance hole) usually had several inches of food left in it. But if I did not replenish the food, the hungry raccoons would keep working until nothing but a few crumbles of dog food were left in the deep box.

I learned what I wanted to know from my tests — that raccoons could scrape the bottom of nestboxes that are 8 inches deep. I also learned that I shouldn't have used nestboxes to make the tests. The raccoons, trained overwinter to feed from nestboxes, raided my trail the next spring for a distance of 6 miles. I'd never had a severe raccoon problem until I trained them!

Many types of entrance hole guards have been used over the years. Some, made of plastic or wire, resemble the cardboard tube inside a roll of toilet paper. They do limit the reach of predators but are not popular with the birds. The tubes make it very difficult for nesting birds to make the hundreds of trips in and out of the box that are necessary every day.

Hole guards that use barbed wire, carpet tack strips, and parapet walls of sharpened nails, are downright dangerous to the birds and trail monitors, as well as to predators. One concept that does work is a deep, large-diameter entrance hole guard. Many variations are possible; I'll describe two. Both should be installed before birds begin nesting. Adding one after nesting begins may cause the nest to be abandoned. If a guard must be added while the birds are nesting, check to see that it is accepted.

Don Hutchings of Winfield, Texas, designed my favorite, a **PVC hole guard and restrictor combination.** The device is made with a flat-topped 4-inch PVC sewer and drainpipe cap and a 6-inch length of 4-inch-diameter PVC pipe. The cap is drilled with two holes, one for bluebirds and one for chickadees. Either hole can be placed over the nestbox entrance hole and the cap screwed to the front of the nestbox.

The 6-inch length of pipe fits into the cap and is held by three short screws that fit through holes drilled into the collar of the cap. The cap and pipe could be glued together, but a screwdriver with an extension would then be needed to attach the device to the nestbox.

Bluebirds in most areas readily accept this guard. In fact, bluebirds sometimes nest in the 4-inch PVC pipes that are attached beside rural mailboxes for local newspaper deliveries.

Don has experimented with different pipe diameters and lengths and found that his birds preferred the 4-inch pipe and that 6-inch lengths of pipe deterred cats and most raccoons. In areas with a severe raccoon problem, 9-inch-long pieces should prove 100 percent effective. With lengths of 12 inches or more, some bluebirds will build their nest at the back of the guard and against the front of the box, preferring this to actually entering the box!

A hardware-cloth guard developed by Jim Noel of Ashland, Illinois, is similar in concept to the PVC guard. The walls are ½-inch-mesh hardware cloth instead of PVC, and Jim makes them rectangular rather than round. Designed to fit the Peterson nestbox, the guard is 3½ inches wide, 5½ inches tall, and 5 inches deep. The vertical sides extend a half-inch deeper and are stapled to the edges of the front panel. Tin snips can be used to cut the hardware cloth.

An adaptation of Jim's hole guard (see picture, p. 102) can be made to work with most wood nestboxes. Start with a 3½-by-5½-inch block of ¾-inch-thick wood. Drill an entrance hole in the block to match the nestbox entrance hole and drill screw holes in each corner of the block for the mounting screws. You can drill two different size entrance holes in the block, as Don Hutchings does in his PVC entrance hole guard. Then if chickadees choose to nest, the guard can be remounted so that the hole restrictor sits over the nestbox entrance.

Staple the hardware cloth around the edges of the wood block. Some people make the guard deeper than Jim's recommended 5 inches to provide added protection from determined long-armed raccoons.

Hole guards for avian predators are needed on some nestbox trails. Starlings, magpies, jays, crows, hawks, and owls are becoming increasingly common predators all across the continent. While these birds are too large to enter a 1%16-inch hole,

A hungry raccoon sticks its paw through a nestbox entrance hole to reach the meal inside. Note that the wood-block hole protector doesn't deter this raccoon!

some can stick their heads into the box for a meal of bluebird eggs or young.

The 1½-inch-thick wood blocks used as hole protectors (p. 117) limit the distance that avian predators can reach into a nestbox, but they may not limit it enough.

A few magpies learned to feed from the nestboxes of Myrna Pearman and other trail operators in Alberta, Canada, one year. By the following year, magpie predation had become epidemic, and a quick, cheap fix had to be developed in a very short time. There were hundreds of nestboxes with young birds at risk.

The magpies would land on the roof of a box and look down over the front edge toward the entrance hole. When the bluebird nestlings raised their heads up to be fed by what they thought were their parents, the magpies would simply pull the young birds through the hole.

Several guards were devised and tried but either failed or were too difficult to implement. The solution proved to be a guard made of 30-gauge sheet metal, commonly called galvanized flashing metal.

The flashing metal was cut the width of the roof and attached so that 5 to 7 inches of it extended over the front edge of the nestbox. When a magpie walked to the edge of the flashing to reach the entrance hole, the metal would collapse and dump the bird off the roof! The flashing would momentarily cover the entrance hole until it sprang back up in the flat position. Magpies have never again been a problem on Myrna's trail.

If you try it, be sure to use steel flashing, not aluminum. Steel retains a "memory" of its flat form and will spring back up after bending. Aluminum flashing will not.

In-Box Traps — Aggressive House Sparrow Control

Each person who provides a nestbox for bluebirds must decide what control methods to use if or when a house sparrow lays claim to the box. There is no way to prevent a house sparrow from entering a bluebird box, but there are passive methods of house sparrow control (p. 78).

Here, I'll describe in-box traps for capturing house sparrows. All the traps use a similar concept: upon entering the nestbox, the house sparrow dislodges a trip wire of some sort, which results in the entrance — or in this case, exit — hole being blocked and the house sparrow trapped inside.

A makeshift trap can be made with nothing more than a scrap of cardboard, a piece of tape, and a blade of grass. Cut the cardboard so that it will cover the hole, and hinge it with a piece of tape to the inside of the box, just above the hole. Prop the trap door open with a stem of dry grass braced against the bottom of the entrance hole. When a bird enters, it will dislodge the grass, and the cardboard will fall, blocking the entrance. It may not take long for a house sparrow to figure out how to lift the cardboard and escape, so a makeshift trap like this must be observed continuously.

All the traps that follow are metal and durable enough to last for many years. They are easy to set and operate, but because they trap any bird that enters the nestbox — bluebirds and chickadees as well as house sparrows — they must never be left unattended for more than a very short time.

The Huber sparrow trap, designed by Joe Huber of Heath, Ohio, is easy to build and works reliably on wooden boxes with vertical fronts and round or oval entrance holes. It is too wide for the Peterson box, and it doesn't work on slot or PVC-pipe boxes.

Instead of using a piece of cardboard to block the entrance, Huber uses a flat plate of steel. A flat strip of aluminum or a piece cut from Plexiglas can be substituted. If you paint the plate a light color, it will contrast with the dark hole, and you will be able to see at a distance whether or not the trap has been tripped.

The plate pivots on a screw attached to the wood panel through a hole in one end. A trip rod fashioned from a brass welding rod holds the other end of the plate in place above the entrance hole. The steel wire used in coat hangers is the same diameter and can be used in place of the brass rod. The rod (or wire) is attached to the box with insulated staples and bent in a Z-like shape so that a bird will trip it when dropping into the box.

When the rod (or wire) is tripped, one end of the steel plate will fall, rotating on its pivot screw until it hits a stop screw. At rest on the stop screw, the plate will cover the bottom two-thirds of the entrance hole, trapping the occupant inside.

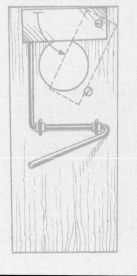

HUBER SPARROW TRAP

Materials
Flat steel plate: 1" x 3" x ⅛"
Brass welding rod: 3/32" dia.
Plywood: 4" x depth of nestbox
Two ½" wood screws
Two insulated electrical staples

Method
1. Attach the metal plate to the plywood with a wood screw as the pivot.
2. Position the second wood screw as a stop for the metal plate.
3. Hinge the welding rod 1½ inches below the entrance hole with insulated staples. The rod must be bent approximately as shown before it is attached. The bottom leg should be bent into the box about 40 degrees from vertical.

The Huber trap is usually constructed on a separate panel rather than permanently affixed to a box. The trap panel is installed behind the entrance panel of whatever nestbox is experiencing a hostile sparrow takeover. You can attach the trap with screws or even Velcro strips.

If your boxes are mounted on lightweight poles that sway in the wind, the motion may repeatedly set off the trap even though no bird has entered the box. In this case, you can substitute a lightweight aluminum welding rod or a wire with a smaller diameter for the brass rod. Motion will have less effect on the lighter trip rod or wire.

Several variations of the Huber trap are available commercially. Some traps designed for use in purple martin houses can also be adapted to bluebird nestboxes.

The Bolt sparrow trap (see picture, right) is similar to Joe Huber's but has a nice added feature. Mel Bolt had trouble removing house sparrows from nestboxes after he had trapped them. He cracked the door open enough to reach into the box and remove the sparrow, only to have it escape around his searching hand.

After visiting Joe Huber and consulting with him, Bolt designed a cage made from ½-inch hardware cloth. A bird entering the trap finds itself in a the cage. The nestbox door can be thrown wide open and the sparrow can't escape. The sparrow is removed through a small door built into the hardware cloth.

After years of manufacturing this fine trap himself, Bolt licensed another bluebirder, David Magness of Jenna Bird (see Resources, p. 124), to continue making and distributing the Bolt sparrow trap.

The Peterson sparrow trap is another modification of the Huber trap. Dick Peterson wanted to create a trap that would fit in his narrow (3½-inch-wide) Peterson box. He also needed to make a plate that would block the box's taller oval entrance hole.

Peterson fitted his trap on a separate panel. It is one of the items that are part of the Peterson "system." Changing door panels to adapt to the situation at hand is quick and easy.

None of the variations of the Huber sparrow trap will work inside the popular PVC-pipe nestboxes made by Steve Gilbertson — so he designed one that would. His **Universal sparrow trap** (see Resources, p. 124) employs the spring steel used in tape measures to block the entrance hole. The 1-inch-wide band is bent away from the hole and restrained by a trip wire. When a house sparrow enters the box and trips the wire, the steel band snaps over the hole.

Because it has a positive action and doesn't depend upon gravity, the universal sparrow trap works on the sloping front of a Peterson box. In fact, it works on all box styles except slot boxes and the Gilwood box.

A **Bolt sparrow trap** is attached inside the door of a wooden nestbox manufactured by David Magness of JennaBird.

The Van Ert sparrow traps utilize a steel door and a small coil spring to block a nestbox entrance hole. Floyd Van Ert produces and sells two models that, between them, will work on any nestbox.

One of the Van Ert sparrow traps is designed for use on nestboxes that have a flat door panel. It is only 3 inches wide, so it will fit on narrow boxes such as the Peterson box.

This Van Ert model also works on the Gilwood box. Other sparrow traps must be mounted above the entrance hole, and that isn't possible on the Gilwood box, which has its entrance right at the roof. The Van Ert trap fits below the entrance hole, and the plate flips up to block the hole.

The same model even works on horizontal slot boxes if the slots aren't much longer than 3 inches, because the plate extends the full 3-inch width of the trap.

The second Van Ert sparrow trap, designed for use on PVC-pipe boxes, attaches with a clip through the entrance hole, so it can be installed in seconds. You can also screw this trap onto wooden boxes with round or oval entrance holes.

Van Ert sticks a bright orange dot — like the kind used for price stickers — on the plate of each of his sparrow traps. Many other sparrow trap builders also incorporate a brightly colored plate or spot that contrasts in color with the box front. It is easy to see the dot at a distance when the trap has been sprung — saving you a lot of fruitless trips back and forth to check the box.

Erv Davis, a nestbox monitor and bird bander in Montana (p. 52), designed and uses **a radio-remote-controlled trap.** It has no trip wire. Davis makes the decision when to flip the switch on the remote control unit that closes the trap.

Because he is in control of the switch, Davis can trap the individual bird he wants. Others he lets come and go as they wish. And that's the advantage of a remote-controlled trap — you don't end up trapping every bird that enters a box. You get the one you want.

Davis mounts his trap mechanism on a panel that fits over the front (door) panel of his nestboxes. It is held in place with bungee cords wrapped around the nestbox. When the trap is activated, the entrance hole is fully blocked by a disk of light plastic at the end of a rotating arm. When the trap is switched off, the arm rotates to uncover the hole. Two screws in the panel serve as stops, limiting the motion of the arm.

A remote-controlled trap is much more expensive to build than any of the other in-box traps, and you must stay and observe any nestbox on which it is used. But it does let you control the action, rather than the bird.

Bait Traps —
Industrial-Strength Sparrow Control

The simplest of the three types of house sparrow bait traps is **the funnel bait trap.** Tomahawk Live Trap Company (see Resources, p. 124) is one of the manufacturers of funnel traps. House sparrows are enticed to the bait through long passages that funnel into the cage. The initial opening is wide, but the passages gradually taper to a small entrance hole that is just big enough for the birds to squeeze

through. Once inside, most sparrows can't distinguish the hole from the surrounding wire mesh.

It takes a smart sparrow to find its way back out of a funnel trap, but some do. It's a good idea to remove captured sparrows daily from a funnel trap.

The Purple Martin Conservation Association (see Resources, p. 124) markets the model ST-1 — a spring-door trap made of wire that is often referred to as **the trio bait trap** because of its three compartments. The center compartment is the holding cell; the two side compartments are traps.

Each trap compartment has a spring-loaded door at the top. When the door is open, sparrows can enter, but when they alight on the perch provided for them to feed from, their weight causes the door to spring shut. Trapped, they look for a way out, but all they can find is a one-way door into the holding cell. House sparrows do not escape from the trio bait trap.

I find that the trio trap works better if a flat piece of lightweight material (a 4-by-4-inch square of thin aluminum, plastic, or even cardboard) is placed on top of the trip levers and the tiny seed cup that are supplied with the trap. Seeds sprinkled on the platform are more easily visible and get a sparrow's attention.

Each time a bird is caught, the trio bait trap must be reset. And because the entrance is large, the trio bait trap will capture large birds such as starlings and grackles, as well as house sparrows and other small birds. However, large birds can't enter the holding cell; you can release them from the trap compartments without releasing any house sparrows that are being held.

The repeating or elevator trap is a popular style of bait trap made by several companies. It is made mostly of wire but has some wooden parts, including a deck below the entrance hole.

A house sparrow standing on the deck can look through the entrance hole and see the bait. When it goes inside to get to the bait, it must step on the elevator, which is a cage that falls to the bottom of the trap under the weight of the sparrow. The only way out for the sparrow is through a one-way door into the holding section of the trap. After the sparrow leaves the elevator cage, the cage rises, and the trap is ready to capture another sparrow.

Repeating traps can capture a dozen or more house sparrows and hold them without being reset. And large birds can't enter the trap, so they never have to be removed.

With all three of these traps, it is very important to provide food and water to any birds trapped inside. Small birds may die in just a few hours inside a trap without water. The best water container is the type used for cage birds — the water bottle is fastened outside the cage, and only a small cup fits inside.

A trio house sparrow trap is baited and awaits customers. The two spring-loaded doors will snap shut behind house sparrows that enter.

CORNELL LAB OF ORNITHOLOGY

The Birdhouse Network
Cornell Lab of Ornithology
159 Sapsucker Woods Rd.
Ithaca, NY 14850
tel: 800 843-BIRD (2473);
(outside U.S.) 607 254-2473
http://birds.cornell.edu/
birdhouse

NORTH AMERICAN BLUEBIRD SOCIETY

North American Bluebird
Society
Box 74
Darlington, WI 53530
http://www.nabluebird
society.org/

NABS AFFILIATES

CANADA

ALBERTA

Calgary Area Bluebird Trail
Monitors
c/o Don Stiles
20 Lake Wapta Rise SE
Calgary, AB T2J 2M9

Ellis Bird Farm Ltd.
Box 5090
Lacombe, AB T4L 1W7
tel: 403 346-2211
contact: Myrna Pearman,
EBF biologist

Mountain Bluebird Trails
Conservation Society
1725 Lakeside Rd. S
Lethbridge, AB TIK 3G9
tel: 403 328-0868
contact: Bob Harrison

BRITISH COLUMBIA

Southern Interior Bluebird
Trail Society
Sherry Linn, President
Box 494
Oliver, BC VOH 1TO
e-mail: goldstrm@vip.net

MANITOBA

The Friends of the
Bluebirds
3011 Park Ave.
Brandon, MB R7B 2K3
tel: 204 727-5102
fax: 204 728-7346
e-mail: smitha@brandonu.ca
contact: Ann Smith

ONTARIO

Ontario Eastern Bluebird
Society
2-165 Green Valley Drive
Kitchener, Ontario N2P 1K3
contact: Bill Read

UNITED STATES

ARKANSAS

Bella Vista Bluebird Society
c/o Jim Janssen
27 Britten Circle
Bella Vista, AR 72714
tel: 501 855-7277

CALIFORNIA

California Bluebird
Recovery Program
2021 Ptarmigan Drive #1
Walnut Creek, CA 94595
tel: 925 937-5974
fax: 925 935-4480
e-mail: cbrp@value.net

COLORADO

Colorado Bluebird Project
c/o Bob Priester
6060 N. Broadway
Denver, CO 80216
tel: 303 291-7253
e-mail: priesterpc@tech
nologist.com

GEORGIA

Bluebirds Over Georgia
5858 Silver Ridge Dr.
Stone Mountain, GA 30087
e-mail: fgsawyer@bell
south.net

IDAHO

Our Bluebird Ranch
152 N 200 E.
Blackfoot, ID 83221
tel: 208 782-9676
e-mail: pjbarnes@micron.net

Rocky Mountain Blues
c/o David Richmond
HC67 Box 680
Clayton, ID 83227
tel: 208 838-2431
e-mail: fowest@custertel.net

ILLINOIS

JoDaviess County, Illinois
Bluebird Recovery
Program (a Natural Area
Guardians program)
c/o Grace Storch
15 Cedar Rim Trail
Galena, IL 61036
e-mail: jbw@galenalink.com

Illinois Bluebird Project
Box 2418
Danville IL 61834
Illinois Audubon Society

INDIANA

Indiana Bluebird Society
Box 356
Leesburg IN 46538
tel: 219 858-9050
e-mail:
bluebird@maplenet.net

The Brown County
Bluebird Society
c/o Dan Sparks
Box 660
Nashville, IN 47448
tel: 812 988-1876
fax: 812 342-3820
e-mail: dansparks_47448@
yahoo.com

IOWA

Johnson County Songbird
Project
c/o Jim Walters
1033 E. Washington
Iowa City, IA 52240-5248
tel: 319 466-1134
e-mail: james-walters@
uiowa.edu

Bluebirds of Iowa
Restoration
c/o Jaclyn Hill
2946 Ubben Avenue
Ellsworth, IA 50075-7554
tel: 515 836-4579
e-mail: hillhome@netins.net

KENTUCKY

Kentucky Bluebird Society
c/o Bob Ivy
Box 3425
Paducah, KY 42002
tel: 270 442-1712
e-mail: kybluebirds@hcis.net

MASSACHUSETTS

Massachusetts Bluebird
Association
Contact: Haleya Priest
89 Pulpit Hill Rd.,
Amherst, MA 01002
tel: 413 549-3937
fax: 413 549-2901
e-mail: MaBlue@gis.net

MINNESOTA

Bluebird Recovery Program
(Audubon Chapter of
Minneapolis)
c/o Dorene H. Scriven
Box 3801
Minneapolis, MN 55403
tel: 612 922-4586
fax: same, call first.
e-mail: scriv001@tc.umn.edu

MISSISSIPPI

Mississippi Bluebirds
c/o Tena Taylor
192 CR 457
Calhoun City, MS 38916
tel: 662 628-1625
fax: 662 628-1625
e-mail: tenataylor@tycom.net

MONTANA

Mountain Bluebird Trails, Inc.
c/o Erv Davis
604 N. Main

Charlo, MT 59824
tel: 406 644-2740
e-mail: ervdavis@black
foot.net

NEBRASKA

Bluebirds Across Nebraska
c/o Connie Finley
6732 K Rd.
Nebraska City NE 68410
tel: 402 873-7550
e-mail: bbcdf@hotmail.com

NEW HAMPSHIRE

New Hampshire Bluebird
Conspiracy
c/o Bruce Burdett
Box 103
Sunapee NH 03782
e-mail: blueburd@srnet.com

NEW YORK

New York State Bluebird
Society (NYSBS)
c/o James Kunz
454 Ashley Road
Maine, NY 13802
tel: 607 862-3410
e-mail: jrfk2@yahoo.com

Schoharie County Bluebird
Society
c/o Kevin Berner
SUNY Cobleskill
Cobleskill, NY 12043
tel: 518 255-5252
e-mail:
bernerkl@cobleskill.edu

NORTH CAROLINA

North Carolina Bluebird
Society
Helen Munro
22 Bobolink Rd.
Jackson Springs, NC 27281
tel: 910 673-6936
e-mail: cbmunro@ac.net

Rutherford County
Bluebird Club
Box 247
Ellenboro, NC 28040
contact: Christopher Greene

OHIO

Ohio Bluebird Society
c/o Doug LeVasseur
20680 Township Road #120
Senecaville, OH 43780
e-mail: emdlev@clover.net

OKLAHOMA

Oklahoma Bluebird Society
Marion Liles
5656 So. 161 W. Ave.
Sand Springs, OK 74063
tel: 918 241-2473
fax: 918 699-3358
e-mail:
sialia@worldnet.att.net

OREGON

Prescott Bluebird Recovery
Project
c/o Pat Johnston
Box 1469
Sherwood, OR 97140
tel: 503 246-1337
e-mail: bluebird@pacifier.com

Audubon Society of
Corvallis
Elsie Eltzroth
6980 N.W. Cardinal Rd.
Corvallis, OR 97330
tel: 541 745-7806
e-mail: eltzroth@peak.org

PENNSYLVANIA

Bluebird Society of
Pennsylvania
Kathy Clark, President
Box 267
Enola, PA 17025-0267
tel: 717 938-4089
fax: 717 938-0455
e-mail: kcbsp@aol.com

Purple Martin Conservation
Association
Edinboro University of
Pennsylvania
Edinboro, PA 16444
tel: 814 734-4420 (Louise
Chambers)
fax: 814 734-5803
e-mail: louise@purple
martin.org

TENNESSEE

Benton County Bluebird
Society of Tennessee, Inc.
c/o Dan McCue
155 Post Oak Avenue
Camden, TN 38320
tel: 901 584-5060
e-mail: dmccue@usit.net

Tennessee Bluebird Trails
c/o Steve Garr
Box 190
Mt. Juliet, TN 37121
e-mail: tnbluebirdtrails
@msn.com

VIRGINIA

The Virginia Bluebird
Society
3403 Carly Lane
Woodbridge, VA 22192
tel: 703 730-1729
e-mail: virginiabluebirds
@home.com
Julie A. Kutruff:
jkutruff@aol.com
Anne Little:
aglmkt@erols.com

WASHINGTON

Cascadia Bluebird and
Purple Martin Society

c/o Dr. Michael Pietro
3015 Squalicum Pkwy #250
Bellingham, WA 98225

WISCONSIN

Bluebird Restoration
Association of Wisconsin
Rt. 1, Box 137 Akron Ave.
Plainfield, WI 54966

Lafayette County Bluebird
Society
14953 Hwy 23
Darlington, WI 53530

SUPPLIERS

Dave Ahlgren (Peterson
nestboxes)
Ahlgren Construction, Inc.
12989 Otchipwe Ave. N.
Stillwater, MN 55082-8564
tel: 612 430-0031

Armstrong's Cricket Farm
(mealworms)
1127 Wood St, Box 125
West Monroe, LA 71294
tel: (inquiries) 318 387-6000
(orders) 800 345-8778
http://www.armstrong
crickets.com/worms.htm

Audubon Workshop (nest-
boxes, feeders, guards,
traps, bluebird banquet)
5200 Schenley Place
Lawrenceburg, IN 47025
tel: 812 537-3583
http://audubonworkshop.com

Ben Meadows Company
(bait traps)
Box 5277
Janesville, WI 53547-5277
tel: 800 241-6401
http://www.benmeadows.com

The Bird's Paradise (nestboxes, bait traps, feeders)
20835 Morris Rd.
Conneautville, PA 16406
tel: 800 872-0103

Cornell Birding Shop
(feeders, nestboxes)
http://www.withoutbricks.
com/cornellbirdingshop

Duncraft (feeders, nestboxes)
102 Fisherville Road
Concord, NH 03303-2086
tel: 800 763-7878
http://store.yahoo.com/dun
craft/index.html

Steve Gilbertson (nestboxes,
in-box traps, feeders)
HC 5, Box 31
Aitkin, MN 56431
tel: 218 927-1953

Grubco (mealworms)
Box 15001
Hamilton, Ohio 45015
tel: 800 222-3563
fax: 888 222-3563
e-mail: sales@grubco.com
http://www.grubco.com

Heath Manufacturing
Company (feeders, nest-
boxes)
140 Mill Street, Box 105
Coopersville, MI 49404
tel: 800 678-8183
http://www.heathmfg.com

Homes For Bluebirds (nestboxes, dogwood berries)
Box 699
Bailey, NC 27807
tel: 800 245-4662
e-mail:
finchnursery@bbnp.com

Joe Huber (plans for
in-box trap)
e-mail: hubertrap@webtv.net

Kness Mfg. Co. (bait traps)
Hwy 5 South, Box 70
Albia, IA 52531
tel: 800 247-5062
http://www.kness.com

Kridler Construction (nestboxes, sparrow and
snake traps)
1902 Ford Drive
Mt. Pleasant, TX 75455
http://www.kridler.net

David Magness (nestboxes,
feeders, in-box traps)
Jenna Bird
Box 328
Whiteford, MD 21160
tel: 800 500-2473
e-mail: Jennabirds@aol.com
http://www.jennabird.com

Nature Society (nestboxes,
bait traps)
Purple Martin Junction
Griggsville, IL 62340
tel: 800 255-2692
http://www.naturesociety.org

Nature's Way (mealworms)
Box 7268
Hamilton, OH 45013-7268
tel: 800 318-2611
fax: 513 737-5421
http://www.herp.com/
nature/nature.html

North American Bluebird
Society online catalog
(feeders, nestboxes)
http://www.nabluebirdsociety
.org/catalog/merchcat.html

Purple Martin Conservation
Association (nestboxes,
bait traps)
c/o Edinboro University of
Pennsylvania
Edinboro, PA 16444
tel: 814 734-4420
e-mail: pmca@edinboro.edu
http://www.purplemartin.org

Rainbow Mealworms
126 E. Spruce St.
Compton, CA 90224
tel: 800 777-9676
e-mail: order@rainbow
mealworms.com
http://www.rainbowmeal
worms.com/mealworm.htm

Gary Springer
Real Bird Homes.com
(nestboxes)
617 Shepherd Road, Box 523
Carnesville, GA 30521
tel: 706 677-3857
www.realbirdhomes.com

Thomas Wildbird Feeders
(nestboxes, feeders)
Aurora, Ontario, Canada
tel: 905 727-3110
e-mail: thomaswbf
@idirect.com

Tomahawk Live Trap Co.
Box 323
Tomahawk, WI 54487
tel: 800 272-8727
http://www.tomahawklive
trap.com

Van Ert Enterprises (feeders, nestboxes, traps)
39755 Highway 92
Carson, IA 51525-4275
tel: 712 484-3479
e-mail: fvanert@aol.com
http://www.hometown.aol.
com/fvanert

Edward and Elaine
Whittemore (log-style
nestboxes)
Box 207
East Ellijay, GA 30539
tel: 888 835-1207

Wild Birds Unlimited, Inc.
(feeders, nestboxes)
find your nearest store:
800 326-4928
http://www.wbu.com

BLOWFLY RESEARCH

Dr. Terry Whitworth
2533 Inter Avenue
Puyallup, WA 98372
tel: 888 959-1818
e-mail: wpctwbug@aol.com
http://www.birdblowfly.com

Page numbers in *italics* indicate photographs. The letter s after a page number refers to a sidebar.